HISTORY: FICTION

MW01228026

The Issue with Baptism of Russia

By Anatoly Fomenko
and Gleb Nosovskiy

DELAMERE PUBLISHING

•

THE ISSUE WITH BAPTISM OF RUSSIA
By Anatoly Fomenko and Gleb Nosovskiy

On the cover: Vasily Perov. *First Christians in Kiev* (1880, fragment). Wikimedia Commons.

Translated from Russian by Mikhail Yagupov
Design and layout by Paul Bondarovski
Project management: Franck Tamdhu

Published by Delamere Resources LLC

THE ISSUE WITH BAPTISM OF RUSSIA

CONTENTS

CONTENTS

*History is a pack of lies about events that never happened
told by people who weren't there.*

GEORGE SANTAYANA

*Be wary of mathematiciens, particularly when
they speak the truth.*

ST. AUGUSTINE

*History repeats itself; that's one of the things
that's wrong with history.*

CLARENCE DARROW

*Who controls the past controls the future.
Who controls the present controls the past.*

GEORGE ORWELL, 1984

From the Publisher

The quadruple baptism of Russia

The official version of Russian history was manufactured in XVIII century by imported by Romanov dynasty German historians Bayer, Miller and Schlezer. It relates the one and only baptism of Russia took place under Prince Vladimir in 986–989 A.D. Envoys of different lands presumably came to Vladimir in 986, offering to convert him into their confessions.

Greek team has won the competition. The actual baptism took place in 989. The Christian ecclesiastical hierarchy was nonexistent prior to that, therefore the priests from Greece got the job of teaching the faith to the pagan Russians. It took several decades under the Prince Yaroslav the Wise to translate the ecclesiastical literature from Greek into Slavic.

Dr. Fomenko *et al.* scratched this polished surface and found out that the Great Catechesis, published in Moscow under Czar Mikhail Fyodorovich Romanov and Patriarch Filaret in 1627 A.D., contains the version of the unique Baptism greatly at odds with the one we're accustomed to.

According to the Great Catechesis, Russia was baptized *four times.* The first baptism was by Apostle Andrew, the second performed by Fotius, Patriarch of Czar-Grad "in the reign of the Greek King, Basil of Macedonia, and Ryurik, Great Prince of Russia, with Princes Askold and Dir regnant in Kiev". The Great Catechesis doesn't give any dates for either Baptism.

Unlike the first two, the third and the fourth baptisms of Russia are dated in the Catechesis. The third one has taken place under the Great Princes Olga, in 963 A.D. The fourth baptism of Russia is the famous baptism of 989 A.D. under Prince Vladimir. The Great Catechesis says: "And so he had ordered to the whole people of Russia to get baptized by the Holy Patriarchs Nikola Khrusovert, or Cicinius, or Sergiy, Archbishop of Novgorod, under Mikhail, the Metropolitan of Kiev".

German team of historians says nothing about any Russian or Greek archbishops in Novgorod or metropolitans in Kiev under Vladimir. For learned Germans, Russia was pagan at that time. Period. Bayer, Miller and Schlezer used the *Povest Vremennyh Let* 'discovered' (written, *sic!*) only in XVIII century as the primary source.

Dr. Fomenko *et al.* refute this version with abundant data that explains the consecutive baptisms of Russia as confession choices during religious schisms of XII–XIV centuries, and not a unique Baptism of pagans took place.

Franck Tamhdu

1.

The baptism of Russia

Modern readers are most likely to be familiar with the history of the baptism of Russia from the *Povest Vremennyh Let* ([716] and [715]). The latter is a source that dates from the early XVIII century, as we demonstrate in Chapter 1 of *Chron4*. According to this chronicle, the one and only baptism of Russia took place under Prince Vladimir in 986-989 A.D. Envoys of different lands presumably came to Vladimir in 986, offering to convert him into their faith ([716] and [715], pages 65-66). This is how the preparations for the baptism started. The actual baptism took place in 989, according to the *Povest Vremennyh Let* ([715], pages 84-85). The Christian ecclesiastical hierarchy is said to have been nonexistent prior to that; when it did appear, it had initially consisted of foreign priests from Greece. The first Russian metropolitan is said to have appeared several decades later, under Yaroslav the Wise, which is also the time when the ecclesiastical literature was translated from Greek into Slavic. This is how the Romanovian version of Russian history relates the baptism of Russia – the one that was created in the XVII-XVIII century. This is also the official version, and one that we're accustomed to.

But let us see how the baptism of Russia, doubtlessly a major event in the ecclesiastical Russian history, was described in the canonical church literature of the early XVII century. Let us consider the Great Catechesis, published in Moscow under Czar Mikhail Fyodorovich Romanov and Patriarch Filaret in 1627 ([86]). This book contains a special section on the baptism of Russia ([86], sheets 27-29). The version it contains is greatly at odds with the one we're accustomed to. According to the Great Catechesis, Russia was baptised four times. The first baptism was by Apostle Andrew, the second performed by Fotius, Patriarch of Czar-Grad "in the reign of the Greek King, Basil of Macedonia, and Ryurik, Great Prince of Russia, with Askold and Dir regnant in Kiev" ([86], sheet 28, reverse). The Great Catechesis doesn't indicate any dates for either baptism – all of this in the early XVII century!

Unlike the first two, the third baptism of Russia is dated in the Catechesis. It is said to have taken place under the Great Princes Olga, in the year 6463 since Adam, or around 955 A.D. We shall withhold from discussing why the Catechesis insists on converting this date into the B.C./A.D. chronology somewhat differently (the book insists on 963 A.D.). This must be explained by the poor correlation between the "Adam era" and the B.C./A.D. chronology, which had still been in a state of flux around that time.

The fourth baptism of Russia is the famous baptism under Prince Vladimir. The Great Catechesis dates it to 6497, which is roughly 989 A.D. This is what we read:

> "And so he had ordered to the whole people of Russia to get baptised by the Holy Patriarchs in the year of 6496 – Nikola Khrusovert, or Cicinius, or Sergiy, Archbishop of Novgorod, under Mikhail, the Metropolitan of Kiev" ([86], sheet 29).

This description rings very odd nowadays. We "know" that Russia had been pagan before the baptism, and that no ecclesiastical hierarchy had existed until Prince Vladimir summoned the first members of the Christian clergy from abroad. Yet the XVII century Catechesis claims the baptism to have happened in the epoch of Sergiy, Archbishop of Novgorod, and Mikhail, Metropolitan of Kiev, which means that two church hierarchies had existed at least – in Novgorod and in Kiev. However, as one may have expected, the Scaligerian and Romanovian version of history knows nothing about any archbishops in Novgorod or metropolitans in Kiev under Vladimir. Nowadays we are told that all of the above is but a "mediaeval fancy" – "fantasies of the Catechesis" in the present case.

One is also instantly confronted with the following question. Could the people in the XVII century have known nothing of substance about the baptism of Russia? Have they never read the *Povest Vremennyh Let*? One must think that if even the authors of the Catechesis possessed no definite information about this event, the rest of the people, those who had used the Catechesis as a learning aid, must have known even less. Therefore, later historians must have been the first to discover "truth about the baptism of Russia" – Bayer, Miller and Schlezer, who had "read about it" in the *Povest Vremennyh Let*. This oeuvre was naturally unknown to their predecessors in the XVII century for the simple reason that the version of this chronicle known to us today had not yet been written; it had only attained its Romanovian and Millerian characteristics in the XVIII century, q.v. in *Chron4*, Chapter 1. As we can see, the history of Russia's baptism in its consensual version also cannot predate the end of the XVII century, since it had still been seen in a totally different light in the early XVII century.

However, let us return to the Great Catechesis, which reveals more curious facts, and begin with the date of the baptism. According to our research, the epoch when Russia was baptised becomes superimposed over the XI and the XV century (see the chronological tables in figs. 2.4 and 2.5 in *Chron4*, Chapter 2). Bear in mind that the XV century is the famous epoch of the Great Schism. According to the New Chronology, this is when the formerly united Christian Church had become divided into several separate branches. This is why the issue of confession choice had been a poignant one for the secular authorities of the XV century. Mark that the baptism of Russia under Prince Vladimir was described in the *Povest Vremennyh Let* as a choice of faith and not a simple baptism ([86]). This explains the several baptisms of Russia, which must indeed look odd if we regard a baptism as the conversion of the pagans into Christianity – we see nothing of the kind in the history of any other country. Who would there remain to baptise? However, if we are to view the consecutive baptisms of Russia as confession choices made during religious schisms, the picture becomes perfectly clear.

Another thing that ceases to look odd is the way the patriarchs are listed – the baptism was supposed to be performed by either Nikola Khrusovert, *or* Cicinius, *or* Sergiy. If the above patriarchs all took part in the baptism of a pagan country, wherefore the *"or"*? "And" would have been more appropriate. If they didn't take part in the baptism, why mention them at all? However, if the baptism of Russia is to be regarded as a choice of confession, everything starts to look normal – different patriarchs must have sided with different branches, and the indication of a chosen confession must have also contained the names of its most distinguished patriarchs. There could have been several; the use of "or" becomes justified if we're to assume that all of them had been in consensus – any of them could have supervised the "confession choice" with the same result. Therefore, the conjunction "or" is used by the Great Catechism in order to hint at the atmosphere of an ecclesiastical schism.

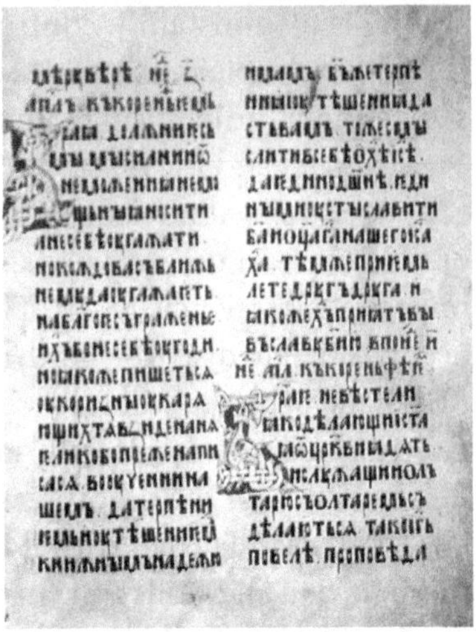

Let us now consider the way the date of the baptism is transcribed in the original – "six thousand УЧ3." It contains the Slavic letter У, which stands for "400." However, in many old texts the letter in question is virtually indistinguishable from Ц, q.v. in fig. 14.123. The difference be-

Fig. 14.123. Page from an old edition of the "Apostle" dated to the alleged XIV century. A specimen of the "ustav" writing style, where the letters of У and Ц are virtually identical to each other. Taken from [745], Volume 8, page 197.

Fig. 14.124. Fragment of the previous illustration. One of letters Ц at the top is highlighted, likewise the three letters У below. It is perfectly obvious that the shape of the two letters is identical.

tween the two had been truly minimal (see fig. 14.124). This is how these letters were written in most of the old texts – all but duplicating one another. Examples of just how similar the two letters had been in writing are abundant in the illustrations to [745].

However, when these letters would actually come up in texts, the letter У would as a rule be accompanied by the letter О – in other words, the sound ОУ was transcribed as two letters. Therefore, the similarity between the letters У and Ц did not usually lead to any confusion in the interpretation of narrative text. However, when used as digits, the letters would immediately become very confusing, since there were no additional О's next to the У's, and the similarity between the shapes of the two letters proved problematic. Both letters also referred to the hundreds place, which would lead to occasional 500-year errors in dating. The matter is that the letter Ц had stood for 900, whereas У had meant 400. In cases when the latter became confused for the former, the dating written in these digits immediately gained 500 years of extra age. Such cases were numerous, since confusion came easy. Thus, if a certain Slavic date has the letter У in the hundreds place, the very same date may have been transcribed with Ц in the old original that it was copied from, and there is a possibility of a 500-year chronological error inherent in the newer copy.

This is the very situation that we have with the date of Russia's baptism. The date in question is 6497 since Adam and is transcribed with the use of the latter У, which stands for 400. If the letter in question were Ц, the dating would become 6997 since Adam, or 1489 A.D. Therefore, it is possible that the original old document had dated the baptism of Russia to 1489 instead of 989, which is the date that we're accustomed to using nowadays. The baptism is thus dated to the end of the XV century, while the previous baptism of Russia instigated by Olga shifts to the middle of the XV century.

However, it is this very century that the largest reform of the Russian Church falls upon, which was in direct connexion with the religious schism, the famous Council of Florence and the failed attempt of a religious union. The story is known to everyone very well, and related in numerous textbooks on ecclesiastical history. Nowadays this reform is presented to us as an important moment in the history of the Russian Church, but not really a crucial one. However, the contemporaries of this event had written some interesting things about it. A. V. Kartashov reports the following: "Simeon of Suzdal in his 'Tale' likens Vassily Vassilyevich not only to his predecessor St. Vladimir, but also Constantine, the great Czar and the 'founding father of the Orthodox faith' considered equal to the Apostles in rank by the Church" ([372], page 374). Vassily Vassilyevich is the Great Prince Vassily II Tyomniy, who had lived in the XV century. Apparently, the *Povest Vremennyh Let* describes this very epoch as the last baptism of Russia under Prince Vladimir. Let us also remind the reader that the given name of Vladimir the Holy had actually been Vassily, which is common knowledge – see the Great Catechesis, for instance ([86], page 29).

However, one is confronted by the natural wish to find out the identities of Nikola Khrusovert, Cicinius and Sergiy, Archbishop of Novgorod, whose faith had been chosen at the baptism of Russia. No archbishop of this name exists anywhere in the epoch of the X century, which is the epoch that the Millerian and Romanovian textbooks place it. Indeed – what Orthodox hierarchy could possibly exist in the pagan Novgorod "before the baptism"?

However, let us turn to the XV century and look for the above-mentioned characters there. We do find them here; moreover, they are actually rather famous.

Nikola Khrusovert is most likely to identify as the famous Nicolaus Chryppfs Cusanus, who had lived in 1401-1464 ([936], Volume 2, page 212). He is known as "the greatest German humanist ... theologian, theologian, mathematician and a public figure, ecclesiastical and secular" ([936], Volume 2, page 212). The nickame Cusanus is presumed to have derived from the village of Cusa, which is where he was born ([936], Volume 2, page 212). We find it odd that he was named after a village that nobody has ever heard of instead of the province or the country that he had hailed from. We believe his nickname to translate as "native of Kazan" – a famous city in the XV century.

The origins of the name Khrusovert as mentioned by the Great Catechesis also become clearer. Nicholas Cusanus had also borne the name Chryppfs, q.v. above, which may have read as "Khrus" in Old Russian. But where does the word *"vert"* come from, and what does it mean? The following explanation is possible. Apparently, Nicholas Cusanus had written a tractate on telluric rotation, no less – "a hundred years before Copernicus," as it is generally assumed ([936], Volume 2, page 212). In this case, the word *"vert"* might refer to his discovery (cf. the Russian word *"vertet"*, "to rotate," and the

Latin *"verto"* – "I turn." Thus, the name Khrusovert might stand for "Khrus, the discoverer of telluric rotation" – or even "the Christian who had discovered the rotation of the Earth." Possibly, khrus+ vert may have stood for "converting to Christianity," especially seeing how the Great Catechesis names him among the founding fathers of the Orthodox Christianity. The nickname Khrus could have stood for "Christian" and been derived from the name Christ, or Horus. As we are beginning to realise, Great Prince Vladimir (aka Vassily) must have baptised Russia while Khrusovert had still been alive, or shortly after his death.

Now, who could the Cicinius character possibly be? He is the ecclesiastical activist mentioned second in the Great Catechesis. The Christianity encyclopaedia ([936]) doesn't mention any known XV characters under that name. However, we did find Zosima, one of the most famous Russian saints and the founder of the famous monastery at Solovki. Zosima died in 1478 ([936], Volume 1, page 562). Could he be the person mentioned in the Great Catechesis as Cicinius? Moreover, it turns out that Gerontiy, the Metropolitan of Moscow, died in 1489, which is the very year of the baptism, and his successor had been Metropolitan Zosima ([372], Volume 1, page 387). The biography of Metropolitan Zosima is complex and very convoluted; his entire life was spent in the atmosphere of a heated ecclesiastical schism. The details aren't known all that well ([936], Volume 1, page 562). It is possible that Cicinius from the epoch of Russia's baptism as mentioned in the Catechesis is Zosima, the Muscovite Metropolitan from the end of the XV century.

What can we say about Sergiy, the Archbishop of Novgorod, who is also mentioned among the actual instigators of Russia's baptism, according to the Great Catechesis? There is but a single person suitable for that role – Sergiy of Radonezh. Although his death is dated to the end of the XIV century nowadays, he was canonised in 1452 ([936], Volume 2, page 553) – the very epoch of the "fourth baptism of Russia" under Prince Vladimir, or Vassily. The lifetime of Sergiy falls on the epoch of the ecclesiastical schism, which had already been in its budding stage around the beginning of the XV century, according to our reconstruction.

A propos, to come back to Nicholas Cusanus (possibly, Nicholas Khrusovert) – it must be pointed out that "in 1453, being deeply impressed by the conquest of Constantinople by the Turks, he had published a tractate ... wherein he had emphasised ... the possibility of a Christian agreement between all the nations. Next he had published a work entitled ... 'Sifting through the Koran' ... which is concerned with pointing out the close ties that exist between Islam and Christianity" ([936], Volume 2, page 212). This demonstrates his positive attitude towards the Ottomans, or the Atamans, which hints at his connexions with the mediaeval Russia, or the Horde. Let us reiterate that the Ottoman = Ataman conquest, had been launched from Russia, or the Horde, according to our reconstruction.

2.

How the Romanovian falsification of documents was reflected in the history of Russian handwriting

Above we have said a great deal about the global falsification of the ancient Russian documents that took place in the epoch of the first Romanovs (starting with the middle of the XVII century, that is). Let us ponder how this tremendous hoax should have affected the history of Russian handwriting. Handwriting styles are subject to change in the course of time; this can greatly affect the manner in which certain letters and combinations of letters are written. As a result, texts written in an archaic and uncommon handwriting are often very hard to read – due to the simple fact that some of the letters will be impossible to recognize at the very least.

However, let us imagine that at some point in history all the documents of the previous epochs were edited and written anew, and the originals destroyed. This shall leave us with a situation where all of the falsified "ancient" documents are written in more or less the same style of handwriting – the one that had been used in the epoch of the falsification. This is the handwriting that the scribes of the late XVII century were taught as children. No matter how hard they may have tried to make the handwriting look "ancient," the manner of writing adopted in the childhood should have affected the end result in one way or another. Thus, the modern reader shouldn't have that many problems with reading the "ancient" (falsified and edited) texts. It suffices to read two or three such "ancient documents" to get accustomed to the manner of writing. The rest of the "ancient" documents shouldn't present any difficulties, since the shape of letters and the manner of writing should remain more or less the same.

This is precisely what we see happen with the history of the Russian handwriting. All of the "ancient" texts allegedly dating from the pre-Romanovian epoch can be read without much trouble. If you can read a text dating from the alleged XVI century, you will find it easy to read the texts from the alleged XI and XII century as well, etc. The same applies to texts dating from the second half of the XVII century. It seems as though the shorthand texts of the first half of the XVII century are the only exception, notwithstanding the fact that the shorthand of the alleged XVI century is usually a lot more accessible. We are quite naturally referring to published specimens exclusively – there is no way of knowing what is concealed in the closed archives.

And so, something strange happened to the Russian handwriting in the first half of the XVII century, or the epoch of the first Romanovs, starting around the beginning of the XVII century and up until 1630. The handwriting in these documents is drastically different from any other handwriting dating from any other historical period. For some mysterious reason it is the epoch of roughly 1613-1630 that had the handwriting one finds particularly hard to interpret, occasionally failing altogether. This is primarily due to the outlandish shape of most letters, which often resemble Arabic script more than they do Slavic characters. In reality, the letters are Slavic – it is only their shape that we find uncommon today. This effect is truly of great interest, and vividly manifest in the series of specimens of Russian handwriting reproduced in the multi-volume edition entitled the *Dictionary of the Russian Language of the XI-XVII century* ([782]-[791]). Twenty-three volumes of the dictionary have been published to date. Each of them contains two different examples of the old handwriting reproduced on the title page. We have chosen twelve handwriting specimens – documents concerning trade for the most part, q.v. in fig. 14.125 – 14.140. Let us point out that the specimens we do not reproduce herein are all written in a perfect calligraphic hand that shall be easy to decipher for any modern reader, despite the several centuries that had passed since the epochs in question.

Fig. 14.125. Page from "Svyatoslav's Almanac" allegedly dating from 1076. Taken from [782], issue 1.

Fig. 14.126. Page from the "Ryazan Nomocanon" allegedly dating from 1284. Taken from [782], issue 1.

Fig. 14.127. A parchment purchase deed allegedly dating from the XIV – early XV century. Taken from [788], issue 8.

Fig. 14.128. Another deed on purchase on parchment allegedly dating from the XIV – early XV century. From [728], issue 8.

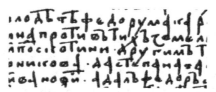

Fig. 14.129. Close-in of a fragment of a parchment purchase deed allegedly dating from the XIV – early XV century.

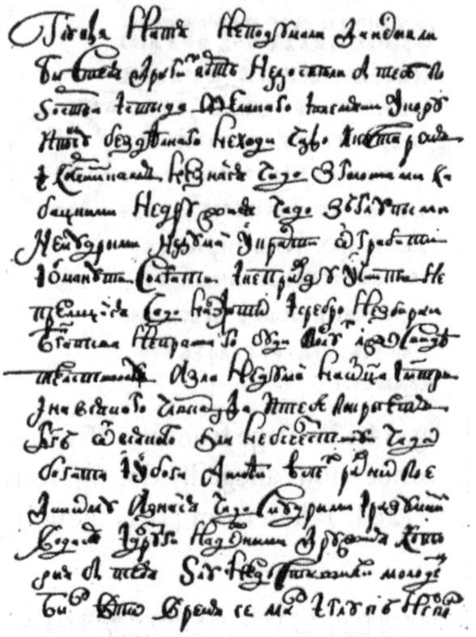

Fig. 14.131. Page from a book entitled *Guard*, dating from the XVI century. Taken from [783], issue 2.

Fig. 14.130. Page from the *Chronicle of Avraamka* allegedly dating from the XV-XVI century. Taken from [784], issue 3.

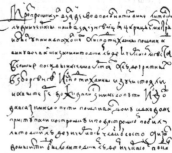

Fig. 14.132. Page of the *Spear Books* allegedly dating from the late XVI – early XVII century. Taken from [783], issue 2.

Fig. 14.133. Document from the *Stroganov Archive*. Dates from "the year of 122," which converts to the modern chronological scale as 1613-1614. Taken from [787], issue 7.

Fig. 14.134. Fragment of the previous illustration: a close-in.

Fig. 14.135. Page from the *Chronicle of Putivl* dating from 1629. Taken from [791], issue 19.

Fig. 14.136. Fragment of the previous illustration: a close-in.

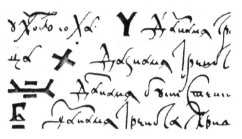

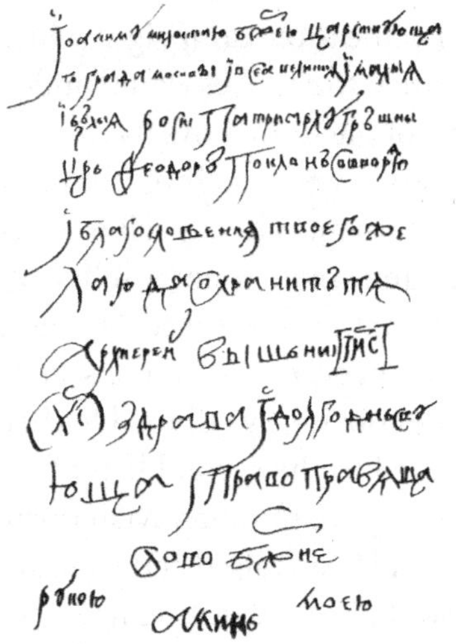

Fig. 14.137. Authentic missive sent by Czar Fyodor Alexeyevich Romanov to the Muscovite Patriarch Ioakim around 1676-1682 A.D. Taken from [785], issue 5.

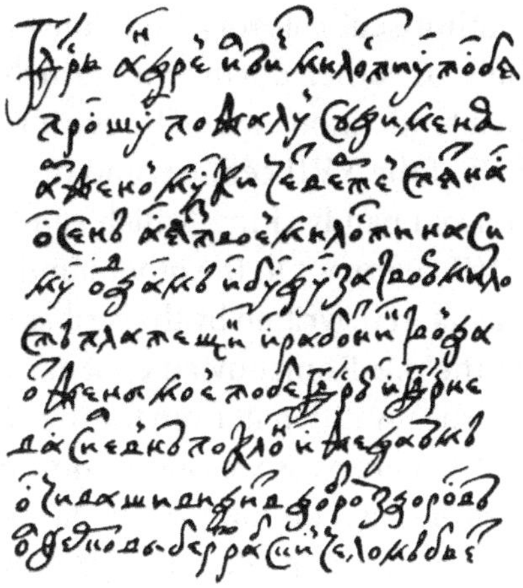

Fig. 14.138. "The letter sent by Olfyorka to A. I. Bezobrazov." XVII century. Taken from [785], issue 5.

Our recommendation to the readers familiar with the Cyrillic alphabet is to try and actually read these specimens, and then estimate which ones are the hardest to decipher. Those are doubtlessly the specimens of shorthand writing dating from 1613-1614 and from 1629. This fact can obviously be explained in a number of ways – however, our reconstruction makes it look perfectly natural. More-

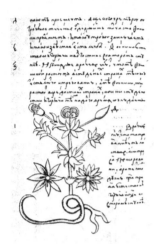

Fig. 14.139. Page from a XVII century *Book of Herbs*. Taken from [791], issue 19.

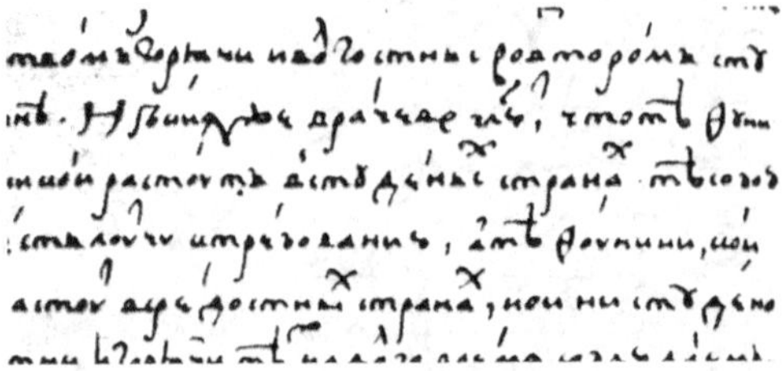

Fig. 14.140. Fragment of page taken from a XVII century *Book of Herbs*: a close-in. Taken from [791], issue 19.

over, it would be strange if things had been any different. Indeed, during the Romanovian document falsification campaign, which falls on the second half of the XVII century, the scribes would understandably enough leave the documents of the Romanovs themselves intact – the ones that dated from the epoch when their dynasty had just come to power. After all, these documents already fell into the "authorised" category, and didn't need any amendments, unlike the bulk of earlier documents, which were either destroyed or edited in a tendentious way. The editing was however done in the second half of the XVII century, and the scribes obviously adhered to their normal handwriting, which can be dated to the second half of the XVII century. On the other hand, the very first Romanovian documents were written by the scribes who had been raised and educated in the pre-Romanovian epoch, and so their handwriting had been drastically different from the one introduced in the second half of the XVII century, as we can see nowadays. Thus, the mysterious handwriting was common in Russia, or the Horde, around the end of the XVI century; the documents of the first Romanovs had fortunately enough preserved some specimens.

We must note that we did manage to read a Russian document dating from 1613-1614, and some fragments of another Russian document dated 1629, q.v. in fig. 14.133 and 14.134, but it had cost us much effort, and it had taken us a long time to get accustomed to the idiosyncratic shape of letters, the peculiar manner of making insets and abbreviations, and the various versions of one and the same letter.

Let us quote the header of the document that dates from 1613-1614:
"*Questioning materials*

In the ркв (122nd) year, on the 14th day of December, Prince Timofei, son of Prince Ivan Obolenskiy, arrived with haste from the Varkharchinskaya Horde to represent the Lithuanians and the Cherkassians."

A curious detail is that year 122 "since Adam" is indicated sans millennia (seven in the thousands place is omitted). This year corresponds to 1614 A.D. on the modern chronological scale, since 7122 = 5508 + 1614. This "millenarian abbreviation" had been used in the old documents as a rule. There is no chronological confusion in the present case – however, if the document had related unfamiliar events, one could easily "extend" Russian history into the distant past, dating it to 614 instead of 1614, for instance.

Another interesting observation is as follows. The Lithuanian and Cherkassian troops are referred to as the Horde; the Russian word used is "*gorda*" and not the more common "*orda*." This spelling might shed some light over the etymology of the English word Horde, for instance. The word "horror" must be of a similar origin – this is how the Horde became reflected by the sweet-sounding "ancient" Latin (see [237], page 480). As for Russian, the word "*gordiy*", or "proud," is also very likely to be a derivative of the word "*gorda*."

Let us however return to the ancient Russian handwriting styles and recollect the fact that many of the ancient coins found in Russian have illegible inscriptions that are declared Arabic (see *Chron5*, Chapter 2). The Arabic origin of these letters can only be estimated from the shape of the letters, that does indeed look Arabic. However, attempts to read the inscriptions as Arabic texts have failed, and that is why they were called illegible in the first place. However, the Russian handwriting of the late XVI – early XVII century, which often strongly resembles the Arabic script visually, brings us to the thought that all these "illegible inscriptions" on coins are in Russian. The unfamiliar characters declared Arabic today must be old Russian letters of the XIV-XVI century, now completely forgotten. Also, inscriptions on coins are a lot more difficult to read than texts on paper. In the former case it is always a short phrase or a single word; also, the use of abbreviations had been a rule in minting. If the shape of the letters is unfamiliar, the inscription is rendered utterly illegible.

We are therefore confronted by a most bizarre tendency. Russian chronicles, books and artwork that are presumed to date from ancient epochs and have de facto been received from the hands of the XVII-XVIII century historians were written in perfectly readable Russian. This makes it very odd indeed that whenever an authentic Russian historical artefact is unearthed, and by authentic we mean one that has fortunately evaded the clutches of the Romanovian editors, we see a completely different picture. The decipherment of such inscriptions always leads to great complications (they literally need to be deciphered), and the obstacles encountered by researchers often prove insurmountable. We are beginning to realise this trait to characterise objects that truly date from pre-Romanovian epochs, and in certain cases also the epoch of the first Romanovs – the destruction of the old Horde tradition had required some time, after all, and so even in case of Romanovian artefacts we occasionally encounter old style lettering. This particularly concerns faraway provinces. Indeed, old traditions die hard.

3.

An example of an obviously counterfeited Russian historical document – a royal decree of Ivan the Terrible

Above we wrote a great deal about the falsification of the old Russian documents in the epoch of the Romanovs. It is a commonly known fact that Russian documents of the pre-Romanovian epoch have either vanished or reached us as XVII century copies, already manufactured under the Romanovs. It is known that in the XVII century many of the ministries were compiling books of copies made from old documents. These "copies" are still about, while the originals have mysteriously disappeared. It is believed that the Romanovian officials had diligently copied all the ancient documents, and the copies in question are therefore regarded as bona fide verbatim copies of the perished originals. However, all that we have already managed to find out makes us strongly doubt the hypothesis that the copying campaign of the first Romanovs had pursued the noble objective of conserving the frail scrolls for posterity. It is more likely to have been the reverse – destruction of the originals and their replacement by copies edited in the necessary manner.

Nevertheless, certain documents, in particular, several decrees of the Czars and the Great Princes are presumed to have reached us in their original form. We are of the opinion that one needs to conduct a new and very meticulous study of the presumably authentic pre-Romanovian Russian documents in order to find out whether they have indeed been preserved in their original form.

Could the documents that we're shown today be Romanovian forgeries? The suspicion that the activity in question did indeed take place is confirmed by the following vivid example. The colour insets from the end of [638] contain a photograph of the royal state seal of Czar Ivan IV the Terrible attached to "a decree dating from a later epoch," according to the commentary of the learned historians ([638]; see fig. 14.141). According to [638], this decree is kept in the Central State Archive of Ancient Documents ([638], page 568).

Let us describe the official seals of state as used in that epoch. Several holes were made in the bottom part of the document, and joined with a piece of thread, whose ends would then be woven together and sealed with wax, lead or some other material. The seal itself could not be attached to another document without getting

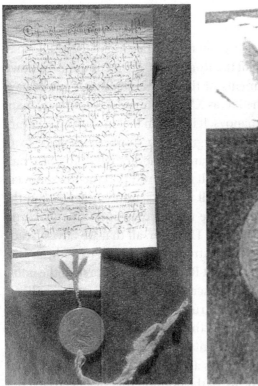

Figs. 14.141 and 14.142. A decree of "Czar Ivan Vassilyevich (The Terrible)," obviously counterfeit. The seal attached to the paper was obviously taken from some other document together with the piece of paper it is attached to, and glued to the present document. The decree is kept in the Central National Archive of Ancient Acts in Moscow. Taken from the colour inset section at the end of [638].

damaged. It is crucial that the holes for the thread were made in the document itself, and not a separate sheet of any kind, which could be easily removed and pasted to another document.

What do we see in the photograph of the royal decree sealed by the seal of Czar Ivan Vassilyevich "The Terrible" (taken from [638])? The seal is quite obviously attached to some small piece of paper or parchment, which, in turn, was pasted to the bottom part of the seal, q.v. in figs. 14.141 and 14.142. Thus, both the seal and the thread were cut from some other document, and pasted to another. This is obviously a counterfeit item.

The first lines of the document say that it was issued by Great Prince Ivan Vassilyevich. This, as well as the fact that historians admit the decree to date from "a later epoch," spells out as a hoax right away, since "Ivan the Terrible" had been the last Russian Czar named Ivan Vassilyevich.

4.

Despite all their attempts, historians never managed to conceal the fact that the Muscovite czars had worn the title of a Great Emperor

Although school textbooks write nothing about it, historians are aware of the fact that the Russian Czar had been referred to as the Great Emperor in the XVI century Western Europe. This is reported by Karamzin, for instance ([362], Volume 8, column 146). Our reconstruction is in complete concurrence with this fact, since the Russian Czars, or Khans, had been the rulers of the entire Great = "Mongolian" Empire, which had included the Western Europe in particular. This is why all the local kings of the Western European countries had acknowledged his higher rank, calling him Emperor. The word originated in the Western Europe; it is used for referring to a single supreme ruler and the liege of the rulers of the imperial provinces, such as kings, dukes, etc.

The fact that the rulers of the Western Europe had once used the title "Great Emperor" for referring to the Russian Czar is known to us from the documents of the XVI century. It irritates the learned historians no end, since it contradicts the picture of the "backwards and savage Russia" that they have painted – a country that had repeatedly tried its best to reach the level of the illuminated Western Europe and failed. However, the fact remains, and historians are forced to explain it in some way. They have found a simple solution, presenting matters as though the use of the title were a result of confusion or a mockery. The implication is that the powerful monarchs of the Western Europe had treated their Eastern and somewhat savage neighbour patronisingly, calling him the "Great Emperor" with a half-smile, using the term as a verbal equivalent of the glass beads that the seafarers from the West had traded for gold and other valuables in their interactions with the ignorant savages, who were only too happy to get swindled. This is how historians present the fact that the monarchs of the Western Europe had called the Russian Czar, or Khan, the Great Emperor.

It isn't all that hard to understand the historians – they have no other option. Let us observe how Karamzin attempts to solve this problem. This is what he writes telling us about the return of the Russian envoy Iosif Nepeya of Vologda from Britain: "Ivan the Terrible had truly enjoyed the kind letters of Mary and Philip, who had addressed him as the Great Emperor; having learnt from Nepeya that the English had treated him with great reverence and sympathy, the court and the people alike, Ivan had made the English welcome guests in Russia… In other words, our relations with Britain, which had been based upon mutual benefits and avoided dangerous political competition … had served as proof of the Czar's wisdom, making his reign even more splendorous" ([362], Volume 8, Chapter 5, column 146).

Karamzin really tried his best. The Czar is "enjoying" the fact that the English call him Great Emperor, the implication being that he is surprised to be addressed in this manner, and uses it as proof of his wisdom, demonstrating the letter from Britain to his boyars so that they would see just how wise their Czar was – recognised as such by the enlightened Britons, no less. It is also implied that the authority of the refined British made the barbaric Russian throne "all the more splendorous" in the eyes of the somewhat savage Russians.

We must state right away that Karamzin is de facto taking part in a hoax here, since he completely misinterprets the old document's evidence of England being subordinate to the Great = "Mongolian" Empire and its Czar, or Khan, in the XVI century. He turns everything upside down, presenting us with a fantasy scenario where the rulers of the Western Europe offhandedly use as serious a title as that of the Great Emperor in official missives in pursuit of short-term benefits.

The above also reveals the location of the imperial capital, or the residence of the Great Emperor – Moscow. The very word Emperor is applied to the ruler of an Empire, and there had been just one

Empire in that epoch – the Great = "Mongolian" Empire. A single empire implies a single emperor – the Czar, or Khan of Russia, also known as the Horde. Russian sources refer to the Empire as to the Russian Kingdom, titling its ruler the Great Prince of All Russia. The Muscovite Principality had been the heart of the Empire, but had by no means comprised all of it. There was a distinction between the two terms, which is reflected even in the documents of the XVII century – the famous *Council Code* of 1649, for instance (see *Chron5*).

During the epoch of the Great Strife in Russia, when the Empire had already fallen apart, the throne went to Dmitriy Ivanovich, who is wrongly accused of having been an impostor nowadays, q.v. above. The documents of that epoch, namely, the Polish diplomatic archive, have preserved the following words that he had addressed to the Polish ambassador. We are quoting them in the rendition of Karamzin, who must have done his best to conceal the rough edges. Dmitriy says the following: "I am not merely a Prince, a Czar and a liege; I am the Great Emperor of my vast domain. This title was given to me by the Lord himself, and isn't a mere word, like the titles of other kings: neither the Assyrian, nor the Median, nor the Roman Caesars had possessed the right to title themselves thus ... am I not addressed as Emperor by every European Monarch?" ([362], Volume 11, Chapter 4, column 155).

The above passage tells us all about the Russian Czar being the Great Emperor, stating it blatantly that no other monarch could claim rights to this title. We also learn that the Emperor's domain had been vast and that every European monarch had addressed him as the Great Emperor.

All of this is in perfect correspondence with our reconstruction, according to which the Great = "Mongolian" Empire had existed up until the early XVII century. Czar Dmitriy, the Khan, had naturally tried to hold on to the title of the Great Emperor in its former meaning. However, the fragmentation of the Empire had already started, and the mutinous local monarchs (including the Poles) were striving for independence from the old rulers of the Horde in Moscow.

5.

The reaction of the Russian nobility to the introduction of the Scaligerian version of the "ancient" history in the XVIII century

R. K. Almayev was kind enough to point out to us a number of curious facts contained in the article of V. V. Dementyeva entitled "Charles Rolain's 'Roman History' as read by a Russian nobleman" published in a special scientific periodical entitled "Vestnik Drevney Istorii" ("Ancient History Courier," [238]).

V. V. Dementyeva tells us the following: "The collection of the State Archive of the Yaroslavl Oblast includes the manuscript entitled 'A Critique of the New Book of 1761 on the Origins of Rome and the Deeds of that Monarchy's Nations.' It contains 47 sheets, whose reverse sides are also covered in writing, or 94 pages... The reverse of the last sheet says: 'Critique by Pyotr Nikiforov of the Krekshin family. 30 September 1762, St. Petersburg'" ([238], page 117). The item number of the chronicle in the State Archive of the Yaroslavl Oblast is 43 (431); see [238].

P. N. Krekshin (1684-1763) had been a prominent government official from the epoch of Peter the Great. In particular, he had "kept the journal of Peter the Great, and sorted through the Czar's papers after Peter's death" ([238], page 119). He had also supervised the works in Kronstadt ([238], page 117). "Krekshin retired in 1726, after the death of Peter the Great, and started to write his works on history, predominantly Russian history" ([238], page 118). The historical oeuvres of P. N. Krekshin were used by such famed Russian historians as V. O. Klyuchevskiy, I. I. Boltin, M. M. Shcherbatov and V. N. Tatishchev ([238], page 118).

After the death of Krekshin, Empress Catherine the Great demanded "to see some of his chronicles, as well as the papers that had belonged to Krekshin, which she studied with great interest; she decided to keep some of them at her disposal" ([238], page 119).

All of the above demonstrates that Krekshin had been a very prominent figure in that epoch, and that his historical works had been followed with great interest. The entire archive of Krekshin was purchased in 1791, after his death, by Count A. I. Moussin-Pushkin, a famous collector" ([238], page 118).

What does Krekshin write in his critique of the "New Book of 1761 on the Origins of Rome"? It has to be emphasised that the book of C. Rolain, a French historian, had been among the first books on the new Scaligerian history published in Russian. It is reported that "the works of Rolain and Crevier had been the first modern textbooks on the ancient history" ([238], page 119).

V. V. Dementyeva tells us further:

"The primary disagreement between P. N. Krekshin and C. Rolain had concerned the claim made by the latter about the invincibility of Rome...

The critique cites a great many sources – Joseph Flavius, Pliny, Tacitus, Ovid, Plutarch, Strabon and Herodotus, as well as the 'Babylonian Chronicle' of Beros and so on... Which nation had been the conqueror of Rome, making her army and her emperors tremble? Krekshin ... claims that Romans had always been defeated by the Slavs, or the Russians. His postulations are as follows:
- 'The Slavs are known as the Muscovites (after Prince Mosokh)',
- the Russians ('named after Prince Ross'),
- 'the same nation is known as the Scythians, named thus after Prince Skif',
- 'under Prince Sarmat they were known as Sarmatians',
- 'the same nation is known as the Goths (after Prince Gott)',
- 'the Vandals are the very same nation',
- 'likewise the Varangians.'

Other names were also used, and all of them identify as 'the Slavic Russian nation as described above....' The rendition of the defeats of Rome is as follows:

- 'In the reign of Augustus Caesar, the Slavic Goths devastated the neighbouring provinces of the Roman Empire';
- 'Attila, Czar of the Huns, known as the Scourge of the Lord, from the land of Russia...';
- 'Odoacer, the Russian Czar, gained control over Italy', etc." ([238], page 120).

Basically, P. N. Krekshin fully confirms our reconstruction of history, Russian as well as international, despite the fact that he uses the erroneous Scaligerian datings. However, Krekshin isn't familiar with the Millerian and Romanovian version of the Russian history, since it was still in the making around the time that he wrote his critique. Millerian and Romanovian history strictly forbids any recollections of the fact that the "ancient" Rome, or Russia as the Horde in the XIV-XVI century, had existed simultaneously with the Muscovite Kingdom of Russian in the Middle Ages. However, this restriction does not apply to Krekshin, despite the fact that he had already been taught the Scaligerian chronology; this is why Russian history stretches far back into the "antiquity."

Could all of the above be seen as nothing else but a personal opinion of Krekshin – wishful thinking, inability to grasp certain details and so on? After all, people's opinions differ greatly. Not remotely so – V. V. Dementyeva reports the most amazing fact. Apparently, "Krekshin's knowledge of ancient history had corresponded to the general level of knowledge in that epoch... Ancient studies as a discipline of the Russian historical science have only existed since the end of the XVIII century" ([238], page 121). Apparently, the studies were conducted even before that, but had not been "scientific" enough. It is quite obvious that the term "scientific" is only used by the modern historians in reference to the works of the Millerian and Scaligerian school.

V. V. Dementyeva enquires rhetorically whether the critique of Krekshin "reflected the level of historical knowledge as it was in the middle of the XVIII century," and answers that it "most definitely did" ([238], page 121). In other words, Krekshin's views were generally shared by the educated part of the Russian society.

We see that up until the end of the XVIII century, the Russians had adhered to the very version of Russian history rendered by Krekshin. This is in perfect concurrence with our reconstruction.

It was only by the end of the XVIII century that the Scaligerian and Millerian version became consensual in Russia as well, and after much effort at that.

Nowadays the Millerian and Romanovian version of the XVIII century is already treated as the only one possible – it is presumed to have existed since time immemorial as a common and obvious chronological system. Obvious to the extent that any piece of information that contradicts it is automatically declared absurd.

However, history is a historical science and has no room for dogma. Every scientific postulation requires proof, or at least some validation if the issue at hand is too complex. If the Russian society had an altogether different notion of history in the middle of the XVIII century, what argumentation do modern historians cite in order to prove that the XVIII century Russians had "thoroughly failed" to understand their own history? The alleged "absurdist concept of Russian history" adhered to by the educated Russians in the XVIII century seems highly implausible.

Modern chronological research leads us to another recollection of the forgotten XVIII century disputes, which had been won by the Scaligerian and Millerian school. However, nowadays it turns out that the consensual version contains tremendous contradictions – it is erroneous through and through. On the other hand, it turns out that the Russian concept of history in its XVII-XVIII century form, which was ruthlessly suppressed in the course of introducing the Scaligerian history, is correct in many instances.

6.

Vehement opposition encountered by the proponents of Romanovian and Millerian history in the XVIII century. Lomonosov and Miller

In Chapter 1 of *The Issue with Russian History* (Book 7 of the present series) we emphasise the amazing fact that the consensual version of Russian history was created in the XVIII century, and by foreigners exclusively – namely, the Germans Miller, Bayer, Schlezer, etc. One must naturally wonder about the Russian scientists and the part they played in this process. How could the educated Russian society permit such a blatant intrusion into a matter as important for the science and culture of Russia as its own history? A foreigner would obviously find it much harder to study Russian history than a Russian.

It would therefore be expedient to remove the veil from the almost forgotten history of acute conflicts amongst the academicians of the XVIII century that were concerned with Russian history. Let us turn to a book by M. T. Belyavskiy entitled *M. V. Lomonosov and the Foundation of the Moscow University*, which was published by the Moscow State University in 1955 to commemorate its 200th anniversary and is rather hard to find these days ([60]). It turns out that the battle for Russian history had been one of the most important ones in the course of struggle for the right of the Russian society to have a science of its own in the XVIII century, which had been in mortal danger. Russian scientists were led by M. V. Lomonosov (see fig. 14.143). Their foreign opponents, eager to suppress the Russian scientific school and enjoying direct support of the Romanovian imperial court, were led by the historian Miller, whose portrait can be seen in Chapter 1 of *Chron1*.

In 1749-1750 Lomonosov stood up against the version of Russian history that was being whipped up by Miller and Bayer in his plain eyesight ([60], page 60). He criticised the freshly published dissertation of Miller entitled *On the Origins of the Russian Nation and its Name*. Lomonosov made the following scalding comment in re Miller's works on the history of Russia: "I believe that he greatly resembles some pagan priest, who puts himself in a trance by burning noxious herbs and spinning

Fig. 14.143. A portrait of Mikhail Vassilyevich Lomonosov. Taken from [60], page 3.

around on one leg and makes obscure, unintelligible, dubious and outright preposterous readings" (quoting according to [60], page 60). This is how an all-out war for Russian history began.

"This is the time when historical issues became just as important for Lomonosov as his natural scientific studies. Furthermore, in the 1750's humanities become the crux of Lomonosov's studies, with an emphasis made on history. He is even forced to lay down his responsibilities of a professor of chemistry… In his correspondence with Shouvalov he refers to his works entitled 'On the Impostors and the Mutinies of the Royal Marksmen', 'On the State of Affairs in Russia during the Reign of Czar Mikhail Fyodorovich', 'A Brief Account of the Czar's Deeds' [Peter the Great – M. B.] and 'Notes on the Deeds of the Monarch.' However, neither these works, nor the numerous documents that Lomonosov had intended for publication as appendices, nor the preliminary research materials, nor the manuscripts of the second and third part of the first volume [of Lomonosov's work under the title of *The Ancient History of Russia* – Auth.] have survived until our age. They were confiscated and vanished without a trace" ([60], page 63).

The first part of *The Ancient History of Russia* did get published nevertheless; however, the history of its publication is bizarre to the extreme: "The publication would be held back in a variety of ways. It commenced in 1758; however, the book only came out after the death of Lomonosov" ([60], page 63). Seven years later at least, that is, since Lomonosov died in 1765. Considering the violent strife around the issue, it is likely that the book that came out under Lomonosov's name has got very little in common with his original work. At best, it was heavily expurgated and edited, if not re-written from scratch. This is all the more plausible since a similar thing happened to the works of the Russian historian Tatishchev around the same time, q.v. in *Chron4*, Chapter 1. Those were published by Miller after Tatishchev's death and based upon some mysterious "drafts" of the latter. The original of Tatishchev's work vanished without a trace. Who could have stopped the victorious Miller from publishing a distorted version of Lomonosov's works if the Romanovs had given him full control over Russian history? One must say that the very method of "caringly" publishing the works of one's opponent after his death is very characteristic for the battles fought over Russian history in that epoch, which had been anything by an abstract academic matter then. The Romanovs needed a distorted version of Russian history, likewise the monarchs of the Western Europe. The publications of Tatishchev's and Lomonosov's works on Russian history known to us today are most likely to be forgeries, q.v. below.

Let us return to the earliest stages of the opposition between Lomonosov and Miller. German historians decided to oust Lomonosov and his supporters from the Academy of Sciences. This "scientific activity" was conducted in Russia as well as abroad, since Lomonosov had been famous internationally. All possible means were used for compromising the scientist's reputation and his works – not just the historical ones, but also those concerned with natural sciences, where his authority had been immense (in particular, Lomonosov had been member of several foreign academies – the Academy of Sweden since 1756 and the Academy of Bologna since 1764" ([60], page 94).

"In Germany Miller would incite public speeches against the discoveries made by Lomonosov, demanding the latter to be expelled from the Academy" ([60], page 61). He didn't succeed then; however, the opponents of Lomonosov managed to get Schlezer appointed Academician of Russian History ([60], page 64). "Schlezer would call Lomonosov ... a 'total ignoramus who knew nothing but whatever was written in his chronicles'" ([60], page 64). Lomonosov was accused of being well familiar with the Russian chronicles, no less!

"Despite all of Lomonosov's objections, Catherine II had appointed Schlezer Academician. Not only did he obtain full control over all the documents kept in the Academy in this manner, but was also granted the right to demand any document he needed from the Imperial library and other institutions. Another right given to Schlezer was that of presenting his works to Catherine directly... After this appointment, Lomonosov wrote the following in a bitter and enraged 'memorandum' of his that accidentally eschewed confiscation: 'There is nothing left to preserve. The madman Schlezer can access anything. There are more secret materials in the Russian National Library'" ([60], page 65).

Miller and his clique were in full control of both the University of St. Petersburg and the gymnasium that prepared university students. The Gymnasium was presided over by Miller, Bayer and Fisher ([60], page 77). "The teachers of the gymnasium spoke no Russian ... the students didn't speak any German. All the studies were conducted in Latin exclusively. Over the thirty years of its existence (1726-1755), the Gymnasium didn't prepare a single university student" (*ibid.*). This had led to the claim that "the only solution would be to bring students over from Germany, since the Russians were allegedly unable to learn" (*ibid.*). Indeed – a savage and illiterate country.

"Lomonosov found himself in the thick of the battle... A. K. Nartov, a prominent Russian engineer who had worked at the Academy, registered an official complaint with the Senate, which was also signed by Russian students, translators and chancellery workers, as well as the astronomer Delisle. Their objective was crystal clear – to stop the Russian Academy of Sciences from being only nominally Russian... The commission gathered by the Senate to study the accusations made by the scholars ended up with Prince Yousoupov as its chairman... The commission had decided that A. Nartov, I. V. Gorlitskiy, P. Shishkaryov, V. Nosov, A. Polyakov, M. Kovrin, Lebedev and their supporters were nothing but ... 'hoi polloi bold enough to rebel against their superiors'" ([60], page 82).

One must say that A. K. Nartov had been a prominent specialist in his field – "the creator of the first mechanical support, an invention that had revolutionised engineering" ([60], page 83). "A. K. Nartov had been an eminent Russian engineer and inventor. His name is associated with the most revolutionary inventions in civil and military engineering... In 1741 Nartov invented a high-speed cannon battery, which is now kept in the Historical Museum of Artillery in St. Petersburg. It consists of 44 small mortars... The mortars would fire one after another, as soon as the fire from a burning gunpowder trail or cord would reach the fuse" ([264], Book 2, page 700). A portrait of A. K. Nartov can be seen in fig. 14.144, and his high-speed cannon is shown in fig. 14.145.

The Russian scientists wrote the following to the Senate: "We have proven our accusations for the first eight points, and we shall prove them for the remaining thirty if we get access to archives"

Fig. 14.144. A. K. Nartov, around 1725. Taken from [264], Book 2, page 699.

Fig. 14.145. The rapid-firing battery cannon of A. K. Nartov. Taken from [264], Book 2, page 700.

([60], page 82). "However ... they were arrested for 'stubborn persistence' and 'insulting the commission.' Some of them were chained and incarcerated, refusing to take any of their accusations back after two years of remaining in this condition. The verdict of the commission was nothing short of the most hideous atrocity – Schumacher and Taubert are to be decorated, Gorlitskiy is to be executed, Grekov, Polyakov and Nosov are to be ruthlessly switched and exiled to

Siberia, while Popov, Shishkaryov and others should remain under arrest until the solution of the matter by the next president of the Academy.

Formally, Lomonosov had not been included in the group of scientists who filed a complaint against Schumacher; however, his behaviour during the process demonstrates that Miller had hardly been errant with his claim that 'adjunct Lomonosov had been among the miscreants who filed a complaint against Council member Schumacher and instigated the creation of the prosecution committee.' Lamanskiy, who claimed Nartov's complaint to have been written by Lomonosov for the most part, must also have been close to the truth. Lomonosov had remained a keen supported of Nartov for the whole time that the commission was active... This is the reason for his violent clashes with some of Schumacher's most industrious minions, such as Winzheim, Truscott and Miller, as well as the entire academic conference... The commission was enraged by Lomonosov's behaviour and arrested him... The report of the commission that was presented to Yelizaveta hardly mentions Schumacher at all; its leitmotivs are the 'ignorance and incapacity' of Nartov and the 'affronting behaviour' of Lomonosov. The commission claimed that Lomonosov was to be punished by death, or at least switching, voidance of all rights and confiscation of property for 'numerous discourteous, dishonourable and vile deeds against the academy, the commission and the German land.' Lomonosov had awaited the verdict for seven months, remaining under arrest... Yelizaveta's edict pronounced him guilty; however, he was made 'exempt from punishment' in order to 'learn a lesson.' However, his salary was halved, and he was made apologise to the professors 'for his horrendous boldness'... Miller had compiled a mocking 'Note of Apology', which Lomonosov had to read and sign in public... This was the first and only time that Lomonosov had to renounce his views in public" ([60], pages 82-84).

The struggle continued until the very death of Lomonosov. "Owing to Lomonosov's efforts, several Russian academicians and adjuncts appeared in the Academy" ([60], page 90). However, "in 1763, after the delation made by Taubert, Miller, Schtelin, Epinous et al, Catherine altogether expelled Lomonosov from the Academy" ([60], page 94). However, the edict about his ousting was soon revoked due to the popularity of Lomonosov in Russia and the acknowledgement of his work by foreign academies (*ibid.*). Nevertheless, Lomonosov was relieved from being head of the Department of Geography and replaced by Miller. There was also an attempt to "hand all of Lomonosov's materials on language and history over to Schlezer" (*ibid.*).

This last piece of information is very significant indeed. If there were attempts to get hold of Lomonosov's archive while he was alive, the fate of this unique collection after his death must have been sealed. As one should expect, Lomonosov's archive was immediately confiscated after his death, and disappears without a trace. "Lomonosov's archive, confiscated by Catherine II, is lost to us forever. The day after his death the library of Lomonosov and all of his papers were rounded up by Count Orlov at the order of Catherine and taken to his palace, which is where they vanished for good" ([60], page 20). A letter of Taubert to Miller has survived, wherein "Taubert reports the death of Lomonosov without bothering to hide his glee, and also says: 'The next day after his death Count Orlov ordered for seals to be put on the doors of his study. It must doubtlessly contain papers that they wish to keep from falling into the wrong hands'" (ibid.).

Apparently, Miller and Schlezer, the "creators of Russian history" managed to lay their hands on the archives of Lomonosov. The archives naturally disappeared as a result. However, seven years later Lomonosov's work on Russian history was published – obviously under total control of Miller and Schlezer, and just the first volume, which must have been re-written by Miller in the manner that he saw fit. The other volumes have "disappeared" – apparently, they were too laborious to process. This is how it came to pass that "Lomonosov's work on history" that we have at our disposal today is, oddly and mysteriously, in total correspondence with the Millerian version of history. One wonders why Lomonosov needed to argue with Miller with such passion and for so many years, accusing him of falsifying the Russian history ([60], page 62), when he so complacently agrees with Miller in every instant in the very book that he is supposed to have published himself, obsequiously agreeing with him throughout the entire text?

We are of the following opinion. The book that came out under Lomonosov's name has got nothing in common with the one that he had actually written. One must think that Miller had greatly enjoyed re-writing the first volume after Lomonosov's death – "diligently preparing it for publication," and destroying the rest. One can certainly tell there were many interesting facts related in the original – something neither Miller, nor Schlezer, nor indeed any other "Russian historian" could bear to see published.

7.
Lomonosov's *History of Russia*: authenticity issue. Lomonosov or Miller?

By A. T. Fomenko, N. S. Kellin and G. V. Nosovskiy

Above we have voiced the hypotheses that the text known as the *Ancient History of Russia* today and attributed to Mikhail Vassily-evich Lomonosov, which came out several years after the death of the author, is either a complete forgery, or a substantially distorted version of M. V. Lomonosov's authentic work on Russian history. We have also made the assumption that the author of the falsification can be identified as G. F. Miller personally, or one of his assistants carrying out his orders.

It has to be pointed out that the manuscript of the *Ancient History of Russia*, which could have served as proof of its authenticity, has not survived ([493]). Seven years after the death of M. V. Lomonosov, his oeuvre on Russian history was finally published, but only its first volume – the rest have gone missing. The publication is most likely to have been supervised by Miller, which leads us to the suspicion that it is in fact a forgery. Firstly, Lomonosov's *Ancient History of Russia* is miraculously in perfect correspondence with the Mille-rian version of history. Secondly, the disappearance of the second volume and the rest of them is very conspicuous – it is unlikely that the discrepancies between the versions of Lomonosov and Miller only started to manifest from the second volume on. One gets the suspicion that Miller just made a falsified version of the first volume and destroyed the rest, his possible motivation being the desire to reduce the amount of labour involved in the hoax.

The hypothesis about Lomonosov's *Ancient History of Russia* being a forgery is verified in the present work with the use of the authorial invariant method, as discovered and developed by V. P. Fomenko and T. G. Fomenko, q.v. in Annex 3 to *Chron2*. We come up with the following results.

1) We have compared the authorial invariant values of the *Ancient History of Russia* with those of Lomonosov's works whose authentic originals are still in existence. The results confirm the hypothesis that the *Ancient History of Russia*, ascribed to Lomonosov today, is a forgery. The hypothesis can therefore be considered proven.

2) We have come up with similar authorial invariant values for the *Ancient History of Russia* and the texts of G. F. Miller ([529]). This fact confirms the assumption that Miller had taken part in the falsification, although it does not prove it.

We are thus faced with the following problem. Is it true that the book published under Lomonosov's name and entitled *The Ancient History of Russia* is substantially different from Lomonosov's actual original? If it is, who was responsible for the falsification?

The solution of this problem can be approached with the use of the method developed in [893] and [METH2]:2, pages 743-778. The method allows to identify the author of a text to some extent, and is based on the authorial invariant algorithm discovered by V. P. Fomenko and T. G. Fomenko, q.v. in *Chron2*, Annex 3. The invariant turns out to be defined as the frequency of function word usage. The calculation of this frequency gives us an opportunity to expose plagiarisms and find authors with similar styles.

Let us briefly explain the readers just what it is that we're referring to presently. The "authorial invariants" of literary works might prove a valuable tool for the solution and research of the authorship problems. Under an authorial invariant we understand a numeric parameter related to the text in question whose value can unambiguously characterise the texts of a single author or a small group of authors, but changes significantly in cases of texts written by different groups of authors. It is desirable to have a large amount of such groups, and to have fewer "similar" authors in a single group as compared to the total amount of authors under study.

Numeric experiments demonstrate that the discovery of numeric characteristics that allow to distinguish between the texts of different authors without ambiguity is anything but an easy task. The matter is that the creation of a narrative text is also affected by factors that can be regulated consciously. For instance, the usage frequency of rare and foreign words characteristic for a given author may reflect the author's erudition to some extent; however, this is a factor that can easily be controlled by the author, which renders this characteristic unusable as an authorial invariant ([893]; see also [Meth2]:2, pages 743-778, and *Chron2*, Annex 3).

Some of the complications also stem from the fact that many numeric characteristics of texts are extremely sensitive to a change of style in the works of one and the same author, namely, they attain significantly different values for the texts written by the author in different periods. Therefore, the estimation of a given author's unique characteristic is quite complex, especially if we want to assess these individual parameters quantitatively. The characteristic that we search needs to satisfy to the following conditions.

1) It needs to be very "general" in order to be beyond the conscious control of an author – in other words, the characteristic needs to manifest as an "unconscious parameter."

2) It needs to be stable for every author, which means that is can only possess a small deviation from some average value, which always remains the same, fluctuating very slightly from text to text.

3) It must be applicable for distinction between several groups of authors – in other words, we need different groups of authors for which the discrepancies between the values of this characteristic are greater than those found within the texts of a single author.

After V. P. Fomenko and T. G. Fomenko had conducted an extensive calculation experiment, it turned out that the numeric parameter of texts that satisfies to the conditions listed above is the relative usage frequency of all function words in the text – prepositions, conjunctions and particles, q.v. in figs. 14.146-14.149 ([893] and [909]). As one proceeds along the text using 16,000 word samples, the function word usage frequency turns out to be more or less constant for all the works of a given author. In other words, the curve that represents the evolution of said frequency becomes an almost even horizontal line. Minimal and maximal values were taken for every author under study; therefore, the parameter in question is useful for distinguishing between various authors. This is why it

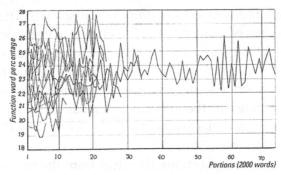

Fig. 14.146. The behaviour of the parameter – function word percentage for 2000-word samples. One sees the resulting curves to be chaotic.

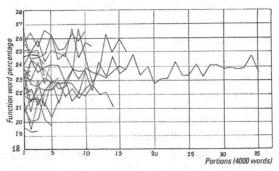

Fig. 14.147. The behaviour of the parameter – function word percentage for 4000-word samples. The curves remain chaotic, but there is a tendency for them to become more even.

was called the authorial invariant. It can be used for attributing anonymous texts as well as hunting out plagiarisms – albeit with a certain degree of caution, since some authors may possess similar invariant values (Fonvizin and Tolstoy, for instance). Moreover, reliable statistical conclusions require the use of voluminous works.

The last condition is met in the case of Lomonosov and Miller. Both have works that can be used for many consecutive 16,000 word samples. The applicability requirements are therefore met for the two authors. Our application of the authorial invariant method in the present case had been as follows.

STEP 1. We have considered all available works of M. V. Lomonosov, whose authentic manuscripts written in his own handwriting are still in existence. Out of those we have selected the ones that contain a required volume of text in words.

50

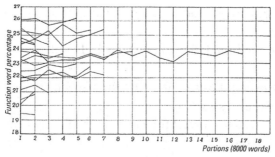

Fig. 14.148. The behaviour of the parameter – function word percentage for 8000-word samples. The curves still intersect occasionally, but they are getting more and more even.

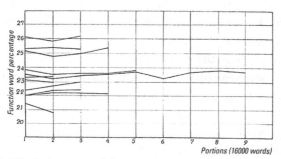

Fig. 14.149. The behaviour of the parameter – function word percentage for 16000-word samples. The curves transformed into more or less straight lines, which means the parameter has stabilised, with significant discrepancies between its value for different authors. The parameter is therefore a "good" one, it is an authorial invariant and can be used for telling different authors apart.

STEP 2. We have calculated the authorial invariant for M. V. Lomonosov, or the evolution of function word percentage, using the method laid out in [893], [909], [Meth2]:2, pages 743-778, and *Chron2*, Annex 3.

STEP 3. Next we calculated the authorial invariant for the *Ancient History of Russia* ascribed to Lomonosov nowadays. The volume of text suffices for the authorial invariant calculations.

STEP 4. We have studied all available works by G. F. Miller. We only specify the ones that contain a sufficient volume of Russian text.

STEP 5. The abovementioned method was then used for calculating the authorial invariant of G. F. Miller, or the evolution of the function word percentage.

51

STEP 6. Finally, we compared the invariant values yielded by our calculations.

We have used the following texts of G. F. Miller as published in [529]:

1) "On Reverend Nestor, the First Russian Chronicler, his chronicles and his successors."

2) "A Proposal to Correct the Errors of the Foreign Authors Writing about Russia."

3) "A Description of Maritime Voyages into the East Sea and the Arctic Ocean Made by the Russians."

4) "News about the Latest Maritime Voyages into the Arctic See and the Kamchatka Sea, Starting with 1743, or the End of the Second Expedition to Kamchatka. From the reign history of the Great Empress Catherine the Second."

5) "On the [Russian] Nobility."

6) "[A Description of towns and cities in the Muscovite province]."

7) "Biography and Reign History of Fyodor Alexeyevich."

8) "[Project to create a historical department of the Academy]."

9) "Important Things and Difficulties Encountered in the Compilation of the Russian History."

10) "An Instruction to the Translator Andreyan Doubrovskiy."

11) "Selected Correspondence."

Only the texts 3-7 possess a sufficient volume of over 16,000 words. Moreover, one needs to leave out the works that weren't originally written in Russian, and may have been translated by someone other than Miller. It applies to work #6; the description of Kolomna is rendered in German. Also, work #6 contains many tables, which complicate the calculations. Works 3 and 4 contain a great number of numeric data, which also complicate the calculations. Text #7 contains many tables and numbers; moreover, we had it rendered in a number of different formats, which is a purely technical complication. This text was also discarded.

We have therefore based our research on text #5. Its volume is over 16.000 words. We have excluded the part of the book that consists of a multitude of tables, namely, pages 197-206. The materials we did process therefore amount to pages 180-197 (beginning of the text before the tables), and pages 206-225 (end of text after tables). Page numeration is given in accordance with [529].

The result of our research is as follows: the authorial invariant of Miller equals 28 per cent.

We must make the following important statement. This invariant value is exceptionally large, q.v. in fig. 14.149. It is the largest of all the invariants calculated for the authors whose texts were analysed in [893] and [909] – see *Chron3*, Annex 3.

Now let us calculate the authorial invariant for M. V. Lomonosov. We have studied the following works by this author:

1) "A Description of the Marksmen's Mutinies and the Reign of Czarina Sofia.

2) "A Brief Account of the Academic Chancellery's History in the Words of the Wise and the Deeds – from the beginning of the present corpus and until our day."

3) "The Ancient History of Russia from the Origins of the Russian Nation to the Death of Great Prince Yaroslav I in 1054, Written by Mikhail Lomonosov, State Council Member, Professor of Chemistry and Member of the Imperial Academy of Sciences in St. Petersburg and the Swedish Royal Academy of Sciences."

Other 44 texts of M. V. Lomonosov published in [493], but we didn't take them into account for various reasons – the ones we listed above for Miller's texts, as well as the fact that about a third of them are written as poetry and not prose. Let us explain that the authorial invariant can only be applied with confidence to prose. The rejection of many other texts is explained by the fact that their originals have not survived until our day, which is the case with the *Ancient History of Russia* that we're concerned with presently; therefore, one cannot be quite certain about attributing them to M. V. Lomonosov. As a result, we ended up with work #2, which meets all the conditions listed above.

The result of the calculation is as follows. The authorial invariant of Lomonosov in work #2 equals 20-21 per cent. This is a very small value of the authorial invariant, and corresponds to the lowest threshold of invariant value if we're to consider all the authors that we have researched (see fig. 14.149).

We see something totally different in case of the *Ancient History of Russia* (work #3). The authorial invariant proved very unstable here – in some samples it equals 27 per cent, whereas in others the amount is 25 per cent. No discrepancies this large have ever been witnessed in case of any text that would belong to the same author. The authorial invariant values for the *Ancient History of Russia* are scattered between 24 and 27 per cent.

The strong fluctuation of the authorial invariant values that we see here implies that work #2 and work #3 listed under Lomonosov's name belong to different authors. However, in case of work #2, the authorship of Lomonosov is indisputable, since it still exists as a manuscript set in Lomonosov's own handwriting. This means that the *Ancient History of Russia* was not written by M. V. Lomonosov. Also, the invariant values for the *Ancient Russian History* ascribed to Lomonosov is in ideal correspondence with the value discovered for the works of G. F. Miller. Strictly speaking, this is not yet sufficient proof that Lomonosov's history was falsified by Miller in particular, since several different authors may possess similar or even identical invariant values ([893]). We have only proven the fact that the work in question is a forgery.

However, previous results make Miller a very likely candidate for having falsified Lomonosov's work on Russian history, all the more so considering that the invariant values of Miller's texts and those of the *Ancient History of Russia* ascribed to Lomonosov are very rare among the Russian authors, q.v. in *Chron2*, Annex 3. This makes chance coincidence between the invariant values for Miller and the hypothetical falsifier of Lomonosov's *Ancient History* a lot less likely, and makes Miller the most conspicuous suspect.

The unnatural invariant value aberration range of the *Ancient History* is therefore explained in a very simple manner. The falsifier had used Lomonosov's original text as a basis. Apparently, the distortion of the original in the process of re-writing was uneven, hence the erratic fluctuations of the invariant and the abnormality of their range.

Let us also emphasise that the authorial invariant values for the *Ancient History of Russia* are drastically different from what we see in case of Lomonosov's authentic works, namely, the fluctuation range equals 3-4 per cent, whereas it is normally confined within the limits of one per cent in the texts of a single author ([803]). It becomes quite obvious that the published version of the *Ancient History of Russia* contains very little of the original text – it is a forgery for the most part.

COROLLARY 1. It has turned out that the authorial invariant of the *Ancient History of Russia* confirms our hypothesis about the original text of Lomonosov's history becoming greatly distorted – virtually written anew before the publication that took place seven years after the death of M. V. Lomonosov.

COROLLARY 2. We have discovered the authorial invariant of the *Ancient History of Russia* to be very close to that of G. F. Miller, a prime suspect for the falsification of the book. This doesn't yet prove that Lomonosov's *History* was corrupted by Miller – we know of texts written by different authors a priori, whose authorial invariants are nonetheless similar to one another (I. S. Tourgenev and L. N. Tolstoy, for instance, q.v. in [893] and [909]). However, in the present case, given the long and arduous struggle between Lomonosov and Miller, the discovery of similar authorial invariants in Miller's text and the *Ancient History of Russia* is most likely to indicate that it was none other but G. F. Miller who had either radically edited or completely falsified the text of M. V. Lomonosov's *History*.

8.
Foreign eyewitnesses of the XVI century located Novgorod the Great on River Volga

Our reconstruction as related above suggests that Novgorod the Great as described in Russian chronicles can identify as either the city of Yaroslavl on the Volga, or a group of famous Russian cities around Yaroslavl. A. I. Karagodov and V. P. Cherepanov from the Saratov State University of Technical Sciences, pointed out to us some direct proof of our reconstruction that has survived in mediaeval texts of the XVI century. Apparently, Taube and Kruse, the presumed eyewitnesses of the events that took place in the epoch of the oprichnina, made direct references to the fact that Novgorod the Great stood on River Volga. We are quoting a passage from [117]:

"Foreign chroniclers and historians of the epoch [the alleged XVI century – Auth.] painted a horrible and repulsive picture of the Oprichnina and its creator [Ivan the Terrible – Auth.]. However, can one really trust the evidence of Taube and Kruse? In their account of the Novgorod murders they locate the city on the banks of the Volga as eyewitnesses of said events" ([117], page 287).

We see that the author, a historian of the Scaligerian school, urges the reader to distrust Taube and Kruse, citing their claim about Novgorod the Great located on the banks of the Volga, which naturally contradicts the Scaligerian and Romanovian history, as an argument. However, this report of Taube and Kruse is in ideal concurrence with our reconstruction. It has fortunately evaded the attention of the Romanovian editors in the XVII-XVIII century, who were very diligent in their attempts to remove every truthful evidence from the annals of Russian history.

By the way, one has no reason at all to doubt the competence of Taube and Kruse, who were well aware of what they wrote about. They weren't mere eyewitnesses of the events that took place in Novgorod on the Volga. It turns out that they were made members of the Oprichnina by Ivan IV: "The Czar didn't just protect the heretics, but also made some of them very close to himself. He made ... I. Taube and E. Kruse members of the Oprichnina" ([775], pages 281-282). One must assume that Taube and Kruse had been well aware of the location of Novgorod, which was destroyed by Ivan IV ("The Terrible").

9.

The Alexandrovskaya Sloboda
as the capital of Russia, or the Horde,
in the XVI century

In *Chron6* we demonstrate that the Muscovite Kremlin, likewise other constructions of Moscow as a capital city, were built in the second half of the XVI century the earliest. We have dated the foundation of the Kremlin in Moscow to the epoch of the Oprichnina, identifying the construction of the city as the famous foundation of Ivan's capital in the epoch of the Oprichnina. We have made the assumption that the royal procession only stopped temporarily in the famous Alexandrovskaya Sloboda en route from Suzdal to Moscow. We must also remind the reader that the Biblical city of Souza is most likely to identify as Suzdal, q.v. in *Chron6*. A further study of the issue revealed the fact that the picture must have been of even greater interest to us as researchers.

It is assumed that the Alexandrovskaya Sloboda (the modern town of Alexandrov in the Vladimir Oblast) had been the capital of Russia in the full meaning of the word for some 20 years, starting with the beginning of the Oprichnina epoch in 1563 ([12], page 17). This appears to be true. Sources report that a luxurious palace complex with a number of secondary constructions had been erected in the Alexandrovskaya Sloboda: "The Czar's court in the Sloboda included the palaces of the Czar and the noblemen, likewise auxiliary constructions, the royal garden, a unique system of ponds and locks, which had served the purpose of filling the moat with water. State services of all sorts were active in the Alexandrovskaya Sloboda, including the Duma of the Oprichnina, the royal court, diplomatic offices and the Ministry of Foreign Relations" ([11], page 7). Apparently, "the best icon artists and builders lived and worked here; they built a magnificent ensemble of palaces and temples, second only to the Muscovite Kremlin in its splendour" ([11], page 5). As we realise today, things are likely to have happened in a different order – the capital in the Alexandrovskaya Sloboda predated the Kremlin, which was built in its image somewhat later, in the XVI century.

The Alexandrovskaya Sloboda had been the place where the Czar met foreign envoys; this fact became reflected in the memoirs of Ulfeldt, the Danish Ambassador, dating to the XVII century: "The impressions of the Alexandrovskaya Sloboda and the Russian Czar (the "cruel Pharaoh") were reflected in the ambassador's book entitled 'A Voyage to Russia of Jacob Ulfeldt, the Danish Envoy'" ([11], page 9). A propos, the fact that the Danish ambassador calls the Russian Czar Pharaoh isn't a mere literary comparison – the Czar had indeed been the Egyptian Pharaoh as described in the Bible; some parts of the Bible were written in this very epoch, q.v. in *Chron6*. The chronicles of the epoch appear to have called used the term "Egyptian Alexandria" for referring to his capital in the Alexandrovskaya Sloboda. The memories of the Library of Alexandria appear to date to the very same epoch, referring to the library of the Alexandrovskaya Sloboda, or the famous library of Ivan the Terrible ([11], page 6). In this case, the demise of the famous "ancient" Library of Alexandria in a blaze might be a legendary reflection of the real destruction of the Alexandrovskaya Sloboda by the Romanovs in the epoch of the XVII century: "During the Great Strife, the palace ensemble was destroyed and pillaged" ([11], page 11). Nowadays, the territory of the former Alexandrovskaya Sloboda is occupied by the Svyato-Ouspenskiy nunnery.

A propos, it is presumed that "prince Ivan [the son of Ivan "The Terrible" – Auth.] died in the Alexandrovskaya Sloboda after a mortal wound inflicted by the Czar in a fit of rage" ([12], page 16). It is further presumed that "the Czar departed from the Alexandrovskaya Sloboda as a result of his elder son's death" ([11], page 11). It is also possible that some of the events reflected in the Biblical book of Esther took place right here, in the Alexandrovskaya Sloboda, in the XVI century, q.v. in *Chron6*.

Modern historians are confronted with the necessity to explain why the capital of Russia was in the Alexandrovskaya Sloboda and not Moscow. They write the following: "Another paradox is that the Oprichnina Court in Moscow, which was constructed in the first months that had followed February, 1565 ... had been an affiliate of the Oprichnina capital, or the Alexandrovskaya Sloboda, in general. All the governing functions became concentrated in the Alexandrovskaya Sloboda towards the autumn of 1565... Starting with 1568, the royal scribes and the publishing house became concentrated here" ([12], page 16; also [11], page 6). Apart from the publication of books, this was also the place where they cast bells" ([11]). And so on, and so forth. Historians "explain" it suggesting that Ivan the Terrible had been an eccentric tyrant, who had decided to transfer the court to the Alexandrovskaya Sloboda from Moscow. We are of a different opinion, which can be encapsulated as follows. The construction of a capital in Moscow had not yet started by that time. At the very beginning of the Oprichnina epoch, the royal capital of Russia and the headquarters of the Czar, or the Khan, became relocated to Alexandrovskaya Sloboda from Suzdal, or the Biblical Souza, and remained there for some 15 years. It is likely that another transfer of the capital was instigated by Khan Ivan Simeon at the end of the XVI century, after the defeat of the Oprichnina, to move it even further westwards by some 100 kilometres. This is how Moscow was built.

The strife flared up again in the beginning of the XVII century. Moscow fell prey to fire, and the Muscovite Kremlin changed hands a number of times. It is presumed that Moscow had been burnt to the ground. Thus, Moscow was either burnt down completely or at least destroyed to a large extent at the very end of the Great Strife, during the epoch of the interregnum and civil wars of the early XVII century, right before the ascension of the Romanovs. This must have resulted in the destruction of the Muscovite Kremlin. According to I. A. Zabelin, even at the end of Mikhail Romanov's reign, in 1645, "the entire Kremlin lay desolate; many layers of bricks were missing from the wall of the citadel and some of the towers, the walls caved in, and the white stones fell out. The domes of some towers were in a decrepit state, or fell in altogether." The reconstruction of the Kremlin began ([284], page 165).

10.

The counterfeited inscription with the name of the monarch on the alleged portrait of Ivan the Terrible dating from the XVII century

We have encountered many occasions when the Russian historical documents dated to the XVI century nowadays underwent a tendentious editing or became falsified all in all. Our experience of dealing with historical materials left us with the impression that it is very difficult to find authentic artefacts of the XV-XVI century that have survived the Romanovian censorship among the documents available to us today and the objects exhibited in museums. This censorship has left a mark on the artefacts exhibited in the museum of the Alexandrovskaya Sloboda and dated to the XVI century in particular. Among other objects from the museum of the Pokrovskaya Church (XVI-XVII century) and the Dining Hall (XVI century), q.v. in figs. 14.150, 14.151 and 14.152) we see a royal portrait (fig. 14.153). It is presumed to depict Czar Ivan Vassilyevich "The Terrible." Modern historians date this portrait to the end of the XVII or the beginning of the XVIII century ([11], page 4). It is often called a "unique XVII century parsuna" ([11], page 9). Therefore, what we have at our disposal is a very rare image of a Russian autocrat.

At the bottom of the portrait we find an inscription that appears to suggest that the Czar in question is indeed Ivan Vassilyevich. By the way, the photograph of the portrait cited in the album ([11], page 4) leaves the inscription out for some reason – we only see the first line and a part of the second. Is there any reason behind this? Let

Fig. 14.150. The Pokrovskaya Church of the XVI-XVII century and the Dining Hall of the XVI century as parts of the ensemble of the royal palace built in Alexandrovskaya Sloboda by Czar Ivan IV.

us turn to the fundamental edition that tells us about the museum of the Alexandrovskaya Sloboda in detail ([1373]). The very first pages of the book contain a reproduction of this portrait; however, an even greater part of the inscription is left out – we only see a vague outline of the first line, and nothing but.

This detail alone would not have been worthy of our attention, if it hadn't been for the fact that the inscription in question is of the utmost interest. We only realised this upon visiting the museum of the Alexandrovskaya Sloboda. We have photographed the entire inscription, which can be seen in figs. 14.154 and 14.155. As we can see, the following is written on the portrait: "Ivan Vassilyevich, Czar and Great Prince of Russia, the wise and valiant ruler. The Czar had conquered three kingdoms – Astrakhan, Siberia and the Land of the Khazars, making them part of his domain; he had also defeated hosts of the Swedes, and taken much of Russia's land back from them. The first one to be crowned and…"

This is where the text ends abruptly; we see some strange squiggle instead of the remaining phrase. The inscription is very interesting indeed.

Firstly, the Kingdom of Kazan is called the Land of the Khazars, which is in perfect concurrence with our reconstruction, according

Fig. 14.151. The Pokrovskaya Church of the XVI-XVII century and the Dining Hall of the XVI century in Alexandrovskaya Sloboda.

to which the famous "ancient kingdom of the Khazars" identifies as the mediaeval Kingdom of Kazan of the XV-XVI century.

Secondly, it is said that the Czar took "much of Russia's land back" from the Swedes. This should ring very odd if we're to follow the Scaligerian and Millerian history. If the Russian Czar had defeated the Swedes, why does it mean that he had taken "much of Russia's land back"? After all, we were taught that the Western Europe, including Sweden, had never been part of Russia or ruled by the Russian Czars. Our reconstruction makes everything crystal clear – the inscription refers to the events of the XVI century, when the Russian (or Assyrian, according to our reconstruction) Czar, or Khan, described in the Bible as Nebuchadnezzar, managed to partially suppress the mutiny in

Fig. 14.152. The dome of the Pokrovskaya Church. Taken from [1373], pages 68-69.

the western lands of the Great = "Mongolian" Empire, restoring his rule over these territories.

It is also quite obvious that this inscription had somehow failed to please the Romanovian editors of history. The strange squiggle at the end of the phrase obviously replaces an obliterated part of the old text. The last line of the text is likely to have been shorter than the previous ones initially, and placed in the middle, with blank spaces to the left and to the right. The phrase "The first to be crowned and..." obviously ends in an abrupt manner; the conjunction "and" indicates that it had been followed by some phrase, which was ruthlessly rubbed out and replaced by a meaningless squiggle that serves the end of

Fig. 14.153. Royal portrait exhibited in the museum of the Pokrovskaya Church and the Dining Hall of the XVI century in Alexandrovskaya Sloboda. Presumably, a portrait of Ivan Vassilyevich "The Terrible." Taken from [11].

making the text more symmetrical than it would have been otherwise, obviously in order to conceal the introduced alterations.

Fig. 14.154. The legend underneath the portrait of "Ivan Vassilyevich" at the museum of the Pokrovskaya Church and Dining Hall of the XVI century. Photograph taken by the authors in 1998.

Fig. 14.155. A close-in. The legend was obviously altered – we see that something else had been written here originally.

However, the most interesting fact is that the name of the Czar is very obviously a forgery. Let us return to the very first line. Take a closer look at the photograph (fig. 14.155). We can clearly see some semi-obliterated phrase underneath the words "Ivan, Great Prince of Russia," which can be seen particularly well in the gap between the words "Ivan" and "Russia." Something else had been written here – another name, or a title. Possibly, "Khan Simeon." However, the obliterated lettering here is unlikely to ever be reconstructed. We haven't managed to make it out, despite having spent a large enough amount of time at the museum. One needs a magnifying glass, laboratory condition, etc. An expertise of the surviving layer of paint is also called for.

And so, the portrait of "Ivan Vassilyevich" that we have at our disposal today has got obvious traces of falsification. The authentic old inscription was erased and replaced by a new one. Could the actual portrait of the Czar have been tampered with as well? This might be the reason why the compilers of the album ([11]) and the author of the book ([1373]) decided to leave the "embarrassing inscription" out and not include it in the photographs of the famous portrait – to preclude the readers from asking unnecessary questions.

Fig. 14.156. Portrait of Czar Alexei Mikhailovich Romanov from the Raspyatskaya Church of Alexandrovskaya Sloboda.

There are other oddities about this portrait. The person painted upon it is presumed to be Ivan the Terrible; it has a distinctive characteristic, namely, an indentation on the bridge of the nose, q.v. in fig. 14.153. However, we see another portrait exhibited in the Raspyatskaya Church nearby, allegedly one of Czar Alexei Mikhailovich Romanov, q.v. in fig. 14.156. We see that it also has an indentation on the bridge of the nose; in general, the faces painted on both portraits look amazingly similar. Could the portrait of "Ivan the Terrible" from the Ouspenskaya Church really be one of Czar Alexei Mikhailovich dating from a later epoch, which the Romanovian historians of the XVII or the XVIII century decided to use in order to manufacture a portrait of "Czar Ivan the Terrible," which would serve to replace some authentic old portrait of the XVI century Czar, or Khan. It is possible that they simply took some portrait of Alexei Mikhailovich, erased the inscription at the bottom and boldly replaced it by the name of Ivan Vassilyevich, wiping out a number of other "embarrassing" words and phrases while they were at it. As we have seen, they didn't bother with extra accuracy – for instant, instead of thinking up some plausible new text to stand at the end of the inscription that they were editing, the hoaxers simply erased a few of the "dangerous words," offhandedly replacing them by a meaningless squiggle, which must have been presumed fit for this purpose.

Apparently, few people paid attention to such phenomena in the epoch of the first Romanovs, and even fewer dared to enquire about the former lettering or the reason why the Czar had suddenly changed his name. All that we have learnt to date implies that such inquisitiveness had hardly been regarded as laudable in that epoch.

11.
Lettering on the neckpiece
of a XVI century chasuble with
a counterfeited name of a Russian czar

The museum of the Ouspenskaya Church in the Alexandrovskaya Sloboda has got a so-called "chasuble neckpiece" up for exhibition (embroidery of 1596. See [11], page 34, and [1373], page 114; also fig. 14.158). The embroidery depicts an Evangelical scene of Jesus Christ administering the communion of bread and wine to his apostles ([11], page 35). It is circumscribed by lettering set in golden and silver thread (see the rectangular strip in fig. 14.158). The entire inscription is represented in five photographs (figs. 14.159-14.163).

It says the following: "The year of ЗРД (7104, or 1596), the reign of Czar and Great Prince [???] Ivanovich and Czarina Irina, to the daughter of Prince Afanasiy Andreyevich Nogayev, Princess Euphimia."

The entire inscription is in a perfect condition, the sole exception being the name of the Czar, which appears to have perished.

The surviving traces lead us to the presumption that the artefact in question fell prey to hoaxers. Someone has made the attempt to make fake traces of the name "Fyodor" here, however the result doesn't look plausible at all. The first part of the name is drafted rather clumsily with a couple of individual stitches; the letters at the end of the name have a strange shape and are likely to have been altered. This concerns the next-to-last letter, Р, and in particular the last letter А. The two previous letters are missing altogether, replaced by some strange blotch (see fig. 14.160). The original lettering is anyone's guess nowadays.

Fig. 14.157. The Ouspenskaya Church at Alexandrovskaya Sloboda (the modern town of Alexandrov). See also [11].

Why is it that "relentless time" chose to erase the name of a XVI century Russian Czar, leaving the rest of the lettering intact? Could its part have been played by the Romanovian editors of the XVIII century?

A propos, the lettering is distinctly at odds with the Russian history as related in Millerian and Romanovian textbooks nowadays. Princess Euphimia as mentioned in the text is referred to as the daughter of Prince Afanasiy Andreyevich Nogayev. However, the only Princess Euphimia known in the Romanovian history of that period is presumed to be the daughter of Vladimir Sergeyevich Staritskiy and Yedvokia Nagaya (q.v. in the alphabetic index of the Russian princes and princesses in [404]).

However, the inscription on the chasuble names Afanasiy instead of Vladimir. Also, the surname Nagoy (Nagaya being its female

Fig. 14.158. The monastic robes of 1596, a fragment. Museum of the Ouspenskaya Church at Alexandrovskaya Sloboda. Taken from [11].

Fig. 14.160. Lettering on the robe continued. The name of the Russian Czar is an obvious forgery; otherwise, the lettering is in good condition.

Fig. 14.159. Fragment of the lettering on the robe. Beginning. Photographs taken by the authors in 1998.

Fig. 14.161. Lettering on the robe continued.

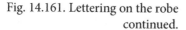

Fig. 14.162. Lettering continued.

Fig. 14.163. Lettering concluded.

form) – or, rather, Nogayev, is worn by Vladimir (or Afanasiy?) Andreyevich himself, and not his wife, as the Romanovian historians are trying to suggest today. The impression is that of total confusion. The epoch in question is a rather recent one – the end of the XVI century; we are presumed to know it in detail, according to the Romanovian historiography.

A propos, the replacement of Nogayey by Nagoy is by no means as harmless as it seems initially. The name Nogayev makes one recollect the famous Nogaiskaya Horde, whose last remnants were destroyed by the Romanovs in the XVIII century (Count Souvorov being the leader of their army), whereas the name Nagoy leads to no such "dangerous associations."

This must be the reason why the Romanovian editors replaced Nogayev by Nagoy, wishing to conceal the relationship existing between the Russian Czars and the Nogaiskaya Horde.

12.

Amazing Russian Biblical scenes on the XVI century frescoes, which have miraculously survived in the Pokrovskaya Church of the Alexandrovskaya Sloboda

We are about to consider the amazing artwork of the Pokrovskaya Church. The dome in its modern condition can be seen in figs. 14.150, 14.151 and 14.152. In fig. 14.164 one sees the reconstruction of the dome as it was in the XVI century made by modern historians. We shall be referring to the scientific publication that contains the article entitled "The Artwork Programme of the Pokrovskaya Church in the Alexandrovskaya Sloboda" by V. D. Sarabyanov, as well as "The Artwork Style of the Pokrovskaya (Intitially Troitskaya) Church of the Alexandrovskaya Sloboda" by V. M. Sorokatiy ([12]) in our analysis of the artwork.

According to V. D. Sarabyanov, "the artwork from the dome of the Pokrovskaya (initially Troitskaya) Church of the Alexandrovksaya Sloboda, dating from the epoch of Ivan the Terrible, is of the utmost interest to us – not just because it dates from the period that has left us but a precious few works of monumental art, but also due to the uniqueness of its iconographic programme" ([12], page 39). Moreover, we learn that "this is the only example of a XVI century Russian church with topical artwork" ([11], page 21). Let us point out right away that this truly amazing artwork has survived quite by chance, invisible under later layers. This is why it has fortunately enough evaded the attention of the Romanovian editors of history in the XVII-XVIII century. Had it been discovered then, it would either be destroyed or falsified – we have seen it happen many a time.

Fig. 14.164. A reconstruction of the dome of the Pokrovskaya (initially Troitskaya) church of Alexandrovskaya Sloboda as it was in the XVI century. Taken from [12], page 80, photograph 2.

The artwork was only discovered in the XX century – in 1925 (see [12], page 55). Its condition is rather poor. Modern historians mark the "poor condition of the artwork, likewise the fact that the murals are at a considerable distance from the viewer... However, one must emphasise the great rarity of the artefact and the role it plays in the correct estimation of the XVI century art" ([12], page 54).

Historians date this artwork to circa 1570 ([12], p. 55). The artwork deteriorates rather rapidly. V. M. Sorokatiy points out that "fortunately, we have a unique source at our disposal, one that reflects the original condition of the artwork upon discovery – incomplete and with numerous defects as it may be, but in much greater detail than we can see today. I am referring to the photographs of 1926, without which no complete evaluation would be possible" (*ibid.*).

One cannot help but wonder about the wanton manner in which the learned historians treat this rarest XVI piece of artwork that has miraculously reached our day and age. According to V. D. Sarabyanov, "the artwork of the Pokrovskaya Church, which was discovered in the beginning of the 1920's, rather unfortunately hasn't been preserved in a proper manner; the substantial deterioration of the layers of plaster and paint over the years that have passed since its discovery make the reconstruction of details and the identification of the saints extremely hard – next to impossible" ([12], page 41).

We haven't managed to study the murals in July 1998, since the church remains closed for visitors of the museum.

In fig. 14.165 one sees the general condition of the artwork as it

Fig. 14.165. General view of the artwork on the dome of the Pokrovskaya (Troitskaya) Church. Modern condition. Taken from [12], page 80, photograph 4.

is today. Fragments of frescoes are reproduced in figs. 14.166 and 14.167. The general concept of the artwork is as follows. Sabaoth the god is at the centre, surrounded by archangels followed by evangelists and Biblical characters together with the Russian princes. For instance, "on the right of St. Vladimir we see the legend 'Vladimir the Great'; we also see the words 'Righteous Prince Gleb' next to St. Gleb" ([12], page 53).

Fig. 14.166. Artwork on the dome of the Pokrovskaya Church: a fragment. Taken from [12], page 80, photograph 7.

Fig. 14.167. Artwork on the dome of the Pokrovskaya Church: a fragment. Taken from [12], page 80, photographs 8 and 9.

It is important that the artwork isn't merely an eclectic collection of individual characters, but rather a rendition of the so-called "Tree of Jesus," or the genealogical tree of Jesus Christ. Sarabyanov points out that the decoration in question "is an interpretation of the decorative and symbolic tree motif, which is very common for mediaeval art. In Byzantine art of the XIII-XIV century this motif was primarily used in the composition entitled "The Tree of Jesus," which had served to represent and glorify the genealogy of Jesus Christ... This triumphal composition ... had served as a basis for a local theme known as 'The Vine of the Nemanich', deifying the Serbian royal dynasty and proclaiming the divine origins of their royal power... This iconography was introduced in the artwork of the Pokhvalskiy side-altar of the Ouspenskiy Cathedral of the Kremlin in Moscow, which dates from 1482 [the dating is apparently erroneous – Auth.], and became widely popular in the second half of the XVI century. The actual 'Tree of Jesus' was among the compositions included in the decoration of the Blagoveshchenskiy Cathedral in 1405 [this dating also appears to be erroneous – Auth.] by Feofan the Greek and recurs in the artwork of 1547-1551, occupying all of the domes and a substantial part of the gallery walls... In the context of the entire artwork, which is largely concerned with the glorification of the regnant Russian dynasty, the 'Tree of Jesus' is doubtlessly parallel to the very same topic, serving to carry across the same concept of royal power being divine in its origin, but more subtly than the 'Nemanich Vine', and referring to the first Russian Czar, who had been crowned shortly before the creation of this artwork" ([12], page 46).

Thus, the artwork of the Pokrovskaya Church depicts several generations of Biblical characters and Russian Czars as an uninterrupted sequence – a genealogical tree of sorts. At the centre of the composition we see the god Sabaoth and not Jesus Christ ([12], page 52). As for the Biblical characters – we see Adam and Eve, a character that is likely to identify as Cyph, the third son of Adam, Abel, Noah, "who is identified unequivocally by the ark that he holds in his hands" ([12], page 42). Next we have Abraham, Isaac, Jacob and "the twelve sons, or the patriarchs of the twelve tribes of Israel. All of them are dressed in princely attires with lavishly decorated neckpieces, sleeves and bottom edges" ([12], pages 42-43). The "tree" also includes twelve Biblical prophets, possibly, Aaron, Isaiah, Daniel and Samuel or Zechariah, likewise King David and King Solomon. Some of the figures cannot be identified as any famous ancient characters at all ([12], pages 42-43).

Finally, "the sixth circle of the artwork ... depicts the saints of the New Testament, predominantly martyrs and Russian princes" ([12], page 43). In particular, we see St. Jacob Perskiy, St. Mina, the Russian princes Vladimir, Boris and Gleb, and so on. The XVI century artists depicted the Biblical characters and the Russian princes as contemporaries, or representatives of the same epoch. Historians write the following about Prince Vladimir, for instance: "His figure is located upon ... the main line of the hierarchy, apparently corresponding to the portraits of the Old Testament patriarchs – Cyph and David the Prophet... The concept of the Muscovite Kingdom being the chosen nation blessed and guarded by the Lord himself, is illustrated in a very obvious manner – the divine grace falling from the heavens is distributed equally ... among the Patriarch Czar, David ... and Prince Vladimir, whom we see in the same row... Prince Vladimir is equalled to the saint kings of the Old Testament, with whole generations of Christian rulers omitted" ([12], page 49).

Modern historians are thus telling us that the global chronology as represented in the artwork on the dome of the Pokrovskaya Church, is greatly at odds with the Scaligerian version. Characters separated from each other by centuries and even millennia within the framework of the Scaligerian history were depicted by the XVI century artists as either contemporaries or representatives of one and the same historical epoch. Likewise, the chronology reflected in the artwork is in perfect correspondence with our reconstruction, according to which the Biblical characters and the Muscovite princes of the XIV-XVI century aren't merely contemporaries, but also often figure as different aliases of a single historical personality. In other words, Russian chronicles describe them as Muscovite princes, whereas the Bible reflected them as Moses, Nebuchadnezzar, King of Assyria, and so on.

The Blagoveshchenskiy Cathedral of the Muscovite Kremlin presents us with just as amazing a picture. Here we also have "the genealogical tree of Jesus Christ painted on the domes of the galleries" ([107], page 147). Historians make the perfectly justified comment that the analysis of the frescoes from the Pokrovskaya Church will be aided by "a comparison of the artwork in question with the most important works of Muscovite art of the XVI century, namely, the murals of the Blagoveshchenskiy Cathedral of the Muscovite Kremlin" ([12], page 60).

A drawn copy of the famous murals from the Blagoveshchenskiy Cathedral made in the early XX century is reproduced in fig. 14.168. Here we also see the Russian Princes alongside Biblical characters from the Old Testament. Moreover, they are depicted in the same chronological sequence as "Virgil, the Roman poet wearing a brimmed hat, Anaxagoras, the Greek philosopher, and Homer, the famous blind poet... It is most peculiar that we also see several Great Princes of Russia alongside the above characters – Daniil Aleksandrovich, Dmitriy Donskoi and Vassily I. This appears to be the genealogical tree of the Muscovite rulers woven into the tree of Christ... The dynastic topic is represented in the context of world history" ([107], pages 148-149).

Nowadays all such mediaeval artwork is regarded as purely symbolic. Historians are trying to convince us that mediaeval artists confused epochs and were ignorant of chronology. Quite naturally,

Fig. 14.168. Fragment of the artwork on the dome of the vestibule of the Muscovite Kremlin's Blagoveshchenskiy Cathedral dating from the XVI century. According to the draft made by V. V. Souslov in the early XX century. Taken from [107], page 148.

modern historians raised on the erroneous chronology of Scaliger and Petavius will regard the attribution of Virgil, Anaxagoras, Homer, Dmitriy Donskoi and other Great Princes of Russia to the same historical epoch as absurd. However, our reconstruction provides an excellent explanation to the mediaeval chronology, which is very demonstrably reflected in the artwork of the Blagoveshchenskiy Cathedral, since, according to the results of our research, all these "ancient" characters had indeed lived in the epoch of the XIII-XVI century. The mediaeval artists who painted the frescoes of the Pokrovskaya Church in the Alexandrovskaya Sloboda had been well aware of this fact, likewise the authors of the more recent artwork of the Muscovite Kremlin's Blagoveshchenskiy Cathedral.

Moreover, these surviving frescoes of the XVI century paint a picture of the mediaeval world that is thoroughly at odds with the one reflected in the modern Scaligerian history textbooks. The XVI century frescoes reflect the supreme position of the Great = "Mongolian" Empire in the mediaeval world.

V. D. Sarabyanov refers to the frescoes of the Pokrovskaya Church in the following manner:

"The theocratic idea that the Muscovite Czars were chosen by God is presented as something that requires no proof whatsoever – an ideological axiom accepted by everyone as the truth... It is perfectly obvious that the artwork is primarily concerned with the concept of the Russian rulers and Russia itself being chosen by the Lord; in the context of the global historical process, the country was regarded as the last truly Christian state... What we see reflected in the artwork is the famous complex of ideas that became the theory of 'Moscow as the Third Rome' and the official doctrine" ([12], page 49).

We are of the opinion that this doctrine only became a "theory" in the works of the Scaligerian and Romanovian historians, starting with the XVII-XVIII century. In the XIV-XVI century it had been reality – not a theory. The Great = "Mongolian" Empire, also known as Assyria, or Russia, covered immense territories – from America to China across Europe, under the power of the Assyrian (Russian) Czar, or Khan, q.v. in *Chron6*.

The Bible describes his power rather magniloquently:

"I will punish the fruit of the stout heart of the king of Assyria, and the glory of his high looks. For he saith, By the strength of my hand I have done it, and by my wisdom; for I am prudent: and I have removed the bonds of the people, and have robbed their treasures, and I have put down the inhabitants like a valiant man: and my hand hath found as a nest the riches of the people: and as one gathereth eggs that are left, have I gathered all the earth; and there was none that moved the wing, or opened the mouth, or peeped" (Isaiah 10:13-14).

Therefore, the authors of the frescoes in the Alexandrovskaya Sloboda and the Muscovite Kremlin were perfectly correct in their reflection of Moscow's role and place in the world history of the XIV-XVI century as that of the Third Rome.

13.

The reason why the megalithic palaces and temples are more common for the Southern countries than for those with a moderate climate

In the Middle Ages, the residential buildings, palaces and temples in Russia were rather small. There were many constructions of stone and wood, but the size of each individual building had been rather small. Construction megalomania had not been characteristic for Russia in that epoch.

On the other hand, gigantesque constructions of stone were often built in the southern parts of the Great = "Mongolian" Empire – large stone temples, for instance. What is the reason for such architectural diversity? There can be a variety of explanations; we believe the primary reason to be the following. The inhabitants of the countries with a moderate climate that had been located at some distance from the seas and the oceans must have found it hard to maintain a warm temperature inside large buildings during cold and snowy winters. The construction materials had nothing to do with it – it is just that a large volume of air inside a huge building requires more heating facilities to get warm, and more fuel.

However, in the south, where the climate is warmer and the winters aren't quite as cold as in the north, the heating issues had not been quite as poignant. On the contrary, hot summers had required the construction of large buildings made of stone, with thick walls, which remained cool inside even in summer heat. This is why we see many gigantic mediaeval temples of stone in Turkey and Egypt, for instance. This is where the so-called megalithic building had flourished. The buildings built in Russia had been much smaller; residential constructions were usually made of wood, since it preserves the warmth better than stone.

The development of technology and industry rendered these considerations obsolete – large buildings of stone and concrete have appeared in Russia and countries with a similar or an even colder climate, whereas the Southerners started to use air conditioning.

14.
A cross with Slavic lettering received as a present from the Patriarch of Jerusalem by Charlemagne

In figs. 14.169 and 14.170 we see the "Jerusalem Cross," which is kept in the treasury of the Hildesheim Cathedral. Its dimensions are as follows: 11 by 10 by 2 centimetres ([292]).

The artefact in question is very famous: "Among the outstanding works of art kept in the Cathedral of Hildesheim there is an artefact that is neither characterised by the finesse of its artwork, nor by great value of materials used in its manufacture. Nevertheless, it is considered a very ancient halidom... It is the so-called "Jerusalem Cross" with holy relics" ([292], page 7). Tradition has it that the Jerusalem Cross was received as a present by the Diocese of Hildesheim from its founder, emperor Louis the Pious, in the first half of the

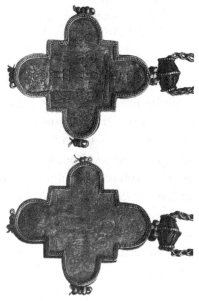

Fig. 14.169. The "Jerusalem cross" (a diptych) from the sacristy of the Hildesheim Cathedral. We see the external part on the photograph. Legend has it, the Patriarch of Jerusalem gave it to Charlemagne as a present. There is Slavonic lettering on the cross. Taken from [292].

Fig. 14.170. Artwork on the reverse of the diptych's back part (Charlemagne's "Jerusalem Cross"). The lettering is Russian. There is no artwork on the front side of the back part. Taken from [292].

alleged IX century A.D. "The first researcher to have studied the cross, I. M. Kratz, presumes it to be of a Greek origin and dates it to the VIII century, indicating that it became part of the royal treasury when Charlemagne, the father of Louis had still been regnant. The cross had been among the halidoms received by him in 799 from John V, the Patriarch of Jerusalem" ([292], p. 7).

One must say that historians instantly run into problems with this artefact, the reason being that neither the cross itself, nor the ancient tradition that surrounds it, correspond to Scaligerian history. The author of the article ([292]), N. Myasoyedov, a historian, writes the following: "Despite the fact that it is impossible to link the name of John V with that of Charlemagne chronologically, seeing as how the former died in 745, when Charles had still been four years of age, the opinion of Kratz about the chronological origins of the cross had not encountered any objections, and was shared by many German authors" ([292], page 7). What we encounter here is a contradiction between the Scaligerian chronology and the historical evidence from the Middle Ages that survived in a number of German documents. The implication is that the Patriarch of Jerusalem had died in 745, and given the cross to Charlemagne in 799, fifty years after his death.

However, the most important detail is as follows. The oddest thing (insofar as the Scaligerian history is concerned) is the fact that the Patriarch of Jerusalem gave Charlemagne a cross covered in Slavic lettering. Scaligerites should naturally find this perfectly outrageous. However, our reconstruction makes it look perfectly natural – moreover, any other kind of lettering on the cross received by Charlemagne from the Patriarch of Jerusalem (Roman, for instance) would appear truly odd to us.

There are Slavic inscriptions on the sides and the reverse side of the cross. The front part of the cross, which is what the visitors usually see, has no inscriptions, which must be the reason why historians only noticed the lettering in the early XX century ([292], page 8). They instantly proclaimed the cross to be a forgery due to its Russian origins, which preclude it from being a "Jerusalem cross." However, N. Myasoyedov, the author of the article in [292], tells us on page 8 that when he visited Hildesheim in 1914, the cross had still been known as the "Jerusalem Cross," despite the vocal protests of learned historians and the fact that the lettering found upon it is Slavic.

Our reconstruction makes the picture perfectly clear. Slavonic had been one of the official languages used in the Great = "Mongolian" Empire. Slavic inscriptions were found all across the vast territories of the Empire. Charlemagne, or simply "The Great King," is most likely to have been one of the Czars, or the Khans, who had ruled over the Empire, and lived in the epoch of the XV-XVI century, during the Ottoman conquest of Europe, or even later.

Let us quote the description of the cross as given in [292].

"The so-called 'Jerusalem Cross' is really a container for holy relics... It is made of gilded silver... The cross would be worn on the chest. The holy relics that had been kept inside the cross initially are listed in the inscriptions found around the portraits of Constantine and Helen: 'This is a Holy Cross; the pall of St. Daniel, the pall of St. Pelagia and St. Savva, the pall of Lazarus, Our Lady and the Lord, the pall of Constantine and Helen, and the pall of John the Baptist'" ([292], pages 9-10).

The lettering on the sides of the cross reads as follows: "Lord help thy servant and all those who glorify Christianity now and in the future, and all the good Christians, amen" ([292], page 14).

Apart from that, the figures on the cross also have Slavic lettering upon them. Myasoyedov points out that the language of the inscriptions is "characterised by several traits that are typically Russian" ([292], page 13).

15.
Mediaeval French kings gave their oaths on a holy book in Church Slavonic

This important fact has been pointed out to us by A. K. Boulygin. It turns out that the French rulers in the Middle Ages had used a holy book written in Church Slavonic for saying their oaths. This fact, quite amazing from the Scaligerian point of view, is usually omitted from textbooks on French history, likewise Russian textbooks. However, it is known to scientists: "Here [in the city of Rheims – Auth.] the French monarchs said their oaths on the holy book, which was in reality a liturgical text in Church Slavonic – the co-called 'Rhemish Fragments'" ([474], pages 64-65).

Our reconstruction makes the picture perfectly clear. Mediaeval French monarchs had still been local representatives of the Great = "Mongolian" Empire, and would naturally say their oaths using a holy book in Church Slavonic, which must have been concealed from the public in the XVII century or even later, when the imperial language (Church Slavonic) was finally banished from France (and, *ex post facto*, from French history), to be replaced by the recently introduced "Holy Latin."

The same process has affected all the other countries in the Western Europe.

16.

The famous Attila the Hun as a contemporary of the renowned Russian Prince Vladimir, according to the evidence of Mediaeval German books. This is a virtual impossibility in Scaligerian chronology

Mediaeval German chronicles generally known as sagas can apparently tell us a great deal about the history of Russia. The picture they paint is radically different from the one reflected in school textbooks. For instance, the famous "Saga of Tidrek" (apparently, Theodoric, aka Frederick) refers to events that took place in Russia and the land of the Great Ones (Wilkinus, Velcinus, Wiltinus, etc.; cf. the Russian *"Velikiy"*, or "great"), q.v. in [126], page 11. The "Great Ones" identify as the "Mongols." The events in question take place on the vast territories between Spain and "the Oriental lands." The Russian cities of Smolensk, Kiev, Polotsk and Souza (Suzdal?) are frequently mentioned, q.v. in [126], page 7, and in [167]. Alongside the protagonists (the konungs, or the Khans) we find the Russian Prince Vladimir and Attila, chieftain of the Huns, mentioned as contemporaries. We learn of the conquest of Russia by the "great ones" (Velcinus, or the "Wiltins"). The term "Russia" must also be used for referring to some of the countries in Western Europe – P-Russia, for instance.

Let us remind the reader that, according to the Scaligerian chronology, Prince Vladimir had lived in the alleged X century A.D., whereas the lifetime of Attila, King of the Huns, is dated to the V century A.D. They are therefore separated by some five centuries. Another historical personality mentioned as their contemporary is Tidrik the konung – most likely, Theodoric the Goth, who had lived

THE ISSUE WITH BAPTISM OF RUSSIA

in the V-VI century A.D., according to the Scaligerian chronology. The name Tidrik (Theodoric = Frederick) is present in the very title of the book ([126]).

We can therefore see that the mediaeval German authors had been of the opinion that several heroes of the "antiquity," whose epochs are separated by centuries in Scaligerian chronology, had been contemporaries.

Let us quote the fragment that describes the conquest of the Western lands by the "Great Ones":

"There was a konung [or a khan – Auth.] known as Wilkin [or the Great One – Auth.], valiant and victorious. He had conquered a land known as the land of the Wilkins [the Great Ones – Auth.], laying it desolate. This land is called Switjod [the holy land, cf. the Russian word *"Svyatoi"*, which translates as "holy" – Auth.] and Gautland [land of the Goths – Auth.]... The domain of Wilkin the konung [the Great Khan – Auth.] had been as vast as the land bearing his name... Having reigned over this land for a while, Wilkon the konung [the Great Khan – Auth.] gathered his troops and set forth towards Poland, accompanied by a great multitude of knights and warriors ... many battles were fought there. Then he was confronted by the army of the konung Gertnit, who had reigned over Russia ... and most of Greece and Hungary, being the ruler of almost the whole of the Eastern kingdom ... together with his brother Girdir. They had fought many a violent battle. Wilking the konung [the Great Khan – Auth.] defeated the Russians every time, laying Poland and all the other kingdoms waste ... to the very salty sea... Then his army set forth towards Russia, conquering many large cities there, including Smolensk and Polotsk" ([126], page 134).

If we are to replace the word "konung" for "Khan" and so forth, we shall end up with the account of the "Mongolian" conquest and the civil wars fought within the empire.

This is what we learn about Attila and Vladimir: "And so it came to pass that Tidrik [Theodoric, or Frederick – Auth.] had summoned Attila the konung [the khan – Auth.] to converse with him and said: 'Do you remember the great disgrace you suffered in Russia from konung Voldemar? [Khan Vladimir – Auth.]... Would you care to revenge yourself upon him, or shall you leave it be?' Attila responded: 'It is certain that I do not want to leave it be, if you promise me assistance...' Then Attila the konung had sent orders to all the parts of his kingdom, for every valiant man eager to help his konung to join him in battle. It didn't take him long to gather an army of ten thousand knights... And before leaving the land of the Huns, he had twenty thousand knights by his side, and many other warriors. He set forth towards Poland and Russia, burning down cities and castles everywhere. And so Attila and his army came to the city known as Polotsk. The fortifications of the city had been formidable; they hardly knew how to conquer it – the city had a sturdy wall of stone, great towers, and moats wide and deep" ([126], pages 183-184). Attila's capital is called Souza – possibly, Suzdal in Russia ([126], pages 180 and 182).

We see references to Attila, Vladimir, Poland and the Russian city of Polotsk. This evidence contained in mediaeval texts is in good concurrence with our reconstruction. The texts in question were telling the truth and describing the mediaeval reality of the XIV-XVI century, and not the events of the "ancient" V-VI century.

We must conclude with the observation that the German sagas weren't mere legends, but rather real chronicles and voluminous oeuvres. As we can see, they deserve a most meticulous study.

17.
The *tugra* as a sign of authenticity used in the royal documents of the Middle Ages

In the present section we shall voice a number of considerations concerning the estimation of authenticity of the mediaeval royal documents. It is presumed that some of the pre-Romanovian royal decrees have reached us as originals – for instance, the decrees of Ivan III, Vassily III, Vassily I, Simeon the Proud, Ivan the Red, Ivan Kalita, etc. ([794] and [330:1]). See figs. 14.171-14.176. For instance, the museum of the Rila Monastery in Bulgaria has the original missive of Ivan IV sent to this monastery up for exhibition, if we are to believe the explanatory sign (see fig. 14.177).

Let us enquire about the methods of protection from forgery used in these documents. It is perfectly obvious that important documents written in the chancellery of the Czar, or the Khan, and indeed every other ruler, must have had an efficacious system of protection from forgery. Nowadays we use watermarks and special signs found on banknotes – special paper and so forth. Otherwise important state documents would be easy to falsify.

What system of protection was used by the mediaeval Russian Czars, or khans, before the Romanovs? If we are to believe the documents that are presented to us as "royal originals" nowadays, there was no such system save the seals. However, seals are easy enough to falsify; if one has the stamp of a seal at one's disposal, it isn't all that hard to produce its replica, which will be all but impossible to tell from the original.

Fig. 14.171. The allegedly authentic testament of Great Prince Ivan Kalita. Approximately dates from 1339. There is no tugra. State Archive of Ancient Acts. Taken from [330:1], page 23.

Let us now consider the protection system used in the documents issued by the sultan of the Ottoman Empire. It turns out that all the letters and decrees of the sultan were marked by the so-called tugra, which is a complex graphical symbol resembling a signature, placed at the beginning of the document. The sultan's tugra would occupy a significant part of the scroll. For instance, in fig. 14.178 one sees a document with the tugra of Suleiman the Magnificent. The tugra occupies most of the page; the text itself is a single line.

We must point out that a document of the sultan is exhibited next to the missive of Ivan IV in the museum of the Rila Monastery. G. V. Nosovskiy saw it in 1998. About two thirds of the scroll are occupied by the tugra of the sultan. It is obvious that manufacturing a counterfeit tugra, which is an extremely complex signature, is a very hard task indeed. Even if one has a copy of the tugra at one's disposal, making its exact representation is next to impossible. It requires a long period of special training, as well as the decipherment of the esoteric system of symbols used in this signature. The appearance of the signature depends on the order and the direction of its complex lines, which were drawn with a quill; this affects the thickness of the lines – it varies from place to place. In general, the sultan's scribes had a great number of secret

Fig. 14.172. The allegedly authentic testament of Great Prince Simeon the Proud. Dates from 1353 [330:1], page 24). No tugra. State Archive of Ancient Acts. Taken from [330:1], page 24).

Fig. 14.173. The allegedly authentic testament of Great Prince Vassily Vassilyevich. Dates from 1461-1462 ([330:1], page 27). We see no tugra. State Archive of Ancient Acts. Taken from [330:1], page 27.

Fig. 14.174. The allegedly authentic gift certificate of Great Prince Ivan III Vassilyevich. Dates from 1504 ([330:1], page 28.

methods that they employed for protecting the documents from forgery. Anyone who tries to reproduce such a signature without the knowledge of all the secrets shall come up with a drawing that shall instantly be exposed as a forgery by the experienced officials of the sultan (or the khan).

Another example of such a tugra can be seen in fig. 14.179 ([1465], page 55). We see the tugra, or the signature, of Sultan Mehmet II. We see a text set in small characters to the left of the tugra, at the bottom. Another complex tugra of Sultan Mehmet II can be seen in fig. 14.180; it comes from a decree issued by Mehmet II.

Fig. 14.175. The allegedly authentic testament of Great Prince Ivan III Vassilyevich. Dates from 1504 ([330:1], page 29.

The tugras were used by other rulers apart from the Ottoman sultans. In the official documents of the XVII century issued by independent rulers from the Western Europe we always see complex strokes in the same place – different versions of the tugras. For instance, in fig. 14.182 we see a charter sent to Czar Mikhail Fyodorovich Romanov by Christian IV, King of Denmark, which is kept in the Russian National Archive of Ancient Documents ([855:1], page 246). We can clearly see a tugra at the top of the document. Another missive, of a later origin, sent by another Danish king to

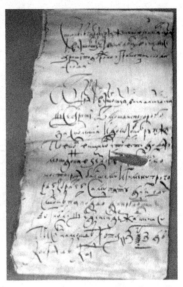

Fig. 14.176. The allegedly authentic testament of Great Prince Vassily III Ivanovich confirming the previous testament and the status of the Novo-devichiy Monastery. Dates from 1523. No tugra. State Archive of Ancient Acts. Taken from [330:1], p. 31.

Fig. 14.177. The allegedly authentic decree of the Russian Czar Ivan IV "The Terrible" kept in the museum of the Rila Monastery in Bulgaria. No tugra. Photograph taken in 1998.

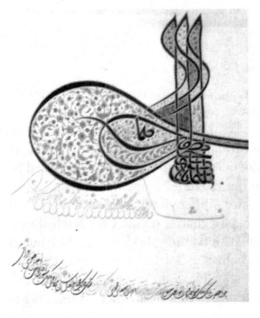

Fig. 14.178. Document with the tugra of Sultan Suleiman the Magnifi-cent. The tugra occupies almost the entire document, whose actual text is a mere line at the bottom of the page. Taken from [1206], page 55.

Fig. 14.179. A complex tugra used by Sultan Mahmoud II as a signature. Taken from [1465], page 55.

Czar Peter the Great in 1697, can be seen in fig. 14.183. It also has a distinctive tugra in the top left corner.

In fig. 14.181 we see a missive sent to Czar Mikhail Fyodorovich Romanov in 1631 by Sultan Amourat IV. At the top of the missive we see the tugra of the sultan set in gold.

Thus, the Danish kings of the XVII century had used tugras to secure their documents from forgery, likewise the Ottoman sultans. Other European monarch did likewise. For instance, the missive of 1633 sent to Czar Mikhail Fyodorovich by the Swedish senators in order to inform him of the demise of Gustav-Adolph, King of Sweden, and the crowning of his daughter Christina, also has a large and complex tugra, q.v. in fig. 14.184. Another tugra can be clearly seen in the missive sent by Friedrich-Ludwig, Duke of Schleswig-Holstein to Czar Peter the Great in 1697, q.v. in fig. 14.185. The missive sent to Peter the Great by the rulers of Hamburg, q.v. in fig. 14.186, also bears a tugra. Thus, even the rulers of Hamburg had used tugras to protect their documents. However, the Russian Great Princes of the pre-Romanovian epoch are said to have used nothing of the kind. At

Fig. 14.181. Missive sent by Sultan Amourat IV to Czar Mikhail Fyodorovich in re the attack on Azov by the Cossacks of Don. We see a luxurious tugra. State Archive of Ancient Acts. Taken from [330:1], page 246.

Fig. 14.180. A decree issued by Sultan Mahmoud II – complete with a tugra. Taken from [855:1], page 27.

Fig. 14.182. Missive sent by Christian IV, King of Denmark, to Czar Mikhail Fyodorovich Romanov in 1631 about the appointment of Maltupel as the envoy to Russia. Complex tugra. State Archive of Ancient Acts. Taken from [330:1], page 246.

Fig. 14.183. Missive sent by Christian V, King of Denmark, to Czar Peter the Great with a promise of support to the Kurfürst of Saxony in his struggle for the Polish throne. 1697. Complex tugra. State Archive of Ancient Acts. Taken from [330:1], page 249.

Fig. 14.184. Missive sent by the Swedish senators to Czar Mikhail Fyodorovich in re the demise of Gustav-Adolph, King of Sweden, and his daughter Christine crowned queen. 1633. Complex tugra. State Archive of Ancient Acts. Taken from [330:1], page 251.

Fig. 14.185. Missive sent by Frederick-Ludwig, Duke of Schleswig-Holstein to Peter the Great with a request to be the godfather of his newborn child. 1697. Luxurious tugra. State Archive of Ancient Acts. Taken from [330:1], page 252.

Fig. 14.186. Missive sent by the Elders of Hamburg to Czar Peter the Great. 1702-1705. We see a splendid tugra. State Archive of Ancient Acts. Taken from [330:1], page 252.

Fig. 14.187. Missive sent by Frederick-Wilhelm, Kurfürst of Brandenburg, to Czar Alexei Mikhailovich. 1656. State Archive of Ancient Acts. Complex tugra. Taken from [330:1], page 242.

least, the "originals" of the documents written by the Great Princes of Russia demonstrated to us nowadays have no tugras upon them, q.v. in fig. 14.171-14.176.

In fig. 14.187 we see a missive sent to Czar Alexei Mikhailovich by Frederick-Wilhelm, Kurfürst of Brandenburg. Once again, we can clearly see a tugra at the top of the document. Let us point out that this document, as well as the ones we cited previously, dates

Fig. 14.188. A very complex and elaborate tugra at the beginning of a document issued by Czar Mikhail Romanov. Kept in the museum of Pafnoutievskiy Monastery, Borovsk, near Moscow. The museum plaque reports it to be a "Land ownership certificate sent by Czar Mikhail Fyodorovich to the Pafnoutiev Monastery in replacement of the papers that perished in the blaze of 1610. 1624." Photograph taken by T. N. Fomenko and A. T. Fomenko in May 1999.

Fig. 14.189. Close-in of a fragment of the document issued by Mikhail Romanov in 1624. We can clearly see a very elaborate tugra. The complexity of this "signature" secured the document from forgery. Photograph taken at the Pafnoutievskiy Monastery in May 1999. Such tugras were usually drawn on authentic documents issued by the Russian Czars and the Ottoman Sultans in the XVI-XVII century. The Turks have kept this tradition for longer. On the other hand, we see no tugras on the XVII-XVIII century forgeries presented to us as authentic documents issued by the Russian Czars in the XVII-XVIII century. It was too complex a task to copy such a pattern. The hoaxers contented themselves with the falsification of seals, which required less skill and effort from their part – all they needed was a print of the real seal.

Fig. 14.190. Missive sent by Czar Mikhail Fyodorovich to Prince D. M. Pozharskiy to confirm the ownership of his estate. Complex tugra. State Archive of Ancient Acts. Taken from [330:1], page 305.

Fig. 14.191. Ownership certificate sent by Czar Alexei Mikhailovich to the Iverskiy Monastery at Valdai. 1657 A.D. Complex tugra. State Archive of Ancient Acts. Taken from [330:1], page 70.

from the epoch of the XVII century; these documents are authentic, unlike the ones that date from the epoch of the XV-XVI century, which either got destroyed after the dissolution of the Empire, or have been replaced by forgeries.

Our opponents might suggest that the Russians had never used tugras, being a backward nation with inexperienced government officials, and that the tugras were a Turkish, or Ottoman invention adopted by the Westerners, unlike the Russians, who had merely used seals. However, this is not true. Let us turn to the documents of the first Romanovs, and we shall instantly see that all the royal documents of that epoch had a complex sigil in their top part – tugras, in other words, although their style differed from that of their Ottoman counterparts.

For instance, let us consider a bestowal certificate issued by Mikhail Romanov in 1624 kept in the museum of the Panfnouti-evskiy Monastery in the town of Borovsk near Moscow, q.v. in figs.

Fig. 14.192. Ownership certificate sent to the Novodevichiy Monastery by Czar Fyodor Alexeyevich. Complex tugra. State Archive of Ancient Acts. Taken from [330:1], page 41.

14.188 and 14.189. At the top of the document we see a huge tugra, complex and exquisite; it occupies a large part of the page.

Another document of Czar Mikhail Fyodorovich Romanov (a missive sent to Prince D. M. Pozharskiy) is kept in the National Archive of Ancient Documents in Moscow. It is reproduced in fig. 14.190. We see a complex tugra in the top part of the document. In fig. 14.191 we present another bestowal certificate sent to the Iversk Monastery of Valday by Czar Alexei Mikhailovich Romanov in 1657. It also bears a complex tugra, likewise a similar certificate sent by the same Czar to the Novodevichiy Monastery, q.v. in fig. 14.192. A most complex multicolour tugra with golden details can be seen in a bestowal certificate issued by Peter the Great, q.v. in fig. 14.193.

Tugras were characteristic for all the missives and decrees written by the Czars. In figs. 14.194 and 14.195 we see a photograph of a royal edict dating from 1705 and issued in the name of Peter the Great, which is kept in the museum of the Alexandrovskaya Sloboda. In figs. 14.196 and 14.197 we see photographs of another royal decree dating from 1718, also issued in the name of Peter the Great. Both decrees have complex tugras at their beginning.

And so, could it really be that the Russian royal documents hadn't used any system of protection from forgery before the XVII century and the epoch of the Romanovs? How could the Russian Czars and Khans have left their documents unprotected, especially seeing as how the XVI sultans of the Ottoman Empire had always used tugras in their documents? Apparently, the tugra was a distinctive characteristic of royal documents and nothing but; decrees issued by other parties did not use tugras, as G. V. Nosovskiy learnt in 1998 from the scientists working in the Ottoman chancellery document

Fig. 14.193. Permission given by Peter the Great to I. Ides for the publication of his book about the diplomatic mission to China. State Archive of Ancient Acts. Elaborate and luxurious tugra. Taken from [330:1], page 248.

department of the Library of Kirill and Mefodiy in Sofia, Bulgaria. They report that only a chosen few janissary commanders had used a certain likeness of the tugra – however, their sigils were a great deal less complex; also, they weren't placed in the top part of a document, whereas the tugra of the sultan was always drawn at the very beginning of a decree, occupying a large part of a page or a scroll.

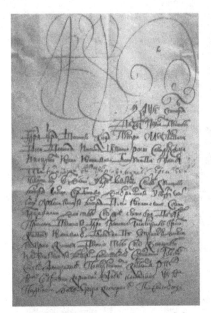

This oddity, namely, the absence of tugras or some similar protection system from the royal documents of the pre-Romanovian epoch, and the fact that they were "first introduced" under the Romanovs in the XVII century, is instantly explained by our reconstruction. It is most likely that such tugras had been mandatory and present in every official document issued in the mediaeval Russia, or the Horde. However, most of the authentic documents dating from that epoch were destroyed by the Romanovs and replaced by forgeries. However, it is all but impossible to reproduce a tugra in its complexity; therefore, the Romanovs decided to use a much simpler method, which is quite obvious. They made counterfeit "originals" of the ancient documents

Fig. 14.194. Authentic decree of the Romanovian epoch exhibited in the museum of Alexandrovskaya Sloboda near Moscow. The photographs were taken by the authors of the book in 1998. We see an official royal decree signed by Peter the Great – complete with a tugra.

without any tugras whatsoever, using nothing but the seals, which were easy to manufacture, since the stamps, and, possibly, the actual seals as well, had been at their full disposal. However, the qualified calligraphists employed by the Khans had died during the Great Strife, and the tradition had ceased to exist. The Romanovian tugras appear to be a lot simpler than the ones used by the old dynasty.

Apparently, a few authentic pre-Romanovian tugras of the Great = Mongolian Empire have nevertheless survived until our day. For instance, there are two odd scrolls exhibited in the Gutenberg Museum (Mainz, Germany). A. T. Fomenko and T. N. Fomenko noticed them when they visited the museum in 1998. The entire space of both scrolls is occupied by a gigantic letter J or I, q.v. in figs. 14.198 and 14.199. The remaining parts of the scrolls are missing. The lavish artwork is very similar to the tugras of the sultans; the fact

Fig. 14.195. Close-in of a fragment of the decree dating from 1705 and exhibited on the previous photograph. The royal tugra is visible perfectly well. It isn't very complex in this case; one must assume, the Royal Chancellery had used several kinds of tugras – simpler ones for regular documents, and more complex ones for the documents of greater importance. It is obvious that the more complex a tugra, the better it protects a document from forgery.

that both sigils are shaped as the letter I (or J) lead us to the presumption that it might be the first letter of the name Ivan, or John. Could the symbol in question really be the Russian tugra of Czar Ivan the Terrible? The dating of the tugra (1597, as provided by the museum staff) pertains to the epoch when the Great = "Mongolian" Empire had still existed as a single entity; therefore, royal decrees with tugras may still have reached the Western Europe in those days. The actual text of the decrees was naturally destroyed during the Reformation mutiny of the XVII century; however, the tugras were preserved due to the beauty of the artwork. The art of making them must have already been forgotten.

This artwork strikes us as the ideal candidate for the role of the tugra. If we are to assume the letters in question to be mere works of calligraphic art, it is unclear just why one would draw a single letter to occupy the whole scroll. Quite naturally, first lines of chapters would often be started with a calligraphic letter; however, this drawing obviously means something else. Let us also pay attention to

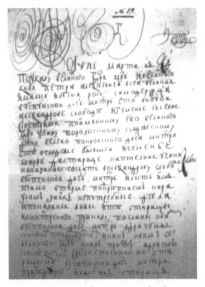

Fig. 14.196. Authentic royal edict of 1718 exhibited in the museum of Alexandrovskaya Sloboda. The photograph was taken by the authors of the book in 1998. We see a complex tugra in the beginning of the document.

the fact that the letter J is drawn upon a scroll; this leads us to the thought that it had once been an important state document. Back in the XVI century, the Khan's documents in the Horde had still looked like scrolls.

We are getting an altogether new concept of the "original" old decrees of the pre-Romanovian epoch exhibited in museums nowadays. They have no tugras, and thus also no means of protecting them from forgery. As we mentioned above, attaching a seal to a counterfeit document wasn't that difficult a task. One would write the text and attach a seal and a piece of thread thereto, using either the stamp of the seal for making a replica or even the seal itself, and then put the resulting "authentic Russian document" into the vaults of an archive for safekeeping. This is how the "authentic testaments of Ivan Kalita" came to existence – not one, but three of them ([794]). And so on, and so forth.

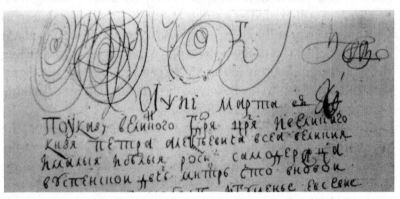

Fig. 14.197. Close-in of the edict of 1718, q.v. in the previous photograph. We see the complex royal tugra that protects the document from forgery.

112

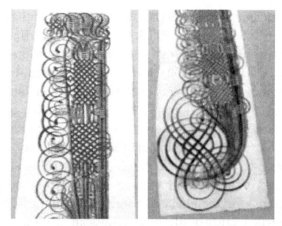

Figs. 14.198 and 14.199. A scroll dated to 1597 from the Gutenberg Museum in Mainz, Germany. The legend says "Kalligraphische Initiale 'J.' 1597. GM/GS 96.61." From a video recording made by T. N. Fomenko and A. T. Fomenko in 1998. Top and bottom parts of the luxurious tugra shaped as the letter "J."

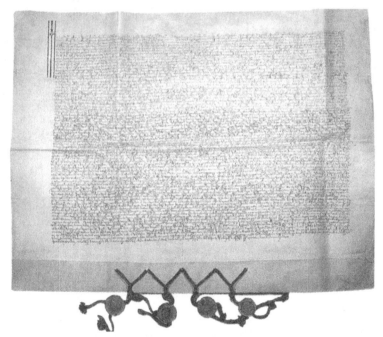

Fig. 14.200. Allegedly authentic pact of 1608 signed between Vassily Shouyskiy, the Russian Czar, and Sigismund III, King of Poland, negotiating a three-year truce. In reality, it is most likely to be a forgery of the Romanovian epoch. We see no tugra. State Archive of Ancient Acts. Taken from [330:1], page 249.

Let us conclude with a reference to the allegedly authentic cease-fire pact signed between the Polish king Sigismund III and Vassily Shouyskiy, the Russian Czar, dating from 1608, or the pre-Romanovian epoch, q.v. in fig. 14.200. Nowadays it is kept in the National Archive of Ancient Documents in Moscow as a precious authentic historical artefact ([330:1], page 249). However, it has nothing remotely resembling a tugra upon it. We believe it to be a forgery, likewise the overwhelming majority of other decrees and edicts demonstrated to us today, which were presumably issued by the Russian Czars of the pre-Romanovian epoch. All of them are most likely to be forgeries manufactured at the order of the Romanovs to distort the true picture of the ancient Russian history.

18.

The "ancient" Achilles as the leader of the Myrmidons – or, according to the chronicler John Malalas, the leader of the Huns and the Bulgarians

According to Scaligerian history, the Myrmidons were a mysterious "ancient" tribe, which had ceased to exist ages ago. Their leader was the legendary hero Achilles, who had fought at the walls of the "ancient" Troy. This is what a modern mythological dictionary tells us about the thoughts of the Scaligerian historians on the matter: "The Myrmidons … were a Thessalian nation, ruled by Achilles; they accompanied him to Troy. The Myrmidons hailed from the Aegina Isle [land of the Huns? – Auth.], where Zeus had transformed ants into people, as the legend has it; hence the name" ([432], page 121).

However, it appears that the mediaeval chroniclers had been of an entirely different opinion on the subject. They knew the true identity of the Myrmidons very well, which had nothing formic about it at all. Of course, modern historians shall say that one should by no means trust the "mediaeval fables" – ants suit them much better. Nevertheless, let us see what the mediaeval chronicler John Malalas has to say on this subject. He refers to "Achilles and his warriors, which had then been known as the Myrmidons – the modern Bulgars and Huns" ([338], page 122).

A propos, the name Myrmidon is most likely to have no formic connotations whatsoever, which is what Scaligerian historians imply, but rather refer to the Sea of Marmara (the Marble Don or the Marble Danube). Bear in mind that the word Don had formerly stood for "river" or "water," q.v. in *Chron5*. The Bulgarians and the

Huns, or the Hungarians, still populate the vicinity of the Danube and the Sea of Marmara.

This is yet another piece of evidence that reveals the extent to which the erroneous Scaligerian chronology distorts the mediaeval reality. According to our reconstruction, the Trojan War was fought at the walls of Constantinople, being the single most important event of the XIII-XIV century A.D. Quite naturally, among the participants there were Bulgarians and the Huns, or the Hungarians, q.v. in *Chron5*.

19.
The Russian *terem* and the oriental *harem* as two different names of the same thing

The word harem is known well enough; it is presumed to be derived from the Arabic *haram*, which stands for "forbidden," and mean the female quarters of a Muslim dwelling ([797], page 276). The harem of a Turkish Sultan was the place where his female kin lived – the mother, the sisters and the wives. Harems were guarded by eunuchs ([1259], page 20). No strangers were ever allowed in harems. The Sultan's harem had a throne hall "where the Sultan would entertain his closest and most trusted friends" ([1465], page 87). Exit from the harem was either altogether forbidden to the women, or largely restricted at the very least. Apart from the sultans, harems were kept by all the affluent Turks. A harem could be part of a residential building, or a separate construction, where the women had lived secluded.

Byzantine emperors also had female harems. For instance, "Teodulf refers to the Byzantine custom of keeping women under guard" ([336], Volume 5, page 63).

It turns out that harems also existed in the ancient Russia, and were called virtually the same – there is the Russian word *"terem"*, which is known to every Russian. The encyclopaedic definition is as follows: "a residential section of a wealthy dwelling with a tall roof. Some of the *terems* were built separately – over basements, gates, etc., connected to the rest of the building with special passages. A *terem* was an important part of any Russian palace, and most

Top part of the building as seen from the outside

The Throne Chamber

The Cruciform Chamber

The Antechamber

Fig. 14.201. The Teremnoy Palace (harem) of the Muscovite Kremlin. Taken from [85], Volume 42, pages 298-299.

often used for housing women, who had lived there in seclusion" ([85], Volume 42, page 298). Thus, a Russian terem served the same purpose as a harem in Turkey or elsewhere in the Orient. The two words differ in the first letter only; also, the Russian letter Г is only marginally different from the letter T, and, if written carelessly, one can be easily confused for the other.

Also, the word *terem* is very similar to the Russian word for "prison" – *"tyurma"*, phonetically as well as semantically, standing for "a guarded house." This corresponds ideally with the meaning of the Arabic word "harem," which is presumed to have been used for referring to something forbidden or closed ([1259], page 20). A propos, we find a quotation from a Russian chronograph in I. Zabelin's *History of Moscow*, where the Teremnoy Palace is called Tyuremniy ("prison palace" in modern translation): "And so he had built a magnificent chamber at his court for Alexei, his son (the Tyuremniy Palace)" ([284], page 164).

One needn't think that the *terems*, or harems, had only existed in "antediluvian Russia." The last royal Terem Palace was built as part of the Muscovite Kremlin in 1635-1636, under the first Romanovs, and exists until the present day ([85], Volume 42, page 298). However, all the artwork on the walls and the domes of the Kremlin terem, or harem, was replaced in the XIX century, namely, in 1837 ([85], Volume 42, page 298). Apparently, the old artwork was destroyed so as to provoke no embarrassing question. The residential chambers of the palace "were situated on the 4th floor, and consisted of four adjacent rooms – the hall, the lobby, the throne room and the bedroom. The fifth floor had housed a spacious and bright 'attic', or terem. It had a tall gilded dome and was surrounded by an open terrace" ([85], Volume 42, page 298). The above description makes the purpose of the Kremlin *terem*, or harem, perfectly obvious – women from the royal family had lived there, and it had also been used by the Czar for the entertainment of his closest friends. Let us also point out that one of the rooms had been a throne room, similarly to the harem of the Turkish sultan, q.v. in fig. 14.201.

In February 2000 we managed to visit the Terem Palace of the Muscovite Kremlin. We have learnt a number of facts from one of the scientists that work at the Kremlin, a professional guide; those facts complement the above picture quite well. Firstly, the history of this palace and the purpose of its construction are presumed to be rather vague these days – it turns out that different historians still haven't reached anything in the way of a consensus on this issue. Some say that the top floors of the Terem Palace had housed the "Czar's study," whereas others insist that they were occupied by children. This rings somewhat strange; could it be that the Czar had signed papers, conferred with the boyars and taken care of the affairs of the state in an "informal setting," playing with the children while he was at it? This is highly unlikely. We believe that there had never been any "study" here – the top floors of the palace had housed the harem, children et al. One must also mention another fact reported by historians in this respect, namely, that the "first Russian emperor-to-be, Peter the Great, was born on the night of 30 May 1672 in the Terem Palace of the Muscovite Kremlin" ([332], page 491). Everything falls into place – Peter the Great was born in a harem, which is perfectly natural.

It turns out that the entrance to the Terem Palace had been anything but easy – there were several circles of guards around it; even the closest associates of the Czar needed to undergo several

Fig. 14.202. The luxurious "Golden Grate" that guards one of the three entrances to the Teremnoy Palace of the Kremlin. Photograph taken by the authors of the book in 2000.

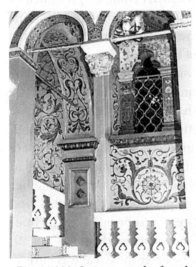

Fig. 14.203. Staircase to the fourth floor of the royal harem (Teremnoy Palace) of the Muscovite Kremlin. Photograph taken by the authors in 2000.

checks before entry. This appears odd for a "study," but more than natural for a harem. Basically, the Czar had been the only male who could enter here freely; hence the numerous guards, who had protected the Czar's wives and his children, future heirs to the throne.

It is also rather curious that the entrance to the old part of the palace was blocked by the so-called "golden grate." A part of the grate, which had blocked one of the entrances, can be seen in fig. 14.202. Obviously, the grate that we see here today isn't the one that had been here in the XVI century; the old pre-Romanovian grate had been wrought of pure gold, q.v. in *Chron5* – apparently, to emphasise the special status of this part of the palace.

After getting through the "golden grate," we can see the altar of the Czar's home church to our right, and a staircase that leads to the fourth floor of the Terem Palace (or the actual harem) to our left, q.v. in fig. 14.203. The walls are covered in floral ornaments exclusively; they resemble the murals in the Cathedral of St. Basil, q.v. in *Chron6*. The guide has told us that these murals date from the XIX century; the old murals were destroyed completely – chiselled off, most

Fig. 14.205. Entrance to the royal bedroom – a faraway room of the Teremnoy (Harem) Palace of the Kremlin. We find a bed there today. Photo taken by the authors in 2000.

Fig. 14.204. Luxurious interiors of the inner chamber of the Teremnoy (Harem) Palace. On the walls and the domes we see a floral ornament, gold, and the mythical phoenix bird. Mark the insignificant number of ecclesiastical themes. Photograph taken by the authors in 2000.

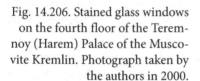

Fig. 14.206. Stained glass windows on the fourth floor of the Teremnoy (Harem) Palace of the Muscovite Kremlin. Photograph taken by the authors in 2000.

probably, despite the fact that they hadn't been all that old, dating from the XVII century originally.

The guide told us further that the purpose of the fourth floor's rooms isn't all that obvious nowadays. When we entered these rooms, we instantly noticed the private nature of these rooms, q.v. in figs. 14.204 and 14.205, including the stained glass windows, which create an exquisite soft light, q.v. in figs. 14.206, 14.207 and 14.208. There are also the lavishly decorated furnaces, q.v. in figs. 14.209 and 14.210.

Fig. 14.207. Internal chambers of the Teremnoy (Harem) Palace of the Muscovite Kremlin. Photograph taken by the authors in 2000.

Fig. 14.208. Internal chambers of the Teremnoy (Harem) Palace.

Fig. 14.209. Luxurious tiled fireplace in the internal chambers of the Teremnoy (Harem) Palace. Photos taken by the authors in 2000.

One of the central rooms is occupied by a large bed (see fig. 14.211). The guide surprised us by his suggestion that it was put here "by mistake." It turns out that the historians of today adhere to the opinion that their predecessors, the restorers of the XIX century, had "misinterpreted" the purpose of the Terem Palace, and put a bed here for some bizarre reason. The guide told us that the bed was placed here, or restored, by an archaeologist named Richter. We were told that Richter made a mistake, since no royal bedroom had ever been here. This was emphasised several times. One gets the impression that different traces of a harem still remain in this part of the palace; however, the numerous Romanovian reforms of the Russian history made the very fact that the Muscovite Kremlin had once housed a harem appear quite preposterous. However, historians occasionally sense certain discrepancies between reality and modern textbooks or find them in old texts, and thus explain to the visitors that the XIX century restorers had been "errant."

We have noticed a very peculiar coat of arms in the Terem Palace of the Muscovite Kremlin, which is integrated into the artwork surrounding one of the windows alongside other coat of arms, q.v. in fig. 14.212. There is a multicolour stained glass window to its left, and the coat of arms of Smolensk above it. In fig. 14.212 we see a bicephalous eagle with a red cross on its chest. Nowadays it is suggested that we should associate such crosses with the "Western European crusaders" of the alleged XI-XIV century exclusively. However, we see this symbol upon a Russian coat of arms, as well as a most peculiar inscription that says "Godynskoy." The first letter is painted over with whitewash, q.v. in fig. 14.213, which leaves us with the word "odynskoy." However, even the original inscription is shifted to the left in a strange manner, and obviously made on top of some old lettering, which is completely illegible nowadays.

Apparently, harems had existed in Russia up until the epoch of Peter the Great, or the XVIII century. Peter had instigated a vehement campaign against the Russian harem customs. German historians of the late XIX century report the following: "Peter had even meddled in the traditions that concerned family and social life. He did not tolerate female *terems* or the old

Fig. 14.210. Another tiled fireplace in the internal chambers of the Teremnoy (Harem) Palace of the Muscovite Kremlin.

Fig. 14.211. The bed that was allegedly "misplaced" by Richter, an archaeologist of the XIX century. The Teremnoy (Harem) Palace of the Muscovite Kremlin. Photos taken by the authors in 2000.

123

Fig. 14.212. Coat of next to a windowpane on the fourth floor of the Teremnoy (Harem) Palace of the Kremlin. We see the word "Godynskoy" with the first letter painted over for some reason.

Fig. 14.213. Close-in of the previous photograph. The lettering was obviously moved to the right; something else had been written here originally. We see distinct traces of other letters. Photos taken by the authors in 2000.

custom of females covering their faces. He insisted that the women should not be kept secluded in the Asian manner, but allowed to walk freely, like their European counterparts" ([336], Volume 5, page 569). By the way, the above passage informs us of the fact that in mediaeval Russia, or the Horde, women had covered their faces, or worn yashmaks of some sort.

The Millerian and Romanovian version of the Russian history naturally rules the existence of harems in Russia right out; we have never been told anything about them. However, we see that the customs of the two former parts of the Great = "Mongolian" Empire (Russia, or the Horde, and the Ottoman Turkey) had also been similar in this respect.

20.

Peculiar names in the old maps of Russia that contradict the Scaligerian version of history

In fig. 14.214 we reproduce an old map of Russia from the *Global Cosmography* of Sebastian Münster, allegedly dating from 1544 ([450], page 325). In the right part of the map, between the Yaik and the Ob, we see a picture of several tents and an inscription that says "kosaki orda," or the Cossack Horde (fig. 14.215). Thus, the old map is telling us directly that the troops of the Cossacks had formerly been known as hordes, which is precisely what we claim in our reconstruction of Russian history.

In fig. 14.216 we see another old map of Russia, allegedly dating from the XVI century. The centre of the map is telling us that the country it depicts is "Tartary, alias Scythia" (*Tartaria, olim Scythia*), q.v. in fig. 14.217. This is a direct reference to the fact that Tartary and Scythia had been synonyms in that epoch. We have mentioned it many times, referring to the ancient authors. Here we see a direct reference to this fact on an old map. The name Tartary, or Scythia, is applied to Russia and no other land. We must also point out the fact that we see the words "Sarmatia Asiatica" to the east of Volga – Asian Sarmatia, in other words. Thus, Russia had also been known as Sarmatia. We also mention this in *Chron5*.

Also, the Northern Caucasus is called Albania. Modern maps tell us nothing of the kind – the only Albania known to us today is in the Balkan Peninsula. However, old maps appear to locate Albania differently.

1038 # De la Cofmographie

mis d'exercer vfures. Plus toft ilz s'appliquent à cultiuer les champs à trafiquer en toutes
fortes de marchandifes,a arrenter les peages et tailles pubilques.D'auantage il y a plufieurs
Armeniens en la ville de Camienne,& femblablement a Leopoly, marchans expertz, qui
trafiquent a Caffe,Conftantinoble,Alexandrie qui eft en Egypte,Au Caire et aux parties d'
Indie,dont aufsi ilz raportent des marchandifes. Les Rutheniens ont leurs propres lettres
approchâtes des lettres Grecques,Et les luifz qui y font,ont leurs characteres Hebraiques,
& font diligens à cognoiftre les artz liberaux,la Medicine,l'Aftronomie. Les Armeniens
aufsi ont leurs façons de faire & leurs lettres à part.Entre tous les fainct ilz honnorent S.Iu-
de.'Apoftre,difans qui ilz ont efté conuertiz par luy a la religion Chreftienne.Ilz ont aufsi
en grand honneur S.Bartholemy,par lequel ilz ont apprins plufieurs articles defia foy com
me ilz afferment.Il y a archeuefche en la ville de Leopoly,fouz laquelle font les Rufsiens &
Lithuaniens. I auoit aufsi autrefois en Kiouie vn fiege archiepifcopal,ayant fouz foy quel-
ques eglifes Grecques,qui font fouz Moldauie & Valachie iufques au Danube.

Mofchouie.

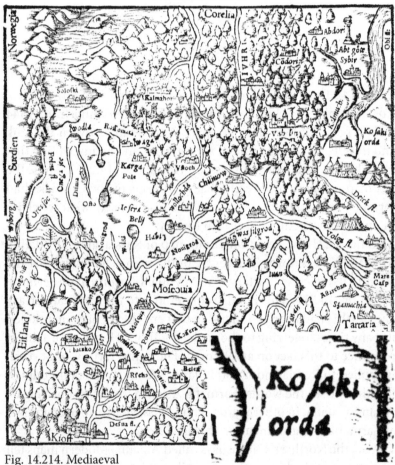

Fig. 14.214. Mediaeval
map of Russia allegedly
dating from the XVI
century.

Fig. 14.215. Fragment of the
map of Russia with the legend
"Cossacks. Horde."

Fig. 14.216. Mediaeval map of Russia allegedly dating from the XVI century. Mark that the modern Straits of Kerch between the Azov Sea and the Black Sea is called the Bosporus for some reason (transcribed as Bosphor), just like the straits where we find Istanbul, or Constantinople. It is therefore possible that some of the Trojan legends apply to the Crimean peninsula and Tauris (Troy). The chroniclers may have confused the two similarly named straits for one another.

Fig. 14.217. Fragment of a map of Russia with the legend "Tartary, aka Scythia." Taken from [267], page 325.

21.

The Russian *subbotniki* sect had been of the opinion that the Biblical Assyria, Egypt and Babylon identified as the Mediaeval Russia

The present section contains an observation made by our readers, which is in good concurrence with our reconstruction.

"Jerusalem Notes," an article by S. Doudakov, which was published in Russian in the magazine "Jews and Slavs," #8, "Oh, Jerusalem!," Pisa-Jerusalem, 1999, contains a reference to a book by T. I. Boutkevich entitled *An Overview of the Russian Sectarians* published in Kharkov in 1910 ([108]). On pages 394-395 T. I. Boutkevich writes about a Russian sect known as *subbotniki* ("the Saturday people"). Doudakov renders Boutkevich's information in the following manner: "They believed their homeland to be Palestine and nor Russia. They refer to Russia as to Assur, reading the name Russa from right to left, the Jewish way... Everything that the Bible says about Babylon, Assyria and Egypt was believed to refer to Russia by the *subbotniki*" (page 286 of Doudakov's article).

This fact is explained perfectly well by our reconstruction, according to which, the name Assyria is used by the Bible in order to refer to Russia, or the Horde, in the Middle Ages, likewise the names Egypt and Babylon, q.v. in *Chron6*. Thus, we see that religious groups with a more correct understanding of the original meaning of certain Biblical texts had existed in Russia up until the end of the XIX century, identifying Russia with the Biblical Assyria, Egypt and Babylon. Those memories must have been rather vague, but the very fact of their existence speaks volumes. It is possible that such religious groups exist until the present day.

One must say that the voluminous encyclopaedic publication entitled *Christianity* ([936]) doesn't utter a single word about this extremely interesting and important belief held by the *subbotniki* in the respective entry, namely, that they identified the Biblical Assyria, Egypt and Babylon as mediaeval Russia.

It is further reported that the *subbotniki* had belonged to the very same tradition as the "Judaist heretics" ([936], Volume 2, pages 653-654), or the famous "Russian Judaism" of the XV-XVI century, which had played an important part in the Russian history of the XVI century, q.v. in *Chron6*. There was a period when the representatives of this confession had come to power at the Russian court of the Czar, or the Khan. According to our hypothesis, the Bible in the modern sense of the word was created around that time, and with their active participation (the early version of the modern Biblical canon, that is). It is little wonder, then, that their followers should remember more about the original meaning of the Biblical terms than any other party.

The *Christianity* encyclopaedia only provides us with the following sparse information about the traditions of the *subbotniki*: "According to the latest research, some of the *subbotniki* had followed the Law of Moses, but refused to revere the Talmud, and had read their prayers in Russian and Church Slavonic; in other regions (the provinces of Irkutsk and Pyatigorsk, for instance) they had worn Russian clothes and adhered to Russian customs in general" ([936], Volume 2, page 654).

The modern *dukhobori* (literally "warriors of the spirit") are considered to be another offshoot of the Russian Judaic Church of the XV-XVI century. The *Christianity* encyclopaedia tells us the following: "The *dukhobori* represent a very old tradition; they are associated with the *strigolniki*, the 'Judaic heretics', Bashkin and Feodosiy Kosoi" ([936], Volume 1, page 495). Let us remind the reader that both Bashkin and Feodosiy Kosoi had been prominent members of the Russian Judaic Church in the XVI century. According to our hypothesis, the Russian Judaic Reformist Church in Russia had been closely tied to the Lutheran Reformist Church in the West – possibly, to the extent of being one of its branches, q.v. in *Chron6*.

However, according to our reconstruction, the epoch of the XVI century, which is when the sect of the *dukhobori* came to existence, became reflected in the Bible as the famous reign of the "Assyrian" King Nebuchadnezzar, q.v. in *Chron6*. It is significant that the *dukhobori* tradition is in total concurrence with this claim that we make – namely, it turns out that "the *dukhobori* themselves trace their tradition to the 'three younglings – Ananiah, Azariah and Misael'" ([936], Volume 1, page 495). They are Biblical characters identified as contemporaries of King Nebuchadnezzar, which dates their lifetimes to the XVI century, according to the New Chronology – precisely the epoch of Bashkin and Feodosiy Kosoi, the founding fathers of the *dukhobori* tradition. According to our reconstruction, the Biblical Assyrian King Nebuchadnezzar can be identified as one of the Czars that had ruled in Russia, or the Horde, during the epoch of Ivan the Terrible. To put it more simply, Nebuchadnezzar can be identified as Ivan the Terrible.

It is even more interesting that some of the researchers who studied the *dukhobori* tradition, identified one of the "three Biblical younglings" as Bashkin, who had lived in the XVI century ([936], Volume 1, page 495). That should indeed make him a contemporary of Ivan the Terrible (or Nebuchadnezzar), as we feel obliged to emphasise.

22.

The old cathedrals of the Western Europe have preserved the style of the XV-XVI century Russian churches

Nowadays we are told that typical Russian churches had looked just the same in the XV-XVI century as they do today – namely, as constructions of a cubic shape with a roof that is almost flat, topped by one or several cylinders that support gilded domes, and a semi-circular altar part on the eastern side (see figs. 14.218 and 14.219). This style is radically different from the churches of the Western Europe – elongated buildings with tall gable roofs, usually topped by a spire, or several spires. The famous gothic Cologne Cathedral is a most typical example (see fig. 14.220). It is presumed that such churches had been built in Europe since times immemorial, whereas the Russian churches had always looked the way they do today – the "cubic" constructions that we know today. We are referring to the Russian churches that are presumed to date from the XII-XVI century nowadays.

However, it turns out that the churches that were built in Russia in the XV, and, most probably, also in the XVI century, had looked exactly like elongated buildings with tall gable roofs; one also gets the impression that this gothic style had been prevalent in Russia in the XV-XVI century. The "cubic" churches that we're accustomed to must have become prevalent as recently as the XVII century.

This suspicion first arose in us after a study of the architecture typical for the churches of Ouglich, a famed Russian city. Let us turn to the guidebook written by N. F. Lavrov ([461]). It describes all the

Fig. 14.218. A typical Russian church of the XVII century. This is the Nikolskaya Church of the Niko-lo-Ouleymenskiy Monastery near Ouglich. We see the eastern wall of the church. It is presumed that most Russian churches of the XII-XVI century had looked like this.

Fig. 14.219. A typical Russian church of the XVII century. We see the northwest view of the Nikolskaya Church, Nikolo-Ouleymenskiy Monastery, Ouglich. Most Russian churches of the XII-XVI century are supposed to have been constructed in the same manner as this one.

churches of Ouglich the way they were in 1869. It turns out that they were either cardinally rebuilt, or built again from scratch, in the XVII century the earliest, with just one exception. The architectural style of these churches looks perfectly normal to us – their primary element is the abovementioned "cube," or its modifications of the XVIII-XIX century. The only exception is the famous Church of St. Alexei, named after the Metropolitan of Moscow, in the Alexeyevskiy Friary of Oug-lich. It is presumed to date from the

Fig. 14.220. The gothic Cologne Cathedral as it looks today. Cologne, Germany. Taken from [1017], photograph 3.

134

Fig. 14.221. Church of Metropolitan Alexei in Ouglich. Southern view. The only church in Ouglich that has survived from the epoch of the XV-XVI century. Photo taken in 2000.

Fig. 14.222. Church of Metropolitan Alexei in Ouglich. View from the southeast. Photo taken in 2000.

Fig. 14.223. Church of Metropolitan Alexei in Ouglich. Western view. Photo taken in 2000.

Fig. 14.224. The Church of Presentation, the Nikolo-Ouleimenskiy Monastery, Ouglich. Northern view. The church is entered via a tall porch that leads directly to the first floor. Photo taken in 2000.

Fig. 14.225. The Church of Presentation, Nikolo-Ouleimenskiy Monastery, Ouglich. Eastern view. A more recent square block topped by a cylinder and also characterised by a semicircular altar part was adjoined to the old building in some later epoch. Photo taken in 2000.

Fig. 14.226. The Church of Presentation, Nikolo-Ouleimenskiy Monastery, Ouglich. View from the southeast. Photo taken in 2000.

XV century – namely, 1482; it is also said to have preserved its original shape ([461], page 110). In figs. 14.222 and 14.223 one sees two modern photographs of this church. It is an elongated building with a tall gable roof; there are three tall spires over the eastern altar part (however, they may have been built later). The entrance to the church is located in its northern part, and it leads to the second floor directly. One cannot help noting that this old Russian church of the XV century strongly resembles the Gothic Cologne Cathedral, q.v. in fig. 14.220.

One must also enquire about the fate of the churches built in the XVI century. Could it be that the residents of Ouglich had abstained from building churches for more than a century? Or have those churches "disintegrated" all by themselves? Oddly enough, there are many XVII century churches in Ouglich. It must be pointed out that the XV century Church of St. Alexei is a huge cathedral, one of the largest churches in Ouglich to date. Having built such a cathedral in the XV century, the people of Ouglich must have also built something in the XVI century. One gets the impression that nearly every church in Ouglich was rebuilt in the XVII century. The Church of St. Alexei must have survived by miracle; therefore, it looks out of place amidst the churches that are said to represent the typical architectural style of the ancient Russia. One must emphasise that all these "typically Russian" churches were built in the XVII century the earliest.

This observation is confirmed by another example. Let us turn to the architecture of the famous Russian Nikolo-Ouleymenskiy Monastery near Ouglich. There are two churches here – the older one is the Church of the Presentation (see figs. 14.224, 14.225 and 14.226). The other is of a more recent origin and known as the Nikolskaya Church (see above, in figs. 14.218 and 14.219). The latter already looks like a "typical" Russian church. However, the older Church of the Presentation is once again an elongated building with a gable roof. It was later complemented by a belfry and a cubic construction in the east; however, these modifications already date from the XVII century. The main part of the church looks more like the gothic cathedrals of the Western Europe than the Greek cubes with cylinders and domes (the more recent type derived from basilicas like the Hagia Sophia in Constantinople = Czar-Grad = Jerusalem).

Fig. 14.227. The Gothic Cathedral of Peter and Paul in Yaroslavl, built in the Old Russian style of the Horde. We see a spire, a gable roof and a first floor entrance. Taken from [996], page 159.

Fig. 14.228. Another photograph of the Gothic Cathedral of Peter and Paul in Yaroslavl. This is precisely the style the West Europeans built their cathedrals in. Taken from [116], ill. 341.

We don't claim that no churches of the Greek type were built in the XV century Russia; we are concerned with whether or not they should be regarded as examples of typical ecclesiastical architecture in Russia when it had still been known as the Horde. The abovementioned facts make one doubt this; one gets the impression that in the XVII century the overwhelming majority of the Russian churches were rebuilt in the "Greek" manner favoured by the Reformists. Moreover, the latter made the claim that Russian churches had always looked like this, which is a blatant lie, as we realise today.

In some regions of Russia, gothic cathedrals were built until the XVIII century – such is the famous Church of Peter and Paul in Yaroslavl, which dates from 1736-1744, q.v. in figs. 14.227 and 14.228. The mosque of the Poyiseyevo village in the Aktanysh region of Tartarstan is built in the same manner (see fig. 14.229). However, the

Fig. 14.229. A mosque in the village of Poiseyevo, Tartarstan. It is built in the Gothic style. Photograph kept in the Funds of the United National Museum of Tartarstan. Taken from [6], page 21.

old gothic style of the Russian churches and the Tartar mosques was eventually cast into oblivion under the Romanovs, either voluntarily or compulsively.

However, there was no such "Greek architectural wave" in the Western Europe of the XVII century, where the churches had still been built in the old Imperial style of the Great = "Mongolian" Empire. Even the word Dom, which is still used for referring to the largest cathedrals of the Western Europe, is obviously derived from the Russian word *"dom,"* translating as "a house." Likewise, name "gothic" is derived from the word "Goth" – the ancient synonym of the word "Cossack." This is the architecture that was brought to the Western Europe by the Cossack troops of the Great = "Mongolian" Empire in the XIV-XV century (see *Chron5* for more details).

In Russia, however, the old Imperial style of the churches fell into disfavour; such churches either got destroyed and rebuilt anew, or became disfigured by later additional constructions. Alternatively, the buildings were converted for non-ecclesiastical purposes, such as the gigantic old building, very tall and with a gable roof, which is part of the Simonov monastery in Moscow, q.v. in figs. 14.230, 14.231 and 14.232. In the XIX century it was used as a grain dryer. The architecture of this building strongly resembles that of the ancient Russian churches. It is therefore most likely to be the old church of the Simonov Monastery. Its size and height could compete with those of the same monastery's cathedral, which must be of a later origin. The entrance to the old building had been on the north and looked like a tall porch. The old porch doesn't exist anymore, and was replaced by a modern metallic construction, q.v. in fig. 14.231. Let us emphasise that this building bears no marks of reconstructions distorting its original architecture – it doesn't even have any spires. Apparently, this is what the old Russian churches really looked like in the XV-XVI century.

Let us point out a distinctive characteristic of the old church of the New Simonov Monastery, which is also typical for many Western European churches. We are referring to the tall column of a semi-circular shape in the corner of the building, which partially protrudes outwards, q.v. in figs. 14.230, 14.231 and 14.232. Similar tower-like columns, which occasionally resemble minarets, can be seen in the Cathedral of St. Cecilia in the French town of Albi, near Toulouse. This cathedral also has an elongated shape; its photograph can be seen in *Chron6*.

One must say that some of the modern specialists in the history of architecture have noticed the few surviving Russian churches built in the Gothic style. However, the pressure of the Scaligerian and Millerian chronology, which has managed to turn a great many historical facts inside out, made them assume that some of the Russian architects had occasionally "used nothing but Gothic elements of the Western European fashion in their pseudo-Gothic constructions... In a number of cases we see intricate decorative 'Gothic decorations', either sculpted or carved in white stone" ([311], page 29). M. Ilyin,

Fig. 14.230. Old building at the New Simonov Monastery in Moscow. The construction is most likely to have been an old Russian church with a gable roof, later converted for drying corn.

Fig. 14.231. Old building at the New Simonov Monastery in Moscow. The tower, or column, integrated into the wall of the building and typical for Western European cathedrals, is visible perfectly well.

Fig. 14.232. Old building at the New Simonov Monastery in Moscow. General view. Photograph taken in 2000.

a renowned expert in the history of architecture, claims that "the composition is based on ancient Russian specimens, modified in accordance with the specifications of the pseudo-Gothic architecture" ([311], page 29). Moreover, it is emphasised that certain Russian architects had "fully mastered ... the entire arsenal of pseudo-Gothic shapes" ([311], page 21). Ilyin cites the "famous church in Bykov" as a typical example on the same page, calling it a "masterpiece." It is emphasised that "although the western part of the temple was rebuilt in the first half of the XIX century, it had played an important part in the history of the Russian pseudo-Gothic style" ([311], page 32).

As we are beginning to realise, all such passages require the removal of the "pseudo" part; one must also mention the fact that the style in question characterises the architecture of the Gothic, or Cossack, Russia, also known as the Horde. Therefore, the Gothic style must have been imported by the Westerners from the East, and not the other way round, as it is presumed in official history.

We reproduce a photograph of the church in Bykovo in fig. 14.233. It is perfectly obvious that its style is the same as that of the ancient Russian Gothic churches listed above. It is likely that in large Russian cities all such constructions, which bore the mark of the old Imperial

Fig. 14.233. Ancient Russian church in the village of Bykovo. It is classified as "pseudo-Gothic" nowadays. Apparently, some of the churches built in the old style of the Horde have survived in small Russian towns and villages. Taken from [311], illustrations at the end of the book.

Fig. 14.234. The principal cathedral of Mozhaysk (the New Nikolskiy Cathedral) was built in the Gothic style. Photograph taken in 2000.

style, were rebuilt under the Romanovs, whereas in smaller towns and villages certain traces of the old tradition have survived. Even in the XVII-XVIII century some of the architects continued to build churches in the old Russian style – Gothic, or Cossack.

The main cathedral of the ancient Russian city of Mozhaysk is also built in the Gothic style – the New Nikolskiy Cathedral of the Mozhaysk Citadel, q.v. in fig. 14.234. This cathedral was built in 1814 by Alexei Nikitich Bakaryov, the architect of the Muscovite Kremlin Architectural Expedition ([536], pages 124 and 80).

The architecture of the cathedral is classified as "pseudo-Gothic" ([536], page 80). It must be for a good reason that in 1806 Bakaryov built the Nikolskaya Tower of the Muscovite Kremlin, which had for a long time housed the Mozhaysk icon of St. Nicholas the Miracle-Worker, in the same Gothic style. Apparently, the memory of the ancient Russian Gothic churches had been kept alive in Mozhaysk for a long time.

Fig. 14.235. The old church at the Louzhetskiy Monastery of Mozhaysk. It is likely to have looked like a Gothic cathedral as well. Photo taken in 2000.

Another ancient church of an elongated shape can be seen in the Louzhetskiy Monastery of Mozhaysk, q.v. in fig. 14.235. It must also have looked like a Gothic cathedral initially, and been rebuilt in the new style in the XVII century. In particular, a cubic church topped by a Greek dome was adjoined to its eastern side; it is clearly visible in fig. 14.235. Moreover, the excavations of 1999-2000, which had uncovered the XVII century layers of the Louzhetskiy Monastery, revealed the fact that mutilated old headstones of the XVI – early XVII century had been used as base stones for the walls and the corners of this later extension.

The old Horde style was preserved in the construction of many Muslim mosques predating the XIX century. For instance, in figs. 14.236 – 14.240 we reproduce photographs of some of the mosques in Tartarstan. It is perfectly obvious that their architecture is virtually the same as that of the Gothic cathedrals in the Western Europe. It has to be pointed out that, according to [760:1], there are a great many such mosques in Tartarstan; we included photographs of only a few of them.

Everything becomes perfectly clear. The Romanovs had tried to forsake the old Russian customs, changing the architectural style of the Russian churches and replacing the headstones in the Russian cemeteries. The old Gothic churches were either rebuilt or demolished, whereas the headstones were destroyed or used as construc-

Fig. 14.236. Mosque at Starye Kiyazly. Republic of Tartarstan. The Western Gothic cathedrals have a similar shape. Taken from [760:1], page 23.

Fig. 14.237. Mosque at Staroye Ibraykino. Republic of Tartarstan. This shape is also characteristic for the Gothic cathedrals of the Western Europe. Taken from [760:1], page 22.

Fig. 14.238. Mosque at Stariy Bagryazh-Yelkhov. Republic of Tartarstan. Gothic cathedrals in the West are shaped similarly. Taken from [760:1], page 46.

Fig. 14.239. Mosque at Asan-Yelg. Republic of Tartarstan. Gothic cathedrals in the West are shaped similarly. Taken from [760:1], page 231.

Fig. 14.240. Mosque at Nizhnyaya Oshma. Republic of Tartarstan. Gothic cathedrals in the West are shaped similarly. Taken from [760:1], page 264.

tion material. This had radically changed the appearance of the Russian graveyards and monasteries. Then it was declared that they had "always looked like this," and that the ancient Russian customs had been the same as the ones introduced under the Romanovs.

Let us return to the work of M. Ilyin. He proceeds to point out additional parallels between the Gothic cathedrals of the Western Europe and the ancient Russian churches: "I was amazed by the similarities between a Czech Gothic church and the Ouspenskiy Cathedral in Moscow, which have made me wonder about the nature of this likeness and the reasons behind it. Quite naturally, one can hardly speak of any direct connexions between the Czech churches and the Muscovite cathedral" ([311], page 97). Ilyin is obviously confused by the erroneous Scaligerian and Millerian chronology. Further he writes: "It is obvious that these similarities reflect some general tendency that was characteristic for the entire mediaeval Europe. In other words, the spatial features of the Ouspenskiy cathedral are related to the Gothic space of the Western cathedrals" (ibid.). Nowadays we understand the reasons behind the similarities noticed by the modern specialists in the history of architecture. Western Europe had been part of the Great = "Mongolian" Empire up until the XVII century; the Gothic (Cossack) style had been prevalent throughout the entire empire.

In fig. 14.241 we see the German church in Mayen, a town located in the vicinity of Bonn. It is called Clementskirche; its dome is shaped very quaintly, as upward spirals. The church was greatly damaged in 1941-1945; however, it was rebuilt in full accordance with the surviving drawings. It is presumed that the construction of the Clementskirche began in 1000, and that the church had then been rebuilt several times, in the XIV century and even later. The unusual spiral shape of the dome was noticed by many specialists in the history of architecture. It is presumed that this cupola was constructed between 1350 and 1360. The reasons why the mediaeval architects chose this peculiar shape appear to be obliterated from memory. The brochure on the history of the church suggests the following amusing legend to explain this architectural peculiarity. Apparently, the inhabitants of the city are said to have addressed the devil with the request to build them a tavern. The blueprints that they gave him

Fig. 14.241. Spiral dome of the German Clemenskirche in Mayen, near Bonn. Taken from the brochure given to visitors at the actual church.

were those of a church, however. The none-too-bright devil had agreed to this, but was surprised to see a church instead of a tavern upon finishing his work. In a fit of anger, he took one of the spires and twisted it into a spiral; it remains in this shape to this very day. The brochure is given to every visitor of the church, which was visited by A. T. Fomenko and T. N. Fomenko in June 2000. Modern commentators and guides usually omit the legend about the horned miscreant, replacing it with an earnest explanation that involves a hurricane, which had struck the city ages ago and twisted the formerly straight spire of the church into a spiral, which has been that way ever since, remaining intact despite the damage inflicted by the hurricane. We believe involved scientific discussions concerning devils and strong winds that blow in Germany to be quite extraneous.

In reality, what we see here is another example of the ancient Russian architecture of the XIV-XVI century. It suffices to compare the dome of the German Clementskirche to the spiral domes of St. Basil's Cathedral in Moscow, q.v. in fig. 14.242, in order to realise that both of them were built in the same architectural style. The spiral domes of St. Basil's look very much like the Ottoman = Ataman turbans. Apparently, such churches were built both in Russia and the

147

Fig. 14.242. Spiral domes of the Cathedral of St. Basil the Blessed in Moscow. Taken from [549], page 35.

Western Europe around the XIV-XVI century, after the colonisation of the latter in the epoch of the Great = "Mongolian" conquest. The Clementskirche sports a similar Ottoman turban-like dome.

Minarets topped with spiral domes also exist in the Orient – for instance, the "spiral minaret of the Mosque of Abu-Dulaf in Samarra (860/61)" ([1210], page 105), as well as the spiral minaret of Üc Serefeli Cami in Edirne ([1210], page 546).

This may shed some light over the legend of the devil, who is presumed to have taken part in the construction of the Clementskirche. As we have already mentioned, everything related to the Great = "Mongolian" Empire was proclaimed evil and "satanic" during the epoch of the Reformation in the Western Europe, including the architecture of the Horde, or the Atamans, characteristic for a number of churches that were later declared to have been built by "the devil." The legend later became part of the folk tradition.

Let us make a brief summary. We are confronted with yet another trace of the large-scale reformation of the ancient Russian customs and architectural styles that took place in the XVII century. The new customs and styles introduced by the Romanovs were later declared "typical for the ancient Russia." This has resulted in a totally warped concept of the Russian history before the XVII century. Most of the allegedly ancient Russian traditions related to architecture, litera-

148

ture, funereal rites, etc. were introduced in the XVII century, or the epoch of the first Romanovs. Another wave of changes swept over Russia under Peter the Great. Nowadays it is presumed that Peter was changing the old Russian customs for Western ones in general and German ones in particular. In most cases, these "ancient Russian" customs had been introduced by his predecessors – the first Romanovs. Precious little is known about the authentic customs of the ancient Russia – what we have is stray bits of information, collected with much effort.

23.

The organs of the Western European cathedrals have preserved the ancient musical culture of the XV-XVI century Russia, or the Horde

The cathedrals of the Western Europe differ from the mosques and the Russian churches in a variety of ways, one of them being that the former are equipped with organs that are played during service. It is presumed that no such instruments have ever existed in Russia. However, this popular opinion is most likely to be erroneous. Organs did exist in Russia. It is also possible that such musical instruments were played in the churches of the Great = "Mongolian" Empire in the XIV-XVI century. As we shall tell the reader in the present section, organs were widely popular in the ancient Russia. They were presumably banned by Peter the Great; possibly – by his predecessors, the first Romanovs, in the course of their struggle against the ancient Russian customs, which had largely proved successful. This is what historians report.

In 1700 Cornelius de Bruin (Brun) came to Moscow from the Western Europe. "In 1711 a book entitled 'Journey to Persia and India via Moscovia' by the Dutch traveller Cornelius de Bruin was published in Amsterdam. Several years later, this amazing oeuvre was translated into nearly every European language" ([537:1], page 52). N. M. Moleva, Doctor of History, gives the following brief summary of the traveller's impressions: "Luxurious houses. Golden and silver dishes galore. Splendorous attires" ([537:1], page 32). De Bruin himself reports the following: "Two gigantic leopards had stood there [in the household of Lefort on River Yaouza – Auth.], with

151

their paws stretched wide, resting on shields with coats of arms, all of it cast in sterling silver; also a globe of silver resting on the shoulders of Atlas, cast in the same metal. Apart from that, there were many large tankards and other vessels, all made of silver" (quotation given in accordance with [537:1], page 56).

"There could however be more music and histrionics at the court. Cornelius de Bruin doesn't mention them anywhere. However, the teenage Italian singer, Philip Balatri, who was in Moscow around the same time, was amazed to discover that there were organs of an original constructions in many households; however, those were concealed in wardrobes for some reason. Later he managed to find out that the organs were banned by Peter the Great as an ancient Russian custom. The wedding of the jester Shanskiy near Kozhuk-hov in 1697 must have been the last Muscovite celebration with 27 organs" ([537:1], page 32).

The construction of the Russian organs isn't described anywhere; we only learn of their "original construction." Let us remind the reader that the organ is a pneumatic instrument equipped by bel-lows with metallic tubes that produce sounds when compressed air is pumped through them. The prototype of the organ must be the bagpipe. There were also small hand organs that produced sounds after the rotation of a roller, with some melody notched upon it ([223], Volume 2, column 1787). This is how the street-organ is constructed, for instance. However, further observations of De Bruin reveal that in some (possibly, most) cases, the instruments in ques-tion were large pneumatic organs.

"Music is just as impressive. De Bruin hears it everywhere – oboes, French horns and timpani played at ceremonial and military proces-sions; whole orchestras of different instruments, including the organ at the Gates of Triumph. Music is heard on the streets and inside houses; finally, he is impressed by the amazing clarity of the choirs. No feast in Moscovia could do without them" ([537:1], page 55).

It is likely that the orchestras that played in squares were accom-panied by large organs with pipes and bellows.

The famous composer Vivaldi had planned to go to Moscow in search of permanent employment. The voyage never came to pass; however, his apprentice Verocagli, a composer and a violinist, did in fact relocate to Moscow ([537:1], page 64). However, the Romanovian version of history is trying to convince us that the musical culture of the ancient Russian had been primitive to the extent of being nonexistent – barbaric dances around smoky fires, primitive folk songs, usually of an obscene character, tambourines, loud horns, squeaky flutes and drunken shouts – a far cry from the refined Versailles, all lace and violins.

N. M. Moleva is correct to point out that "the black decade of Biron and the reign of Peter the Great, void of all music, is a textbook reality."

However, in the XVII century there were organs all across Moscow – and not just Moscow, as De Bruin reports; no work on the history of music mentioned it until very recently. French horns and oboes were the favourite instrument among the street musicians of the epoch, and not just their colleagues at the court of the Czar. Academic publications only mention gusli (a horizontal folk harp) and wooden horns. However, there was a whole state-subsidised school of trumpet players in Moscow in the middle of the very same century; this fact is reflected in the name of the Troubnikovskiy Lane in Moscow [the Russian word for "trumpet" is "truba" – Transl.], whereas every reference book written in accordance with the Romanovian version of history claims that only foreign musicians who came to Russia from the Western Europe could play those instruments, let alone train musicians.

All of this became apparent very recently (the book of N. M. Moleva was published in 1997), when dozens of documents containing the above evidence were discovered in archives. This leads us to yet another question. What became of this highly evolved musical culture, this necessity for music that wasn't felt by the royal court, which had adhered to the same protocol as Europe, but a whole nation? What unimaginable cataclysm could have wiped them out from half a century of Russian history at least? Could the episode with Vivaldi and Verocagli really mean that the real situation had differed from the one described in all the general tractates on the Russian culture? See [537:1], pages 65-66.

Fortunately, "civil records had remained in existence. Few historians have the stamina required for working with them, let alone specialists in the history of fine arts. It is too strenuous to sort through hundreds of thousands of faceless names... However, we had no other option.

The records spoke volumes. For instance, we learned that the foundation of St. Petersburg resulted in plummeting numbers of organists in the ranks of freelance musicians. There were organists in Moscow, but hardly any in St. Petersburg. The fashion and the private tastes of Peter the Great are to blame for this. Also, the old Kremlin organ and clavichord workshop, which had functioned excellently, perished in the blaze of 1701. Nobody ever bothered to rebuild it – Peter had other plans for the Kremlin. No new workshop was ever founded, either. The numbers of musicians in the ranks of the Muscovite landowners had dwindled as well – possibly, due to unemployment and the resulting poverty. This is easy to verify by other civil records – the buying and selling records. All such transactions were registered meticulously and subject to taxation. We learnt that the organists had been busy looking for alternative means of sustaining themselves" ([537:1], pages 67-68).

However, it turns out that certain cities of the Western Europe had made organs and exported them to Russia up until the early XVIII century ([537:1], pages 72-73). This is apparently another trace of the old tradition of the "Mongolian" empire, whose different regions specialised in the production of various industrial products for the Empire in the XV-XVI century. For example, some of the pipe organs for the musical centres of the Empire were produced in the Western Europe. In particular, "Theophilus Anzey Volkmar had been the organist of the 'main church in the old part of Danzig – St. Catherine's', and also a middleman involved in the buying and selling of the most expensive instruments, which became scarcer with the day – organs and clavichords. This was reported by the 'Vedomosti of St. Petersburg' in 1729... Why did the Polish organist look towards Russia as a prospective market for his instruments? Due to lack of experience, or hope for blind luck? This isn't the case – the books of the City Magistrate of Gdansk dating from the late 1720's and early 1730's testify to the opposite. Volkmar had been an experienced middleman, and some of his most important sales were made in Russia. Advertisements in the St. Petersburg newspaper reaped dividends, despite the high cost of the instruments offered" ([537:1], pages 72-73).

Let us point out another peculiar detail. "Finally, a substantial proof of our vague and timid presumptions – archive materials containing the list of the court's employees for 1731. There were more than 90 players of instruments there – quite amazing! The string group included over 30 players, six trumpets and an equal number of French horns, not to mention the oboes and the timpani... This was doubtlessly a symphony orchestra, and a large one, at that, even by modern standards – the orchestra of the Bolshoi Theatre amounts to some 120 musicians nowadays... All of this 70 years earlier than it is generally assumed in the history of the Russian music!

In this case, there might be little fantasy in the rumour that the Venetian abbot Vivaldi had been ready to accept the offer to travel to Moscow, and the only reasons that he never did were his age and his abbot's cloak?... There were no 'empty' decades and no dark age of culture. The great ... tradition of the Russian musical culture had borne new fruits in the new century" ([537:1], pages 81-82).

A propos, we must note that accordions are still very popular in Russia. Their history is generally presumed to date back to the early XIX century the earliest ([797], page 276). However, the accordion is constructed similarly to the organ – compressed air from the bellows is pumped through the pipes of the instrument, which produces differently pitched sounds. The accordion (harmonium) and the organ may be two variants of the same instrument. The accordion is small and portable; it could be used at folk festivals, whereas the larger organs were installed in churches and large buildings. The words "harmonium" and "organ" may be similar, given the frequent flexion of M and N. The word "harmonium" is virtually identical to the Old Russian word *"garniy,"* which stands for "good" or "beautiful," and is still used in Ukrainian (see [223], Volume 1, column 848). The word *garniy* may have been used in Russia for referring to a sweetly sounding instrument. Could the word "organ" be of the same root? Bellows have existed in Russia for a long time, since they were widely used by blacksmiths and metallurgists. The construction of the organ may also be based on military trumpets and hunters' horns, which had been widely used in Russia as well. The Horde, or the Russian army, had often used military trumpets, which are mentioned in the *Tale of the Kulikovo Battle*, for instance, q.v. above.

The so-called "horn music" had still existed in Russia under the Romanovs for some time. Several musicians blew into large horns, mounted upon special supporting constructions ([711:1], pp. 75-76).

Thus, according to the evidence of the XVII century, organ music was very popular in Old Russia. However, the Romanovs banned them in the course of their struggle against the cultural heritage of the Horde Empire, and introduced a new style of musical culture.

Organs are most likely to have been outlawed under the first Romanovs, during the reform of the Russian church in the beginning of the XVII century. However, the old musical culture of the Horde must have proved so resilient that it took decades to wipe it out completely. We have seen that Peter the Great was already concentrated on banning organs from Russian households, where they had still been preserved. As a result, ecclesiastical services had lost musical instruments to accompany the vocals. The contemporaries of Peter the Great observed that "the Czar [Peter – Auth.] was delighted by vocal numbers sans accompaniment – a cappella" ([537:1], page 32). Everything is perfectly obvious – the "a cappella" tradition resulted from the withdrawal of organs, much to the pleasure of Peter. We see that in Romanovian Russia the organs and the accordions were expunged from the official musical culture. Accordions, or harmoniums, were declared a folk instrument dating from the beginning of the XIX century. However, in the West the Gothic cathedrals, formerly mosques, and the organs inside them, have survived until the present day, declared to be of purely Western origins a posteriori.

About the Authors

Fomenko, Anatoly Timofeevich (b. 1945). Full Member (Academician) of the Russian Academy of Sciences, Full Member of the Russian Academy of Natural Sciences, Full Member of the International Higher Education Academy of Sciences, Doctor of Physics and Mathematics, Professor, Head of the Moscow State University Section of Mathematics of the Department of Mathematics and Mechanics. Solved Plateau's Problem from the theory of minimal spectral surfaces. Author of the theory of invariants and topological classification of integrable Hamiltonian dynamic systems. Laureate of the 1996 National Premium of the Russian Federation (in Mathematics) for a cycle of works on the Hamiltonian dynamical systems and manifolds' invariants theory. Author of 200 scientific publications, 28 monographs and textbooks on mathematics, a specialist in geometry and topology, calculus of variations, symplectic topology, Hamiltonian geometry and mechanics, computer geometry. Author of a number of books on the development of new empirico-statistical methods and their application to the analysis of historical chronicles as well as the chronology of antiquity and the Middle Ages.

Nosovskiy, Gleb Vladimirovich (b. 1958). Candidate of Physics and Mathematics (MSU, Moscow, 1988), specialist in theory of probability, mathematical statistics, theory of probabilistic processes, theory of optimization, stochastic differential equations, computer modelling of stochastic processes, computer simulation. Worked as researcher of computer geometry in Moscow Space Research Institute, in Moscow Machine Tools and Instruments Institute, in Aizu University in Japan. Faculty member of the Department of Mathematics and Mechanics MSU.

What mainstream historians say about the New Chronology?

The **New Chronology** is a fringe theory regarded by the academic community as pseudohistory, which argues that the conventional chronology of Middle Eastern and European history is fundamentally flawed, and that events attributed to the civilizations of the Roman Empire, Ancient Greece and Ancient Egypt actually occurred during the Middle Ages, more than a thousand years later. The central concepts of the New Chronology are derived from the ideas of Russian scholar Nikolai Morozov (1854-1946), although work by French scholar Jean Hardouin (1646-1729) can be viewed as an earlier predecessor. However, the New Chronology is most commonly associated with Russian mathematician Anatoly Fomenko (b. 1945), although published works on the subject are actually a collaboration between Fomenko and several other mathematicians. The concept is most fully explained in *History: Fiction or Science?* book series, originally published in Russian.

The New Chronology also contains *a reconstruction*, an alternative chronology, radically shorter than the standard historical timeline, because all ancient history is "folded" onto the Middle Ages. According to Fomenko's claims, the written history of humankind goes only as far back as AD 800, there is almost no information about events between AD 800–1000, and most known historical events took place in AD 1000–1500.

The New Chronology is rejected by mainstream historians and is inconsistent with absolute and relative dating techniques used in the wider scholarly community. The majority of scientific commentators consider the New Chronology to be pseudoscientific.

History of New Chronology

The idea of chronologies that differ from the conventional chronology can be traced back to at least the early XVII century. Jean Hardouinthen suggested that many ancient historical documents were much younger than commonly believed to be. In 1685 he published a version of Pliny the Elder's *Natural History* in which he claimed that most Greek and Roman texts had been forged by Benedictine monks. When later questioned on these results, Hardouin stated that he would reveal the monks' reasons in a letter to be revealed only after his death. The executors of his estate were unable to find such a document among his posthumous papers. In the XVII century, Sir Isaac Newton, examining the current chronology of Ancient Greece, Ancient Egypt and the Ancient Near East, expressed discontent with prevailing theories and proposed one of his own, which, basing its study on Apollonius of Rhodes's *Argonautica*, changed the traditional dating of the Argonautic Expedition, the Trojan War, and the Founding of Rome.

In 1887, Edwin Johnson expressed the opinion that early Christian history was largely invented or corrupted in the II and III centuries.

In 1909, Otto Rank made note of duplications in literary history of a variety of cultures:

> "... almost all important civilized peoples have early woven myths around and glorified in poetry their heroes, mythical kings and princes, founders of religions, of dynasties, empires and cities—in short, their national heroes. Especially the history of their birth and of their early years is furnished with phantastic [sic] traits; the amazing similarity, nay literal identity, of those tales, even if they refer to different, completely independent peoples, sometimes geographically far removed from one another, is well known and has struck many an investigator." (Rank, Otto. *Der Mythos von der Geburt des Helden.*)

Fomenko became interested in Morozov's theories in 1973. In 1980, together with a few colleagues from the mathematics department of Moscow State University, he published several articles on "new mathematical methods in history" in peer-reviewed journals. The articles stirred a lot of controversy, but ultimately Fomenko failed to win any respected historians to his side. By the early 1990s, Fomenko shifted his focus from trying to convince the scientific community via peer-reviewed publications to publishing books. Beam writes that Fomenko and his colleagues were discovered by the Soviet scientific press in the early 1980s, leading to "a brief period of renown"; a contemporary review from the journal *Questions of History* complained, "Their constructions have nothing in common with Marxist historical science." (Alex Beam. "A shorter history of civilization." *Boston Globe*, 16 September 1991.)

By 1996, his theory had grown to cover Russia, Turkey, China, Europe, and Egypt [Emp:1].

Fomenko's claims

According to New Chronology, the traditional chronology consists of four overlapping copies of the "true" chronology shifted back in time by significant intervals with some further revisions. Fomenko claims all events and characters conventionally dated earlier than XI century are fictional, and represent "phantom reflections" of actual Middle Ages events and characters, brought about by intentional or accidental misdatings of historical documents. Before the invention of printing, accounts of the same events by different eyewitnesses were sometimes retold several times before being written down, then often went through multiple rounds of translating and copyediting. Names were translated, mispronounced and misspelled to the point where they bore little resemblance to originals.

According to Fomenko, this led early chronologists to believe or choose to believe that those accounts described different events and even different countries and time periods. Fomenko justifies this approach by the fact that, in many cases, the original documents are simply not available. Fomenko claims that all the history of the ancient world is known to us from manuscripts that date from the XV century to the XVIII century, but describe events that allegedly happened thousands of years before, the originals regrettably and conveniently lost.

For example, the oldest extant manuscripts of monumental treatises on Ancient Roman and Greek history, such as *Annals* and *Histories*, are conventionally dated c. AD 1100, more than a full millennium after the events they describe, and they did not come to scholars' attention until the XV century. According to Fomenko, the XV century is probably when these documents were first written.

Central to Fomenko's New Chronology is his claim of the existence of a vast Slav-Turk empire, which he called the "Russian Horde", which he says played the dominant role in Eurasian history before the XVII century. The various peoples identified in ancient and medieval history, from the Scythians, Huns, Goths and Bulgars, through the Polyane, Duleby, Drevliane, Pechenegs, to in more recent times, the Cossacks, Ukrainians, and Belarusians, are nothing but elements of the single Russian Horde. For the New Chronologists, peoples such as the Ukrainians, Belarusians, Mongols, and others who assert their national independence from Russia, are suffering from a historical delusion.

Fomenko claims that the most probable prototype of the historical Jesus was Andronikos I Komnenos (allegedly AD 1152 to 1185), the emperor of Byzantium, known for his failed reforms; his traits and deeds reflected in 'biographies' of many real and imaginary persons (A. T. Fomenko, G. V. Nosovskiy. *Czar of the Slavs* (in Russian). St. Petersburg: Neva, 2004.). The historical Jesus is a composite figure and reflection of the Old Testament prophet Elisha (850-800 BC?), Pope Gregory VII (1020?-1085), Saint Basil of Caesarea (330-379), and even Li Yuanhao (also known as Emperor Jingzong, or "Son of Heaven", emperor of Western Xia, who reigned in 1032-1048), Euclides, Bacchus and Dionysius. Fomenko explains the seemingly vast differences in the biographies of these figures as resulting from difference in languages, points of view and time frame of the authors of said accounts and biographies.

Fomenko also merges the cities and histories of Jerusalem, Rome and Troy into "New Rome" = Gospel Jerusalem (in the XII and XIII centuries) = Troy = Yoros Castle (A. T. Fomenko, G. V. Nosovskiy. *Forgotten Jerusalem: Istanbul in the light of New Chronology* (in Russian). ?oscow: Astrel, AST, 2007). To the south of Yoros Castle is Joshua's Hill which Fomenko alleges is the hill Calvary depicted in the Bible.

Fomenko claims the Hagia Sophia is actually the biblical Temple of Solomon. He identifies Solomon as sultan Suleiman the Magnificent (1494–1566). He claims that historical Jesus may have been born in 1152 and was crucified around AD 1185 on the hill overlooking the Bosphorus.

On the other hand, according to Fomenko the word "Rome" is a placeholder and can signify any one of several different cities and kingdoms. He claims the "First Rome", or "Ancient Rome", or "Mizraim", is an ancient Egyptian kingdom in the delta of the Nile with its capital in Alexandria. The second and most famous "New Rome" is Constantinople. The third "Rome" is constituted by three different cities: Constantinople (again), Rome in Italy, and Moscow. According to his claims, Rome in Italy was founded around AD 1380 by Aeneas, and Moscow as the third Rome was the capital of the great "Russian Horde." Similarly, the word "Jerusalem" is actually a placeholder rather than a physical location and can refer to different cities at different times and the word "Israel" did not define a state, even not a territory, but people fighting for God, for example, French St. Louis and English Elizabeth called themselves the King/Queen of Israel.

He claims that parallelism between John the Baptist, Jesus, and Old Testament prophets implies that the New Testament was written before the Old Testament. Fomenko claims that the Bible was being written until the Council of Trent (1545–1563), when the list of canonical books was established, and all apocryphal books were ordered to be destroyed. Fomenko also claims that Plato, Plotinus and Gemistus Pletho are one and the same person; according to him, some texts by or about Pletho were misdated and today believed to be texts by or about Plotinus or Plato. He claims similar duplicates Dionysius the Areopagite, Pseudo-Dionysius the Areopagite, and Dionysius Petavius. He claims Florence and the House of Medici bankrolled and played an important role in creation of the magnificent 'Roman' and 'Greek' past.

Specific claims

In volumes 1, 2, 3 and 4 of *History: Fiction or Science?* Fomenko and his colleagues make numerous claims:

- Historians and translators often "assign" different dates and locations to different accounts of the same historical

163

events, creating multiple "phantom copies" of these events. These "phantom copies" are often misdated by centuries or even millennia and end up incorporated into conventional chronology.

- This chronology was largely manufactured by Joseph Justus Scaliger in *Opus Novum de emendatione temporum* (1583) and *Thesaurum temporum* (1606), and represents a vast array of dates produced without any justification whatsoever, containing the repeating sequences of dates with shifts equal to multiples of the major cabbalistic numbers 333 and 360. The Jesuit Dionysius Petavius completed this chronology in *De Doctrina Temporum*, 1627 (v. 1) and 1632 (v. 2).

- Archaeological dating, dendrochronological dating, paleographical dating, numismatic dating, carbon dating, and other methods of dating of ancient sources and artifacts known today are erroneous, non-exact or dependent on traditional chronology.

- No single document in existence can be reliably dated earlier than the XI century. Most "ancient" artifacts may find other than consensual explanation.

- Histories of Ancient Rome, Greece and Egypt were crafted during the Renaissance by humanists and clergy - mostly on the basis of documents of their own making.

- The Old Testament represents a rendition of events of the XIV to XVI centuries AD in Europe and Byzantium, containing "prophecies" about "future" events related in the New Testament, a rendition of events of AD 1152 to 1185.

- The history of religions runs as follows: the pre-Christian period (before the XI century and the birth of Jesus), Bacchic Christianity (XI and XII centuries, before and after the life of Jesus), Christianity (XII to XVI centuries) and its subsequent mutations into Orthodox Christianity, Catholicism, Judaism, and Islam.

- The *Almagest* of Claudius Ptolemy, traditionally dated to around AD 150 and considered the cornerstone of classical history, was compiled in XVI and XVII centuries from astronomical data of the IX to XVI centuries.

- 37 complete Egyptian horoscopes found in Denderah, Esna,

and other temples have unique valid astronomical solutions with dates ranging from AD 1000 and up to as late as AD 1700.

- The Book of Revelation, as we know it, contains a horoscope, dated to 25 September - 10 October 1486, compiled by cabbalistJohannes Reuchlin.
- The horoscopes found in Sumerian/Babylonian tablets do not contain sufficient astronomical data; consequently, they have solutions every 30–50 years on the time axis and are therefore useless for purposes of dating.
- The Chinese tables of eclipses are useless for dating, as they contain too many eclipses that did not take place astronomically. Chinese tables of comets, even if true, cannot be used for dating.
- All major inventions like powder and guns, paper and print occurred in Europe in the period between the X and the XVI centuries.
- Ancient Roman and Greek statues, showing perfect command of the human anatomy, are fakes crafted in the Renaissance, when artists attained such command for the first time.
- There was no such thing as the Tartar and Mongol invasion followed by over two centuries of yoke and slavery, because the so-called "Tartars and Mongols" were the actual ancestors of the modern Russians, living in a bilingual state with Turkic spoken as freely as Russian. So, Russia and Turkey once formed parts of the same empire. This ancient Russian state was governed by a double structure of civil and military authorities and the hordes were actually professional armies with a tradition of lifelong conscription (the recruitment being the so-called "blood tax"). The Mongol "invasions" were punitive operations against the regions of the empire that attempted tax evasion. Tamerlane was probably a Russian warlord.
- Official Russian history is a blatant forgery concocted by a host of German scholars brought to Russia to legitimize the usurpingRomanov dynasty (1613-1917).
- Moscow was founded as late as the mid-XIV century. The battle of Kulikovo took place in Moscow.

- The tsar Ivan the Terrible represents a collation of no fewer than four rulers, representing two rival dynasties: the legitimate Godunov rulers and the ambitious Romanov upstarts.
- English history of AD 640–1040 and Byzantine history of AD 378–830 are reflections of the same late-medieval original.

Fomenko's methods

Statistical correlation of texts

One of Fomenko's simplest methods is statistical correlation of texts. His basic assumption is that a text which describes a sequence of events will devote more space to more important events (for example, a period of war or an unrest will have much more space devoted to than a period of peaceful, non-eventful years), and that this irregularity will remain visible in other descriptions of the period. For each analysed text, a function is devised which maps each year mentioned in the text with the number of pages (lines, letters) devoted in the text to its description (which could be zero). The function of the two texts are then compared. (*Chron1*, pp. 187–194.)

For example, Fomenko compares the contemporary history of Rome written by Titus Livius with a modern history of Rome written by Russian historian V. S. Sergeev, calculating that the two have high correlation, and thus that they describe the same period of history, which is undisputed. (*Chron1*, pp. 194–196.) He also compares modern texts, which describe different periods, and calculates low correlation, as expected. (*Chron1*, pp. 194–196.) However, when he compares, for example, the ancient history of Rome and the medieval history of Rome, he calculates a high correlation, and concludes that ancient history of Rome is a copy of medieval history of Rome, thus clashing with mainstream accounts.

Statistical correlation of dynasties

In a somewhat similar manner, Fomenko compares two dynasties of rulers using statistical methods. First, he creates a database of rulers, containing relevant information on each of them. Then, he creates "survey codes" for each pair of the rulers, which contain a number which describes degree of the match of each considered property of two rulers. For example, one of the properties is the way of death: if two rulers were both poisoned, they get value of +1 in their property of the way of death; if one ruler was poisoned and another killed in combat, they get -1; and if one was poisoned, and another died of illness, they get 0 (Fomenko claims there is possibility that chroniclers were not impartial and that different descriptions nonetheless describe the same person). An important property is the length of the rule. (*Chron1*, pp. 215–223.)

Fomenko lists a number of pairs of unrelated dynasties – for example, dynasties of kings of Israeland emperors of late Western Roman Empire (AD 300-476) – and claims that this method

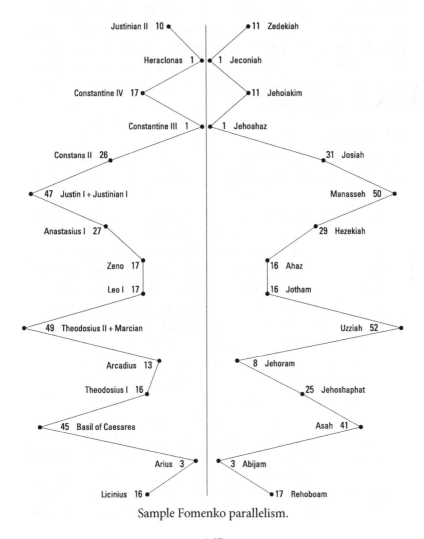

Sample Fomenko parallelism.

demonstrates correlations between their reigns. (Graphs which show just the length of the rule in the two dynasties are the most widely known; however, Fomenko's conclusions are also based on other parameters, as described above.) He also claims that the regnal history from the XVII to XX centuries never shows correlation of "dynastic flows" with each other, therefore Fomenko insists history was multiplied and outstretched into imaginary antiquity to justify this or other "royal" pretensions.

Fomenko uses for the demonstration of correlation between the reigns exclusively the data from the *Chronological Tables* of J. Blair (Moscow, 1808-1809). Fomenko says that Blair's tables are all the more valuable to us since they were compiled in an epoch adjacent to the time of Scaligerian chronology. According to Fomenko these tables contain clearer signs of "Scaligerite activity" which were subsequently buried under layers of paint and plaster by historians of the XIX and XX centuries.

Astronomical evidence

Fomenko examines astronomical events described in ancient texts and claims that the chronology is actually medieval. For example:

- He says the mysterious drop in the value of the lunar acceleration parameter D" ("a linear combination of the [angular] accelerations of the Earth and Moon") between the years AD 700–1300, which the American astronomer Robert Newton had explained in terms of "non-gravitational" (i.e., tidal) forces. By eliminating those anomalous early eclipses the New Chronology produces a constant value of D" beginning around AD 1000. (*Chron1*, pp. pp.93-94, 105-6.)
- He associates initially the Star of Bethlehem with the AD 1140 (±20) supernova (now Crab Nebula) and the Crucifixion Eclipse with the total solar eclipse of AD 1170 (±20). He also believes that Crab Nebula supernova could not have exploded in AD 1054, but probably in AD 1153. He connects it with total eclipse of AD 1186. Moreover he holds in strong doubt the veracity of ancient Chinese astronomical data.
- He argues that the star catalog in the *Almagest*, ascribed to the Hellenistic astronomer Claudius Ptolemy, was compiled

in the XV to XVI centuries AD. With this objective in sight he develops new methods of dating old stellar catalogues and claims that the *Almagest* is based on data collected between AD 600 and 1300, whereby the telluric obliquity is well taken into account.

- He refines and completes Morozov's analysis of some ancient horoscopes, most notably, the so-called Dendera Zodiacs—two horoscopes drawn on the ceiling of the temple of Hathor—and comes to the conclusion that they correspond to either the XI or the XIII century AD. Moreover, in his *History: Fiction or Science?* series finale, he makes computer-aided dating of all 37 Egyptian horoscopes that contain sufficient astronomical data, and claims they all fit into XI to XIX century timeframe. Traditional history usually either interprets these horoscopes as belonging to the I century BC or suggests that they weren't meant to match any date at all.

- In his final analysis of an eclipse triad described by the ancient Greek Thucydides in *History of the Peloponnesian War*, Fomenko dates the eclipses to AD 1039, 1046 and 1057. Because of the layered structure of the manuscript, he claims that Thucydides actually lived in medieval times and in describing the Peloponnesian War between the Spartans and Athenians he was actually describing the conflict between the medieval Navarrans and Catalans in Spain from AD 1374 to 1387.

- Fomenko claims that the abundance of dated astronomical records in cuneiform texts from Mesopotamia is of little use for dating of events, as the astronomical phenomena they describe recur cyclically every 30–40 years.

Rejection of common dating methods

On archaeological dating methods, Fomenko claims:

> "Archaeological, dendrochronological, paleographical and carbon methods of dating of ancient sources and artifacts are both non-exact and contradictory, therefore there is not a single piece of firm written evidence or artifact that could be reliably and independently dated earlier than the XI century." (*Chron1*.)

Dendrochronology is rejected with a claim that, for dating of objects much older than the oldest still living trees, it isn't an absolute, but a relative dating method, and thus dependent on traditional chronology. Fomenko specifically points to a break of dendrochronological scales around AD 1000.

Fomenko also cites a number of cases where carbon dating of a series of objects of known age gave significantly different dates. He also alleges undue cooperation between physicists and archaeologists in obtaining the dates, since most radiocarbon dating labs only accept samples with an age estimate suggested by historians or archaeologists. Fomenko also claims that carbon dating over the range of AD 1 to 2000 is inaccurate because it has too many sources of error that are either guessed at or completely ignored, and that calibration is done with a statistically meaningless number of samples. Consequently, Fomenko concludes that carbon dating is not accurate enough to be used on historical scale.

Fomenko rejects numismatic dating as circular, being based on the traditional chronology, and points to cases of similar coins being minted in distant periods, unexplained long periods with no coins minted and cases of mismatch of numismatic dating with historical accounts. (*Chron1*, pp. 90-92.)

He fully agrees with absolute dating methods for clay tablets or coins like thermoluminescence dating, optically stimulated luminescence dating, archaeomagnetic, metallographic dating, but claims that their precision does not allow for comprehensive pinpointing on the time axis either.

Fomenko also condemns the common archaeological practice of submitting samples for dating accompanied with an estimate of the expected age. He claims that convergence of uncertainty in archaeological dating methods proves strictly nothing per se. Even if the sum S of probabilities of the veracity of event produced by N dating methods exceeds 1.00 it does not mean that the event has taken place with 100% probability.

Reception

Fomenko's historical ideas have been universally rejected by mainstream scholars, who brand them as pseudoscience, but were popularized by former world chess champion Garry Kasparov. Billington writes that the theory "might have quietly blown away in the wind tunnels of academia" if not for Kasparov's writing in support of it in the magazine *Ogoniok*. Kasparov met Fomenko during the 1990s, and found that Fomenko's conclusions concerning certain subjects were identical to his own regarding the popular view (which is not the view of academics) that art and culture died during the Dark Ages and were not revived until the Renaissance. Kasparov also felt it illogical that the Romans and the Greeks living under the banner of Byzantium could fail to use the mounds of scientific knowledge left them by Ancient Greece and Rome, especially when it was of urgent military use. However, Kasparov does not support the reconstruction part of the New Chronology. Russian critics tended to see Fomenko's New Chronology as "an embarrassment and a potent symbol of the depths to which the Russian academy and society have generally sunk ... since the fall of Communism." Western critics see his views as part of a renewed Russian imperial ideology, "keeping alive an imperial consciousness and secular messianism in Russia."

In 2004 Anatoly Fomenko with his coauthor Gleb Nosovsky were awarded for their books on "New Chronology" the anti-prize of the Moscow International Book Fair called "Abzatz" (literally 'paragraph', a euphemism for a vulgar Russian word meaning disaster or fiasco) in the category "Esteemed nonsense" ("Pochotnaya bezgramota") awarded for the worst book published in Russia.

Critics have accused Fomenko of altering the data to improve the fit with his ideas and have noted that he violates a key rule of statistics by selecting matches from the historical record which support his chronology, while ignoring those which do not, creating artificial, better-than-chance correlations, and that these practices undermine Fomenko's statistical arguments. The new chronology was given a comprehensive critical analysis in a round table on "The 'Myths' of New Chronology" chaired by the dean of the department of history of Moscow State University in December 1999. One of the participants in that round table, the distinguished Russian archaeologist, Valentin Yanin, compared Fomenko's work to "the sleight of hand trickery of a David Copperfield." Linguist Andrey Zaliznyak argued that by using the Fomenko's approaches one can "prove" any historical correspondence, for example, between Ancient Egyptian pharaohs and French kings.

James Billington, formerly professor of Russian history at Harvard and Princeton and currently the Librarian of Congress placed Fomenko's work within the context of the political movement of Eurasianism, which sought to tie Russian history closely to that of its Asian neighbors. Billington describes Fomenko as ascribing the belief in past hostility between Russia and the Mongols to the influence of Western historians. Thus, by Fomenko's chronology, "Russia and Turkey are parts of a previously single empire." A French reviewer of Billington's book noted approvingly his concern with the phantasmagorical conceptions of Fomenko about the global "new chronology."

H. G. van Bueren, professor emeritus of astronomy at the University of Utrecht, concluded his scathing review of Fomenko's work on the application of mathematics and astronomy to historical data as follows:

> "It is surprising, to say the least, that a well-known (Dutch) publisher could produce an expensive book of such doubtful intellectual value, of which the only good word that can be said is that it contains an enormous amount of factual historical material, untidily ordered, true; badly written, yes; mixed-up with conjectural nonsense, sure; but still, much useful stuff. For the rest of the book is absolutely worthless. It reminds one of the early Soviet attempts to produce tendentious science (Lysenko!), of polywater, of cold fusion, and of modern creationism. In brief: a useless and misleading book." (H. G. van Bueren, *Mathematics and Logic*.)

Convergence of methods in archaeological dating

While Fomenko rejects commonly accepted dating methods, archaeologists, conservators and other scientists make extensive use of such techniques which have been rigorously examined and refined during decades of use.

In the specific case of dendrochronology, Fomenko claims that this fails as an absolute dating method because of gaps in the record. However, independent dendrochronological sequences beginning with living trees from various parts of North America and Europe extend back 12,400 years into the past. Furthermore, the mutual consistency of these independent dendrochronological sequences has been confirmed by comparing their radiocarbon and dendro-chronological ages. These and other data have provided a calibration curve for radiocarbon dating whose internal error does not exceed ±163 years over the entire 26,000 years of the curve.

In fact, archaeologists have developed a fully anchored dendro-chronology series going back past 10,000 BCE. "The absolutely dated tree-ring chronology now extends back to 12,410 cal BP (10,461 BC)."

Misuse of historical sources and forced pattern matching

Critics of Fomenko's theory claim that his use of historical sources is highly selective and ignores the basic principles of sound historical scholarship.

"Fomenko ... provides no fair-minded review of the historical lit-erature about a topic with which he deals, quotes only those sources that serve his purposes, uses evidence in ways that seem strange to professionally-trained historians and asserts the wildest specula-tion as if it has the same status as the information common to the conventional historical literature."

They also note that his method of statistically correlating of texts is very rough, because it does not take into account the many pos-sible sources of variation in length outside of "importance." They maintain that differences in language, style, and scope, as well as the frequently differing views and focuses of historians, which are manifested in a different notion of "important events", make quanti-fying historical writings a dubious proposition at best. What's more, Fomenko's critics allege that the parallelisms he reports are often derived by alleged forcing by Fomenko of the data – rearranging, merging, and removing monarchs as needed to fit the pattern.

For example, on the one hand Fomenko asserts that the vast ma-jority of ancient sources are either irreparably distorted duplicate accounts of the same events or later forgeries. In his identification of Jesus with Pope Gregory VII (*Chron2*, p. 51) he ignores the oth-erwise vast dissimilarities between their reported lives and focuses on the similarity of their appointment to religious office by baptism. (The evangelical Jesus is traditionally believed to have lived for 33 years, and he was an adult at the time of his encounter with John the Baptist. In contrast, according to the available primary sources, Pope

Gregory VII lived for at least 60 years and was born 8 years after the death of Fomenko's John-the-Baptist equivalent John Crescentius.)

Critics allege that many of the supposed correlations of regnal durations are the product of the selective parsing and blending of the dates, events, and individuals mentioned in the original text. Another point raised by critics is that Fomenko does not explain his altering the data (changing the order of rulers, dropping rulers, combining rulers, treating interregna as rulers, switching between theologians and emperors, etc.) preventing a duplication of the effort and effectively making this whole theory an ad hoc hypothesis.

Selectivity in reference to astronomical phenomena

Critics point out that Fomenko's discussion of astronomical phenomena tends to be selective, choosing isolated examples that support the New Chronology and ignoring the large bodies of data that provide statistically supported evidence for the conventional dating. For his dating of the Almagest star catalog, Fomenko arbitrarily selected eight stars from the more than 1000 stars in the catalog, one of which (Arcturus) has a large systematic error. This star has a dominant effect on Fomenko's dating. Statistical analysis using the same method for all "fast" stars points to the antiquity of the Almagest star catalog. Rawlins points out further that Fomenko's statistical analysis got the wrong date for the Almagest because he took as constant Earth's obliquity when it is a variable that changes at a very slow, but known, rate.

Fomenko's studies ignore the abundance of dated astronomical records in cuneiform texts from Mesopotamia. Among these texts is a series of Babylonian astronomical diaries, which records precise astronomical observations of the Moon and planets, often dated in terms of the reigns of known historical figures extending back to the VI century BCE. Astronomical retrocalculations for all these moving objects allow us to date these observations, and consequently the rulers' reigns, to within a single day. The observations are sufficiently redundant that only a small portion of them are sufficient to date a text to a unique year in the period 750 BCE to 100 CE. The dates obtained agree with the accepted chronology. In addition, F. R. Stephenson has demonstrated through a systematic study of a large number of Babylonian, Ancient and Medieval European, and Chinese records of eclipse observations that they can be dated consistently with conventional chronology at least as far back as 600 BCE. In contrast to Fomenko's missing centuries, Stephenson's studies of eclipse observations find an accumulated uncertainty in the timing of the rotation of the earth of 420 seconds at 400 BCE, and only 80 seconds at 1000 CE.

Magnitude and consistency of conspiracy theory

Fomenko claims that world history prior to 1600 was deliberately falsified for political reasons. The consequences of this conspiracy theory are twofold. Documents that conflict with New Chronology are said to have been edited or fabricated by conspirators (mostly Western European historians and humanists of late XVI to XVII centuries). The lack of documents directly supporting New Chronology and conflicting traditional history is said to be thanks to the majority of such documents being destroyed by the same conspirators.

Consequently, there are many thousands of documents that are considered authentic in traditional history, but not in New Chronology. Fomenko often uses "falsified" documents, which he dismisses in other contexts, to prove a point. For example, he analyzes the Tartar Relation and arrives at the conclusion that Mongolian capital of Karakorum was located in Central Russia (equated with present-day Yaroslavl). However, the Tartar Relation makes several statements that are at odds with New Chronology (such as that Batu Khan and Russian duke Yaroslav are two distinct people). Those are said by Fomenko to have been introduced into the original text by later editors.

Many of the rulers that Fomenko claims are medieval doppelgangers moved in the imaginary past have left behind vast numbers of coins. Numismatists have made innumerable identifications of coins to rulers known from ancient sources. For instance, several Roman emperors issued coinage featuring at least three of their names, consistent with those found in written sources, and there are frequent examples of joint coinage between known royal family members, as well as overstrikes by kings who were known enemies.

Ancient coins in Greek and Latin are unearthed to this day in vast quantities from Britain to India. For Fomenko's theories to be correct, this could only be explained by counterfeit on a very grand

and consistent scale, as well as a complete dismissal of all numismatic analyses of hoard findings, coin styles etc.

Popularity in forums and amongst Russian imperialists

Despite criticism, Fomenko has published and sold over one million copies of his books in his native Russia. Many internet forums have appeared which aim to supplement his work with additional amateur research. His critics have suggested that Fomenko's version of history appealed to the Russian reading public by keeping alive an imperial consciousness to replace their disillusionment with the failures of Communism and post-Communist corporate oligarchies.

Alexander Zinoviev called the New Chronology "one of the major scientific breakthroughs of the XX century."

(Wikipedia text retrieved on 2nd August, 2015)

Afterword from the publisher

Dr. Fomenko *et al* as scientists are ready to recognize their mistakes, to repent and to retract on the condition that:

- radiocarbon dating methods pass the black box tests, or
- astronomy refutes their results on ancient eclipses, or
- US astrophysicist Robert Newton was proved wrong to accuse Ptolemy of his crime.

At present, historians do not, can not, and will not comply. The radiocarbon dating labs run their very costly tests only if the sample to be dated is accompanied with an idea of age pronounced by historians on basis of ... subjective ... mmm ... gutfeeling ... and the history books they have been writing for the last 400 years. Radiocarbon labs politely bill for their fiddling and finetuning to get the dates "to order" of historians. *Circulus vitiosus* is perfect.

Bibliography

Separate books on the New Chronology

Prior to the publication of the seven-volume *Chronology*, we published a number of books on the same topic. If we are to disregard the paperbacks and the concise versions, as well as new re-editions, there are seven such books. Shortened versions of their names appear below:

1. *Introduction.*
2. *Methods 1-2.*
3. *Methods 3.*
4. *The New Chronology of Russia, Britain and Rome.*
5. *The Empire.*
6. *The Biblical Russia.*
7. *Reconstruction.*

• **BOOK ONE.** *Introduction.*

[*Intro*]:1. Fomenko, A. T. *New Experimental Statistical Methods of Dating Ancient Events and their Application to the Global Classical and Mediaeval Chronology.* Pre-print. Moscow, The State Television and Radio Broadcast Committee, 1981. Order #3672. Lit. 9/XI-81. No. BO7201, 100 p.

[*Intro*]:2. Fomenko, A. T. *Some New Empirico-Statistical Methods of Dating and the Analysis of Present Global Chronology.* London, The British Library, Department of Printed Books, 1981. Cup. 918/87. 100 p.

[*Intro*]3. Fomenko, A. T. *A Criticism of the Traditional Chronology of the Classical*

Age and the Middle Ages (What Century Is It Now?). Essay. Moscow, Publishing House of the Moscow State University Department of Mechanical Mathematics, 1993. 204 p.

[*Intro*]:4. 2nd edition, revised and expanded. Fomenko, A. T., and G. V. Nosovskiy. *A Criticism of the Traditional Chronology of the Classical Age and the Middle Ages (What Century Is It Now?).* Moscow, Kraft-Lean, 1999. 757 p. Kraft Publications released a concise version of this book in 2001. 487 p.

[*Intro*]:5. Another revision. Fomenko, A. T., and G. V. Nosovskiy. *What Century Is It Now?* Moscow, AIF-Print Publications, 2002. 511 p.

- **BOOK TWO, PART ONE:** *Methods-1.*

[*Meth1*]:1. Fomenko, A. T. *The Methods of Statistical Analysis of Narrative Texts and their Chronological Applications.* (The identification and dating of dependent texts, statistical chronology of the antiquity, as well as the statistics of ancient astronomical accounts.) Moscow, MSU Publishing House, 1990. 439 p.

[*Meth1*]:2. 2nd revised edition came out in 1996 as *The Methods Of Mathematical Analysis of Historical Texts. Chronological applications.* Moscow, Nauka Publications, 1996. 475 p.

[*Meth1*]:3. Several chapters of the book came out in 1996, revised and extended, as a separate book: Fomenko, A. T. *The New Chronology of Greece. Antiquity in the Middle Ages,* Vols. 1 and 2. Moscow, MSU Centre of Research and Pre-University Education, 1996. 914 p.

[*Meth1*]:4. The English translation of the book, extended and revised to a large extent, was released under the following title: Fomenko, A. T. *Empirico-Statistical Analysis of Narrative Material and its Applications to Historical Dating.* Vol. 1, *The Development of the Statistical Tools.* Vol. 2, *The Analysis of Ancient and Mediaeval Records.* The Netherlands, Kluwer Academic Publishers, 1994. Vol. 1: 211 p. Vol. 2: 462 p.

[*Meth1*]:5. A Serbian translation titled *Статистичка хронологија. Математички поглед на историју. У ком смо веку?* was published in 1997. Belgrade, Margo-Art, 1997. 450 p.

[*Meth1*]:6. The book was published in a revised and substantially extended version in 1999 as Volume 1 in a series of two: Fomenko, A. T. *The Methods of Statistical Analysis of Historical Texts. Chronological Applications.* Vol. 1. Moscow, Kraft and Lean, 1999. 801 p.

[*Meth1*]:7. A revised version of the book was published as two volumes (the first two in a series of three) in 1999 in the USA (in Russian) by the Edwin Mellen Press. Fomenko, A. T. *New Methods of Statistical Analysis of Historical Texts. Applications to Chronology,* Vols. 1 and 2. The publication is part of the series titled *Scholarly Monographs in the Russian Language,* Vols. 6-7. Lewiston, Queenston, Lampeter, Edwin Mellen Press, 1999. Vol. 1: 588 p. Vol. 2: 564 p.

- **BOOK TWO, PART TWO:** *Methods-2.*

[*Meth2*]:1. Fomenko, A. T. *Global Chronology.* (A Research of the Classical and Mediaeval History. Mathematical Methods of Source Analysis. Global Chronology.) Moscow, MSU Publications, 1993. 408 p.

[*Meth2*]:2. A revised and substantially extended version of the book as the second volume in a series of two: Fomenko, A. T. *The Methods of Statistical Analysis of Historical Texts. Chronological Applications*, Vol. 2. Moscow, Kraft and Lean, 1999. 907 p.

[*Meth2*]:3. A revised version of the book was published as the last volume in a series of three in the USA (in Russian) under the title: Fomenko A. T. *Antiquity in the Middle Ages (Greek and Bible History)*, the trilogy bearing the general name: Fomenko A. T. *New Methods of the Statistical Analysis of Historical Texts and their Chronological Application*. The publication is part of the series titled *Scholarly Monographs in the Russian Language*. Lewiston, Queenston, Lampeter, The Edwin Mellen Press, 1999. 578 p.

• **BOOK THREE:** *Methods-3.*

[*Meth3*]:1. Fomenko, A. T., V. V. Kalashnikov, and G. V. Nosovskiy. *Geometrical and Statistical Methods of Analysis of Star Configurations. Dating Ptolemy's Almagest.* USA: CRC Press, 1993. 300 p.

[*Meth3*]:2. The Russian version of the book was published in 1995 in Moscow by the Faktorial Publications under the title: Kalashnikov V. V., Nosovskiy G. V., Fomenko A. T. *The Dating of the Almagest Star Catalogue. Statistical and Geometrical Analysis.* 286 p.

[*Meth3*]:3. A substantially extended and revised version of the book: Kalashnikov, V. V., G. V. Nosovskiy, and A. T. Fomenko. *The Astronomical Analysis of Chronology. The Almagest. Zodiacs.* Moscow, The Delovoi Express Financial Publications, 2000. 895 p.

[*Meth3*]:4. Fomenko, A. T., and G. V. Nosovskiy. *The New Chronology of Egypt. The Astronomical Dating of Ancient Egyptian Monuments. Research of 2000-2002.* Moscow, Veche Press, 2002. 463 p.

• **BOOK FOUR:** *Russia, Britain and Rome.*

[*RBR*]:1. Fomenko, A. T., and G. V. Nosovskiy. *The New Chronology and Conception of the Ancient History of Russia, Britain, and Rome. Facts, Statistics, Hypotheses.* Vol. 1, *Russia.* Vol. 2, *Britain and Rome.* Moscow, MSU Centre of Research and Pre-University Education. Two editions, 1995 and 1996. 672 p.

[*RBR*]:2. A somewhat adapted and revised version of the book came out in 1997: Fomenko, A. T., and G. V. Nosovskiy. *Russia and Rome. How correct is our understanding of Eurasian history?* Vols. 1 and 2. Moscow, Olymp Publications, 1997. 2nd edition 1999. The next three volumes from this series of five were published in 2001. Vol. 1: 606 p. Vol. 2: 621 p. Vol. 3: 540 p. Vol. 4: 490 p. Vol. 5: 394 p.

[*RBR*]:3. A revised version of the first volume was published in 1997 as a separate book: Fomenko, A. T., and G. V. Nosovskiy. *The New Chronology of Russia.* Moscow, Faktorial Publications, 1997. Re-editions 1998 and 1999. 255 p.

[RBR]:4. A new, substantially extended and revised version of the first two-volume edition as a single volume: Fomenko, A. T., and G. V. Nosovskiy. *The New Chronology of Russia, Britain and Rome*. Moscow, Anvik, 1999. 540 p.

[RBR]:5. A new revised version of this book came out as a single volume: Fomenko A. T., and G. V. Nosovskiy. Moscow, The Delovoi Express Financial Publications, 2001. 1015 p.

• **BOOK FIVE:** *The Empire.*

[Emp]:1. Fomenko, A. T., and G. V. Nosovskiy. *The Empire (Russia, Turkey, China, Europe, Egypt. The New Mathematical Chronology of Antiquity).* Moscow, Faktorial, 1996. Re-editions 1997, 1998, 1999, 2001 and 2002. 752 p.

• **BOOK SIX:** *The Biblical Russia.*

[BR]:1. Fomenko, A. T., and G. V. Nosovskiy. *The Mathematical Chronology of the Biblical Events*. Moscow, Nauka Publications, 1997. 407 p.

[BR]:2. A substantially revised and extended version: Fomenko, A. T., and G. V. Nosovskiy. *The Biblical Russia. The Empire of Horde-Russia and the Bible. The New Mathematical Chronology of Antiquity.* Vols. 1 and 2. Moscow, Faktorial, 1998. Vol. 1: 687 p. Vol. 2: 582 p.

[BR]:3. A somewhat condensed version, which nevertheless contained some important new material: Fomenko, A. T., and G. V. Nosovskiy. *Horde-Russia on the Pages of the Biblical Books*. Moscow, Anvik Publications, 1998. 430 p.

[BR]:4. Fomenko, A. T., and G. V. Nosovskiy. *The Biblical Russia. Selected Chapters I (The Empire of Horde-Russia and the Bible. The New Mathematical Chronology of Antiquity. History of the Manuscripts and Editions of the Bible. The Events of the XI-XII Century A.D. in the New Testament. The Pentateuch.).* Moscow, Faktorial, 1999. 173 p.

[BR]:5. Fomenko, A. T., and G. V. Nosovskiy. *The Biblical Russia. Selected Chapters II (The Empire of Horde-Russia and the Bible. The New Mathematical Chronology of Antiquity. History of the XIV-XVI Century in the Last Books of the Kings. The History of the XV-XVI Century in the Last Chapters of the Books of the Kings. History of the XV-XVI Century in the Books of Esther and Judith. The Reformation Epoch of the XVI-XVII Century).* Moscow, Faktorial Press, 2000. 223 p.

• **BOOK SEVEN:** *Reconstruction.*

[Rec]:1. Fomenko, A. T., and G. V. Nosovskiy. *A Reconstruction of Global History (The New Chronology).* Book 1. Moscow, Delovoi Express, 1999. 735 p.

[Rec]:2. Fomenko, A. T., and G. V. Nosovskiy. *A Reconstruction of Global History. The Research of 1999-2000 (The New Chronology).* Moscow, Delovoi Express, 1999. 615 p.

[Rec]:3. Fomenko, A. T., and G. V. Nosovskiy. *A Reconstruction of Global History. Joan of Arc, Samson, and the History of Russia.* Moscow, The Delovoi Express Financial Publishers, 2002.

We have to point out that the publication of our books on the New Chronology has influenced a number of authors and their works where the new chronological concepts are discussed or developed. Some of these are: L. I. Bocharov, N. N. Yefimov, I. M. Chachukh, and I. Y. Chernyshov ([93]), Jordan Tabov ([827], [828]), A. Goutz ([220]), M. M. Postnikov ([680]), V. A. Nikerov ([579:1]), Heribert Illig ([1208]), Christian Blöss and Hans-Ulrich Niemitz ([1038], [1039]), Gunnar Heinsohn ([1185]), Gunnar Heinsohn and Heribert Illig ([1186]), Uwe Topper ([1462], [1463]).

Our research attracted sufficient attention to chronological issues for the Muscovite publishing house Kraft to print a new edition of the fundamental work of N. A. Morozov titled Christ, first published in 1924-1932.

Sources in Russian

[1]. Abalakin, V. K. *The Essential Ephemeris Astronomy.* Moscow, 1979.

[2]. Abbas, Shalabi. *The Entire Egypt, from Cairo to Abu-Simbel and Sinai.* 2nd extended Russian edition. Florence, Bonechi, 1996.

[2:1]. Avadyaeva, E., and L. Zdanovich. *The Hundred Great Afflictions.* Moscow, Veche, 1999.

[3]. Agathius. *The Reign of Justinian.* Moscow-Leningrad, USSR Academy of Sciences Publications, 1953. See also Agathius, Scholasticus. *Agathiae Myrinaei Historiarum libri quinque.* Berolini, 1967.

[4]. Mez, Adam. *The Muslim Renaissance.* Moscow, Nauka, 1966. German edition: Mez, A. *Die Renaissance des Islams.* Heidelberg, 1922.

[5]. Azarevich, D. I. *The History of the Byzantine Law.* Yaroslavl, 1876-1877.

[6]. Aydarova-Volkova, G. *The Priceless Experience. A Cultural Dialogue. Looking Across the Centuries.* The *Kazan* magazine, Issue 9-10 (1999): 13-21.

[7]. Acropolite, George. *The Chronicle of the Great Logothete George Acropolite.* St. Petersburg, 1863.

[8]. *The Historical Acts Compiled and Published by the Archaeographical Commission.* St. Petersburg, The State Document Preparation Expedition Typography. Vols. 1 and 2. 1841.

[9]. Nazarov, V. D., ed. *The Acts of the State of Russia. Archives of the Muscovite Monasteries and Cathedrals.* The XV – early XVII century. Moscow, The Ladomir Research and Publication Centre, 1998.

[10]. *Alexandria. A Novel about Alexander the Great Based on a Russian Chronicle of the XV century.* Moscow-Leningrad, Nauka, 1966.

[11]. Petrukhno, A. S., N. I. Shirinya, S. A. Gleybman, and O. V. Zavgorodniaya. *Alexander's Village (Alexandrovskaya Sloboda, or, literally, "The Freemen's Village of Alexander"). An Album.* The Russian Federation Ministry of Culture.

City of Alexandrov. The State Museum of Art, History, and Architecture of Alexander's Village. The City Council of the City of Alexandrov. 1996.

[12]. *Alexander's Village (Alexandrovskaya Sloboda)*. The materials of a scientific and practical conference. Vladimir, Golden Gate Publications, 1995.

[13]. Alexandrovsky, M. I. *A Historical Reference Book for the Churches of Moscow*. Moscow, The State Museum of History, Department of Visual Arts, the Architectural Graphics Fund, 1917 (with an additional written before 1942).

[14]. Alexeyev, M. P. *On the Anglo-Russian Relations in the Time of Yaroslav the Wise*. The Scientific Bulletin of the Leningrad State University (4, 1945): 31.

[15]. Alexeyev, Y. *My Monarch Sent Me to the Sultan*. The *Rodina* magazine, No. 2 (1997): 31-36.

[16]. Alessandro, Angelini. *Piero della Francesca*. The *Great Italian Masters* series. Moscow, Slovo, 1997. The Italian edition: Italy, Scala, Instituto Fotografico Editoriale, 1995.

[16:1]. *[Altarpieces]* Caterina Limentani Virdis and Mari Pietrogiovanna. *Altarpieces. The Art of the Early Renaissance*. Translated from Italian. Byely Gorod, 2002. Arsenale editrice, Italy, 2001.

[17]. *The Alphabetic Syntagm of Matthew Vlastar*. Translated from Greek by Rev. Nikolai Ilyinsky, a teacher from the Seminary School of Tauris. Simpheropol, 1892. A new edition: Moscow, Galaxy Publications, 1996.

[18]. Alberti, L. *Leon Battista Alberti*. A collection of essays. Moscow, the USSR Academy of Sciences, Nauka, 1977. *Complete ed*. Oxford, Phaidon, 1977.

[19]. Amalrik, A. S., and A. L. Mongayt. *The Essential Archaeology*. Moscow, Prosveshchenie, 1963.

[19:0]. [Amartoles, George]. Matveyenko, V., and L. Shchegoleva. *The Chronicle of George the Monk*. Russian text, comments, indications. Moscow, Bogorodskiy Pechatnik, 2000.

[19:1]. The catalogue of the exhibition *500 Years Since the Discovery of America*. The Hermitage. Russian National Library. St. Petersburg, Slavia-Interbook, Inc., 1993.

[20]. Amousin, I. D. *The Dead Sea Scrolls*. Moscow, Nauka, 1960.

[21]. Amphitheatrov, A. *Collected Works in 8 Volumes*. Vol. 4. St. Petersburg, Prosveshchenie, 1911.

[22]. Anastasov, L. *A New Direction in Science? Be careful!* The *Science and Technology* magazine (Moscow), No. 8 (1983): 28-30.

[23]. Müller, V. K., comp. *The English-Russian Dictionary*. 70,000 words. Moscow, The State National and Foreign Dictionary Publishing House, 1961.

[24]. Andreyeva, V., V. Kuklev, and A. Rovner. *An Encyclopedia of Symbols, Signs, and Emblems*. Moscow, Lokid/Myth/Ad Marginem, 1999.

[25]. Anninskiy, S. A. *The News of the Tartars in Europe Brought by the Hungarian Missionaries*. Included in *The Historical Archive*, 71-112. Moscow-Leningrad, The RAS Institute of History, RAS Publications, 1940.

[26]. *Antwerp and its Sights*. Antwerp, Editions THILL S.A. Brussels, 1999. In Russian.

[27]. Antonov, A. V. *Genealogical Murals of Late XVII Century.* The Archaeographical Centre. The Russian State Archive of Ancient Acts. *The Russian
Historical Research,* No. 6. Moscow, Archaeographical Centre Publications.

[28]. Antonova, V. I., and N. E. Mneva. *The Catalogue of Ancient Russian Art
from the Tretyakov Gallery.* Moscow, 1963. Vol. 1: p. 256; Vol 2: pp. 413 and
421.

[29]. *The Apocryphal Jesus, Holy Family, and Christ Witness Legendry.* Sventsits-
kaya, I. S., and A. P. Skogorev, comp. Moscow, Kogelet, 1999.

[30]. Apollodorus. *The Mythological Library.* Leningrad, Nauka, 1972. English
edition: Apollodorus. *The Library.* London-New York: Loeb Classical Library,
1921.

[30:1]. Arago, F. *The Biographies of the Famous Astronomers, Physicists, and
Geometricians.* Books 1 and 2 (Vols. 1-3). Translated by D. Perevoshchikov.
Moscow-Izhevsk, The Scientific Research Centre for Regular and Chaotic
Dynamics, 2000.

[31]. Arenkova, Y. I., and G. I. Mekhova. *The Don Monastery.* Moscow, Iskusstvo, 1970.

[32]. Aristaenetus. *The Love Epistles.* Eustathius, Macrembolites. *The Story of Ismene and Istmenias.* Moscow-Leningrad, Nauka, 1965. Also see Aristaenetus.
The Love Epistles. In W. Kelley. *Erotica.* London, Bohn's Classical Library, G.
Bell & Sons, 1848. Eustathius, Macrembolites. *Ismene and Istmenias.* London,
1788.

[33]. Zdanovich, G. B., ed. *Arkaim. Research. Prospects. Findings.* A collection
of essays. From the series titled *The Historical Pages of Southern Ural.* The
Arkaim Reserve works, State University of Chelyabinsk, the Specialized
Arkaim Nature and Landscape Centre of History and Archaeology. The State
Reserve of Ilmen. Chelyabinsk, the Kamenny Poyas Creative Group, 1995.

[34]. Arnold, Y. *El Señor Kon-Tiki.* Moscow, Mysl, 1970.

[35]. Aronov, V. *The Elseviers (A History of Literary Art).* Moscow, Kniga, 1975.

[36]. *The Chronicler of Archangelsk. A complete collection of Russian chronicles,*
Vol. 37. Leningrad, Nauka, 1982.

[37]. Archangelskiy, Leonid. *The Samurai Steel.* An article for the magazine
called *Magnum. The New Magazine on Arms* (November-December 1998):
18-21.

[38]. Avdousina, T. D., and T. D. Panov. *Archaeological Antiquities: The Muscovite Kremlin.* The Moscow Kremlin State Museum and Reserve for History
and Culture. Moscow, 1996.

[39]. Serge, Archbishop. *The Complete Oriental Menology.* Vols. 1-3. Vladimir,
Typography & Lithography of V. A. Parkov in Vladimir, 1901. Reprinted
Moscow, Orthodox Encyclopaedia Centre of Ecclesiastic Research, Palomnik
Publications, 1997.

[40]. Archimedes. *The Works.* Moscow, Fizmatgiz, 1962. English edition: Archimedes, *The Works of Archimedes.* Cambridge, Cambridge University Press,
1912.

[40:0]. Asov, A. I. *The Book of Veles.* Moscow, Menedzher, 1995, 2nd edition.

[40:00]. Asov, A. I., Konovalov, M. Y. *The Ancient Aryans. The Slavs. Russia.* Moscow, Veche, 2002.

[40:1]. Gentili, Augusto, William Barcham, and Linda Whiteley. *The National Gallery of London.* From the *The Great Museums of the World* series. Moscow, Slovo, 2001. A translation of the Italian edition Udine: Magnus Edizioni, 2000.

[41]. Nikitin, Afanasiy. *Voyage over the Three Sees. Published in the Literary Monuments of Old Russia. 2nd Half of the XV Century.* Moscow, Khudozhestvennaya Literatura, 1982.

[42]. Nikitin, Afanasiy. *Afanasiy Nikitin's Voyage over the Three Sees. 1466-1472.* Foreword, translation, text preparation and commentary by N. I. Prokofiev. Moscow, Sovietskaya Rossiya, 1980.

[43]. Akhmanova, O. S., and others. *Precise Methods of Language Study.* Moscow, 1961.

[44]. Bayev, K. L. *Copernicus.* From the *Celebrity Biographies* series, Issue 7 (55). Moscow, The Magazine and Newspaper Consociation, 1935.

[45]. Beyer, Rolf. *The Queen of Sheba.* From the *Mark In History* series. Rostov-on-Don, Fenix Publications, 1998. A translation from the German original by Beyer, Rolf. *Die Königin von Saba.* The *Question Mark* series, Gustav Lübbe Verlag GmbH, Bergisch Gladbach. 1987.

[46]. Balandin, R. K. *A Miracle or a Scientific Enigma? Science and Religion Discussing the Shroud of Turin.* Moscow, Znaniye, 1989. The *Question Mark* series, Issue 1, 1989.

[47]. Balandin, R., and L. Bondarev. *Nature and Civilization.* Moscow, Mysl, 1988.

[48]. Baldin, V. I., and T. P. Manushkina. *The Laura of Serge and The Trinity. The Architectural Set and the Collections of Ancient Russian Art of the XIV-XVII Century.* Moscow, Nauka, 1996.

[49]. Baranov, V. *Logic Isn't Facts.* The *Science & Technology* magazine (Moscow), No. 4 (1983): 24-28.

[50]. Baronius, C. *The Ecclesial and Secular Annals from the Birth of Christ and until the Year 1198.* Typography of P. P. Ryabushinsky, from Baronius, *Annales ecclesiastici a Christo nato ad annum 1198.* Moscow, 1913.

[51]. Bartenev, S. *The Moscow Kremlin in the Antiquity and Nowadays.* Moscow, Synodal Typography, 1912.

[52]. de las Casas, Bartólome. *History of the Indias.* Leningrad, Nauka, 1968.

[53]. Baskakov, N. A. *Russian Names of Turkic Origin.* Moscow, Nauka, The Main Oriental Literature Editing Board, 1979.

[54]. Magarichev, Y. M., ed. and comp. *The Cultural and Historical Reserve of Bakhchisaray.* Simferopol, Tavria, 1995.

[55]. Bakhshi, Iman. *Jagfar Tarikhy. A Collection of Bulgarian Manuscripts from 1680.* Russian translation of the Bulgarian text by I. M. K. Nigmatoullin. Orenburg, The Orenburg Press Contact, KOPF, editorial board of the *Bulgaria Courier*, 1993.

[56]. Bashmakova, I. G., and G. S. Smirnova. *The Naissance and the Development of Algebra.* Published in the *Aperçus on the History of Mathematics* edited by B. V. Gnedenko. Moscow, MSU Publications, 1997.

[57]. Belenkiy, M. S. *Judaism.* Moscow, Gospolitizdat, 1966.

[58]. Bellosi, Luciano. *Giotto.* Moscow, Slovo Press, 1996. Translated from the 1995 Italian edition by Scala, Istituto Fotografico Editoriale.

[59]. Belova, A. G. *The Historical Morphology of the Arabic Language.* Moscow, 1994.

[59:0]. Belova G. A, Sherkova T. A. *Russians in the Land of Pyramids. Travellers, Scientists, Collectioners.* Moscow, Aleteya, 2003.

[59:1]. Belyavsky, V. A. *Legendary and Historical Babylon.* Moscow, Mysl, 1971.

[60]. Belyavsky, M. T. *M. V. Lomonosov and the Foundation of the Moscow University (1755-1955).* Edited by M. N. Tikhomirov. Moscow, MSU Publications, 1955.

[61]. Belyaev, D. V. *Byzantine. Essays, Materials and Notes concerning Byzantine Antiquity.* Book III. St. Petersburg, 1891-1906.

[62]. Belyaev, L. A. *The Ancient Monasteries of Moscow According to Archaeological Data.* Moscow, The Russian Academy of Sciences, Institute of Archaeology. Research and materials concerning the archaeology of Moscow. Vol. 6. 1995.

[63]. Belyaev, Y. *100 Monsters of Antiquity.* An illustrated encyclopaedia of mythology. Moscow, Raritet, 1997.

[64]. Bémont, C., and G. Monod. *The Mediaeval History of Europe.* Petrograd, 1915. French edition: Bémont, C., and G. Monod. *Histoire de l'Europe au Moyen Âge.* Paris, 1921.

[64:1]. Berg, L. S. *The Discovery of Kamchatka and Bering's Expedition.* Moscow-Leningrad, The USSR Academy of Sciences Press, 1946.

[64:2]. Berg, L. S. *Essays on the History of Russian Geographical Discoveries.* Moscow-Leningrad, The USSR Academy of Sciences Press, 1946.

[65]. Berry, A. *Concise History of Astronomy.* Translated by S. Zaimovskiy. Moscow-Leningrad, GITTL, 1946.

[66]. Archimandrite Nicephor. *The Biblical Encyclopedia (The Full Illustrated Biblical Encyclopedia).* Moscow, The A. I. Snegiryova Typography, 1891. A modern reprint was published by the Laura of St. Serge and the Holy Trinity in 1990.

[67]. *The Bible.* 10th edition. St. Petersburg, 1912.

[68]. *The Bible. Books from the Old and the New Covenant in Russian Translation with Anagoges and Appendices.* Moscow, Moscow Patriarchy Press, 1968. There are numerous re-editions in existence, for instance, the one published by the Russian Biblical Society in Moscow, 1995.

[69]. *The Bible. Books of the Holy Writ from the Old and the New Covenant.* Russian translation with appendices. 4th edition. Brussels, Life with God Press, 1989.

[70]. *The Bible, or the Books of the Holy Writ from the Old and the New Covenant*

with Anagoges. 2nd edition. St. Petersburg, Synodal Typography, 1900. Reprinted by the Russian Biblical Society in Moscow, 1993. (This version of the Bible dates to the 1st half of the XVIII century and is therefore occasionally called Elizabethan.)

[71]. *Scorina's Bible.* A facsimile edition of the Bible published by Francisco Scorina in 1517-1519. Volumes 1-3. Minsk, The Petrus Brovka Byelorussian Sovetskaya Encyclopaedia Press, 1990.

[72]. Bickerman, E. *Chronology of the Ancient World.* Moscow, Nauka, 1975. Translated from the English edition published in London by Thames & Hudson, 1968-1969.

[73]. Biroulia, Y. N. *Russian Naval Charts of 1701-1750. Copies from originals (Atlas).* St. Petersburg, The Military Navy Publications, 1993.

[74]. *The Book of Good Tidings. Interpretations of the Holy Gospel by St. Theophilactus, the Archbishop of Bulgaria. The Gospel According to Mark Interpreted.* St. Petersburg, P. P. Soykin's Publications. Repr. St. Petersburg, Satis Press, 1993.

[75]. Blazhko, S. N. *A Course of Practical Astronomy.* Moscow, Nauka, 1979.

[76]. Blair, G. *Chronological Tables Spanning the Entire Global History, Containing Every Year since the Genesis and until the XIX Century, Published in English by G. Blair, a Member of the Royal Society, London.* Vols. 1 and 2. Moscow University Press, 1808-1809. The English edition: *Blair's Chronological and Historical Tables, from the Creation to the Present Time, etc.* London, G. Bell & Sons, 1882.

[77]. Bobrovnitskaya, T. A. *The Royal Regalia of the Russian Rulers. The Kremlin in Moscow. Published to Commemorate the 500th Anniversary of the State Coat of Arms and the 450th Anniversary of the Inauguration of the First Russian Czar Ivan the Terrible.* Moscow, The Moscow Kremlin State Museum and Reserve for History and Culture, 1997.

[78]. Bobrovnitsky. *The Origins and the Process of the Roman Catholic Liturgy.* Kiev, 1873.

[79]. Bogdanov, Ivan. *Name Lists of the Bulgarian Khans.* Sofia, Otechestvenia Front Press, 1981.

[80]. Gousseva, E., A. Lukashov, and others. *Our Lady of Vladimir.* A collection of materials. Exhibition catalogue. The State Tretyakovskaya Gallery, The Moscow Kremlin State Museum and Reserve for History and Culture. Moscow, Avangard Press, 1995.

[80:1]. Boguslavskiy, V. V. *The Slavic Encyclopaedia.* Vols. 1 and 2. Moscow, OLMA-Press, 2001.

[81]. Bozhilov, Ivan. *The Asen Dynasty (1186-1460). Genealogy and Prosopography.* Sofia, Bulgarian Academy of Sciences Press, 1994.

[82]. Bolingbroke. *Epistles on Historical Studies and their Utility.* Moscow, Nauka, 1978.

[83]. Bolotov, V. V. *Lectures on Ancient Ecclesial History.* Vols. 1-4. Published posthumously under the editorship of Prof. A. Brilliantov. St. Petersburg, 1907. Reprinted Moscow, Spaso-Preobrazhensky Monastery of Valaam, 1994.

[84]. Bolkhovitinov, E. A. (Metropolitan Eugene). *The Concise Chronicle of Pskov*. Pskov, Otchina Press, 1993.

[85]. *The Great Soviet Encyclopaedia*. Vols. 1-51. 2nd edition. Moscow, The Soviet Encyclopaedia Press, 1949-1957.

[85:1]. *The Great Soviet Encyclopaedia*. Vols. 1-30. 3rd edition. Moscow, 1969-1978. (Electronic version on 5 CD-ROMs.)

[86]. *The Great Catechism*. Moscow, 7135 (1627 ad). Reprinted by the Royal Grodno typography in 7291 (1683 AD).

[87]. *The Great German-Russian Dictionary*. 2nd edition, Stereotyped. Moscow, Russkiy Yazyk, 1980.

[87:1]. *The Great Turkish-Russian Dictionary*. 20,000 words and word groups. The RAS Institute for Oriental Studies. 2nd edition. Moscow, Russkiy Yazyk, 1998.

[88]. *The Great Encyclopaedic Dictionary*. Moscow, The Great Russian Encyclopaedia Press, 1998.

[89]. Borisov, N. S. *Ivan Kalita*. The *Celebrity Biographies* series. Moscow, Molodaya Gvardia, 1995.

[90]. Borisovskaya, N. *Engraved Ancient Maps and Plans of the XV-XVIII century. Cosmography, Maps, Star Charts, City and Battle Plans. From the Pushkin State Museum of Art Collection*. Moscow, Galaktika Press, 1995.

[91]. *Bosch, Hieronymus*. Self-titled album of reproductions. Moscow, Uniserv, 1995.

[91:1]. *Botticelli*. An album from the *Masters of Art* series. Text by Elena Carpetti. 1997, Giunti Gruppo Editoriale, Florence, 2002. Russian edition by Byely Gorod, Moscow, 2001.

[92]. Beaufort, Louis de. *Dissertation sur l'incertitude des cinq premiers siècles de l'histoire Romaine*. Utrecht, 1738. Republished Paris, Blot, 1886.

[93]. Bocharov, L. I., N. N. Yefimov, I. M. Chachoukh, and I. Y. Chernyshev. *The Conspiracy Against Russian History. (Facts, Mysteries, Versions)*. Moscow, Anvik, 1998.

[93:1]. Brant, Sebastian. *Ship of Fools*. Part of the The *World Literature Bibliothèque* series (Series 1, Vol. 33). Moscow, Khudozhestvennaya Literatura, 1971.

[94]. Brownley, C. A. *Statistical Theory and Methodology in Science and Technology*. Moscow, Nauka, 1977.

[95]. Brashinskiy, I. B. *Looking for the Scythian Treasures*. Leningrad, The USSR Academy of Sciences, Nauka, 1979.

[96]. Brodsky, B. *Kremlin – The Heart of the Fatherland*. Moscow, Izobrazitelnoye Iskusstvo, 1996.

[97]. Bronstein, I. N., and K. A. Semendyaev. *A Reference Book on Mathematics*. Moscow, Nauka, 1986.

[98]. Bronsten, V. A. *Claudius Ptolemy*. Moscow, Nauka, 1988.

[99]. Brugsch, Heinrich. *History of the Pharaohs*. Translated by G. K. Vlastov. Published in the series titled *The Chronicles and the Monuments of the*

Ancient Egypt. St. Petersburg, I. I. Glazounov's Typography, 1880. English edition: *Egypt under the Pharaohs. A History Derived Entirely from the Monuments.* London, J. Murray, 1891.

[99:1]. *Bruges: its Sights and Delights. City Plan.* (Russian version). E.E.C., Editions Thill S. A., Brussels, 1997.

[100]. Bryusova, V. G. *Andrei Rublev.* Moscow, Izobrazitelnoye Iskusstvo, 1995.

[101]. Bouganov, V. I. *Razin and his Followers. Documents, Accounts of the Contemporaries.* Moscow, Nauka, 1995.

[102]. Bouganov, S. I. *Native Historiography of Russian Chronicles.* Moscow, Nauka, 1975.

[103]. Bouzeskoul, V. P. *An Introduction into Greek History. Lectures.* Vol. 1. Petrograd, 1915.

[104]. Boukreyeva, T. N. *The Basel Museum of Arts.* Moscow, Izobrazitelnoye Iskusstvo, 1987.

[105]. Boulatov, A. M. *The Historical Plans of Moscow.* Release III. Moscow, Zhiraf, 2000.

[106]. Burian, Y., and B. Moukhova. *The Enigmatic Etruscans.* Moscow, Nauka, 1970.

[107]. Bouseva-Davydova, I. L. *The Temples of the Muscovite Kremlin: Holy Relics and other Antiquities.* Moscow, The Nauka Int'l Academic Publishing Co., 1997.

[108]. Boutkevich, T. I. *An Overview of Russian Sects.* Kharkov, 1910.

[109]. Boutkov, P. *Defending the Russian Chronicle of Nestor from the Vituperation of the Sceptics.* St. Petersburg, 1840.

[110]. Boutomo, S. I. *Radionuclear Datings and the Construction of an Absolute Chronological Scale of Archaeological Monuments.* In *Archaeology and Natural Sciences.* Moscow, Nauka, 1965. 35-45.

[111]. Boutromeyev, V. *Global History in Individual Personalities. Late Middle Ages.* Moscow, Olma, 1999.

[112]. Kalougin, V. I., comp. *Folk Tales and Legends.* Moscow, Sovremennik, 1991.

[113]. Bychkov, A. A., A. Y. Nizovsky, and P. Y. Chernosvitov. *The Conundrums of Ancient Russia.* Moscow, Veche, 2000.

[114]. Bychkov, V. V. *The Mediaeval Aesthetics of Russia. XI-XVII century.* Moscow, Mysl, 1992.

[114:1]. Bauval, Robert, and Adrian Gilbert. *The Orion Mystery. Unlocking the Secrets of the Pyramids.* Russian translation. Moscow, Veche, 1996.

[115]. *Bulgaria. A Traveller's Map.* Scale: 1:530000. Sofia, Datamap Revue, 1997.

[116]. Wagner, G. K. *Soviet Union and its Famous Works of Art. Old Cities of Russia. A traveller's guide.* Moscow, Iskusstvo, Edizion Leipzig, 1980.

[116:1]. Weinstein S., and M.Kryukov. *The Saddle and the Stirrup.* The *Znaniye-Sila* (Knowledge is Power) magazine (Moscow), August 1985, 24-26.

[117]. Valishevsky, K. *Ivan the Terrible.* Moscow, IKPA-press, 1989. Reprinted from Moscow, Obshchestvennaya Polza Typography, 1912.

[118]. Valishevsky, K. *Ivan the Terrible*. Moscow, Svarog, 1993.

[119]. Valishevsky, K. *The First Romanovs*. Moscow, Kvadrat, 1993.

[120]. Vasiliev, A. A. *The History of Byzantium. The Fall of Byzantium. The Palaeiologi Epoch (1261-1453)*. Leningrad, Academia, 1925.

[121]. *An Introduction into Special Historical Disciplines*. Moscow, MSU Publications, 1990.

[122]. Weber, George. *Universal History*. Moscow, 1892. English edition: Weber, G. *Outline of Universal History from the Creation of the World to the Present Time*. London, 1851.

[122:1]. *Hungarian-Russian Dictionary*. 40,000 words. Moscow-Budapest, Russkiy Yazyk, The Hungarian Academy of Sciences Publishing House, 1974.

[123]. Weisman, A. D. *Greek-Russian Dictionary*. 5th edition. St. Petersburg, published by the author, 1899. Reprinted Moscow, Graeco-Latin Department of Y. A. Shichalin, 1991.

[124]. Weisman, A. D. *Latin-Russian Dictionary*. St. Petersburg: published by the author, 1899. Reprinted Moscow, Graeco-Latin Department of Y. A. Shichalin, 1991.

[125]. Venelin, Y. *News of the Varangians as Related by Arab Scribes; their Alleged Crimes as Seen by the Latter*. The Imperial Moscow University Society for History and Russian Antiquities Readings, Book IV, Section V: 1-18. 1870.

[125:1]. Vereshchagin V. V. *Vereschagin, the Artist. Napoleon I in Russia, 1812*. Tver, the Sozvezdie Agency of Tver, 1993.

[125:2]. Vermoush, G. *Diamonds in World History and Stories about Diamonds*. Moscow, Mezhdunarodnye Otnosheniya, 1988.

[126]. Veselovsky, A. N. *Russians and Veltins in the Saga of Tidrec of Berne (Verona)*. St. Petersburg, Typography of the Imperial Academy of Sciences, 1906. A separate engraving from the *Russian Language and Belles Lettres Department Courier*, Vol. XI (1906), Book 3: 1-190.

[127]. Veselovsky, I. N. *Aristarchus of Samos – The Copernicus of the Antiquity*. Historical and astronomical research. Issue 7: 44. Moscow, Nauka, 1961.

[128]. Veselovsky, S. B. *A Research into the History of Oprichnina*. Moscow, 1963.

[129]. *The Russia Academy of Sciences Courier*, Vol. 68, No. 10 (October 1998). Moscow, Nauka.

[129:1]. Palaudirias, S. A., Editorial Escudo de Oro. *The Entire Antwerp*. In *The Entire Europe* Collection. Antwerp, published in Russian. Barcelona, 1998.

[129:2]. Bersnev, P. V., comp. *The Old Testament Apocrypha. The Book of the Jubilees. Testaments of the Twelve Patriarchs*. Translated by A. V. Smirnov. Published in the *Alexandrian Library* series. St. Petersburg, Amphora, 2000.

[129:3]. Vzdornov, G. I. *Book Art in Old Russia. Handwritten Books in the North-Eastern Russia in the XII – Early XV century*. Moscow, Iskusstvo, 1980.

[130]. Widukind of Corvea. *The Deeds of the Saxons*. Moscow, Nauka, 1975. See also Widukind. *Sächsische Geschichten*. Translated by R. Schottin, foreword by W. Wattenbach. GV. Leipzig, 1882. Also see: Widukind. *Sächsische Geschichten*. New revision by Paul Hirsch. GV, Bd. 33, Leipzig, 1931.

[131]. *The Byzantine Book of the Eparch.* Moscow, Oriental Literature Publications, 1962. Also see *The Book of the Eparch. Le livre du préfet,* with an introduction by Prof. Ivan Dulcev. "Reprint of ... the publication (by Jules Nicole)
of the *Book of the Eparch,* to which is added ... a facsimile of the complete
manuscript and Freshfield's English translation." 1970.

[132]. *Byzantine Historians. Dexippos, Eunapius, Olympiodorus, Malchus, Peter
the Patrician, Menander, Candides, Nonnos, Theophanes the Byzantine.* St.
Petersburg, 1858.

[133]. *Byzantine Legends.* Leningrad, Nauka, 1972.

[134]. Vilinbakhov, G. V. *The State Coat of Arms of Russia. 500 Years.* St. Petersburg, Slavia. The State Hermitage. The Presidential State Heraldry Commission. The Moscow Kremlin State Museum and Reserve for History and
Culture, 1997.

[135]. Vilinbakhov, G., and T. Vilinbakhova. *St. George and his Image as Used in
Russia.* St. Petersburg, Iskusstvo, 1995.

[136]. de Villehardouin, Geoffroy. *The Conquest of Constantinople.* Moscow,
Nauka, 1993.

[137]. Vinogradov, V. K. *Theodosia. A Historical Aperçu.* Yekaterinodar, Kilius
& Co Typography, 1902. (A reprint of the first part of the book is given in
the historical and literary almanac titled *Okoyem [Horizon],* No. 2 for 1992,
Theodosia.)

[138]. Vittorio, Serra. *The Entire Rome. (Flowers. Churches. Museums. Monuments. Fountains. The Vatican. The Sistine Chapel. Tivoli. Ostia Antica).*
Bonechi Edizioni "Il Turismo." Florence, 1994.

[139]. Vladimirov, L. I. *The Omnified Literary History.* Moscow, Kniga, 1988.

[140]. Vlasov, Sergei. *The Deeds of Constantine the Great.* First Experimental
Typography of the State Committee of Russian Federation, Eleemosynary
Institution "The Order of Constantine the Great", 1999.

[141]. Vnouchkov, B. C. *The Prisoner of Schliesselburg.* Yaroslavl, the Upper
Volga Publications, 1988.

[142]. Voyekova, I. N., and V. P. Mitrofanov. *Yaroslavl.* From the series titled
Museum Cities. Leningrad, Avrora, 1973.

[143]. *The Military Topographic Map of Moscow and its Environs* (1860). The
map was published in the *Rarities of Russian Cartography* series. Moscow,
Kartair, the scientific and editorial publishing house of I. R. Anokhin, 1998.

[144]. *Around the Coliseum.* The *Izvestiya* newspaper, 18 May 1977.

[145]. *The Vologda Chronicle.* The Anthology of Ancient Russian Literature, Vol.
37. Leningrad, Nauka, 1982.

[145:1]. *The Land of Volokolamsk. Dedicated to 400 Years of Glorifying the Most
Reverend Joseph of Volotsk.* Under the general editorship of Pitirim, the Metropolitan of Volokolamsk and Yurievsk. Moscow, Prosvetitel, 1994.

[146]. Volfkovich, S. I. *Nikolai Alexandrovich Morozov as a Chemist (1854-1946).*
The Journal of the USSR Academy of Sciences, Department of Chemistry,
No. 5 (1947).

[147]. Volfkovich, S. I. *Nikolai Alexandrovich Morozov. His Life and Works on Chemistry.* The *Priroda (Nature)* magazine, No. 11 (1947).

[148]. Voronikhina, L. N. *Edinburgh.* The *Cities and Museums of the World* series. Moscow, Iskusstvo, 1974.

[149]. Vostokov, A. *A Description of the Russian and the Slovenian Manuscripts of the Rumyantsev Museum as Compiled by Alexander Vostokov.* St. Petersburg, Typography of the Imperial Academy of Sciences, 1842.

[150]. *The Chronicle of Ivan Timofeyev.* Prepared for printing, translated and commented by O. A. Derzhavina. Moscow-Leningrad, 1951.

[151]. *Global History.* 10 volumes. Moscow, USSR Academy of Sciences, The Socio-Economic Literature Department Publications, 1958.

[152]. *The Unified Library of Russia, or the Book Catalogue for an Exhaustive and Detailed Description of our Fatherland.* 2nd extended edition. Moscow, 1845.

[153]. Maggi, G. and Valdes, G. *The Entire Turkey.* Florence, Casa Editrice Bonechi, 1995.

[154]. Wooley, L. *Ur of the Chaldees.* Moscow, Oriental Literary, 1961 (1972). English edition: Wooley, L. *Ur of the Chaldees.* London, Benn, 1950. See also: Wooley, L. *Excavations at Ur. A Record of Twelve Years.* London, Benn, 1955.

[155]. Galfridus Monmutensis. *History of the Brits. The Life of Merlin.* Moscow, Nauka, 1984. English edition: *Histories of the Kings of Britain by Geoffrey of Monmouth.* Translated by L. A. Paton. London-New York, 1912. See also: Giles, J. A., ed. *Six Old English Chronicles.* London, 1848.

[156]. Garkavi, A. Y. *The Accounts of the Slavs and the Russians as Given by Muslim Authors (from mid-VII century until the End of the X century AD).* St. Petersburg, 1870 (1872).

[157]. Genova, E., and L. Vlakhova. *24 Church Plates from the Rila Monastery.* Sofia, Bulgarsky Khudozhnik, 1988.

[158]. *GEO.* A monthly magazine. No. 1 (January, 2000). Moscow, Gruner and Yar Ltd.

[159]. *Geographical Atlas.* Moscow, The General Council of Ministers, Department of Geodetics and Cartography. 1968.

[160]. Herberstein. *Baron Sigismund Herberstein. Notes on the Affairs of the Muscovires.* St. Petersburg, A. S. Souvorin's Press, 1908. *Rerum moscoviticarum commentarii.* Wien, S. l. et d., 1549. *Rerum moscoviticarum commentarii.* Basiliae, 1551. *Rerum moscoviticarum commentarii.* Basiliae, 1556. *Moscovia, der Hauptstat in Reissen.* Wien, 1557. Major, R. H., ed. *Notes upon Russia.* 2nd edition. New York, London Hakluite Society, 1963. Vol. 10: 1-116; Vol. 12: 3-174.

[161]. Herberstein, Sigismund. *Notes on Moscovia.* Moscow, MSU Publications, 1988.

[161:1]. Herberstein. *Ziga Herberstein. Sigismund Herberstein – the Warrior, Statesman, Diplomat and Peacemaker.* An edition of the Dr. F. Preshern Society for Contact Development between Slovenia and Russia. Moscow Byelye Alvy Press, Bilio, Humar Press, 2000.

[162]. von Winkler, P. P., comp. *Coats of Arms of Cities, Provinces, Regions and Towns of the Russian Empire Included into the Complete Collection of Laws and Regulations between 1649 and 1900.* St. Petersburg: published by the book salesman Iv. Iv. Ivanov, 1899. New edition: Moscow, Planeta, 1990.

[163]. Herodotus. *History.* Leningrad, Nauka, 1972. English edition: *The History of Herodotus.* From the series *Great Books of the Western World.* Vol. 5. Chicago, Encyclopaedia Britannica, Inc., The University of Chicago, 1952 (2nd edition 1990). See also: Herodotus. *The Histories of Herodotus, etc.* London and New York, Everyman's Library, 1964.

[164]. Herzen, A. G., and Y. M. Mogarichev. *The Fortress of Gems.* Kyrk-Or, Chufut-Kale. Published as part of the series *The Archaeological Monuments of the Crimea.* Simferopol, Tavria, 1993.

[165]. Herzen, A. G., and Y. M. Mogarichev. *Salachik. The Ouspensky Monastery. Bakhchisaray.* The State Museum and Reserve for History and Culture of Bakhchisaray. 1991.

[165:1]. Hertzman, Yevgeni. *The Lost Centuries of Byzantine Music.* The XX International Congress of Byzantine Scholars. St. Petersburg, The Humanitarian Academy Publishing Centre, 2001.

[166]. Gerchouk, Y. Y. *History of Drawing and Book Art.* Moscow, Aspect, 2000.

[167]. Gililov, I. *A Passion Play of William Shakespeare, or the Mystery of the Great Phoenix.* Moscow, "Artist. Rezhissyor. Teatr" Publications, 1997.

[168]. Glazounov, I. *Russia Crucified.* The *Our Contemporary* magazine, Issues 1-5, 7-9, 11 (1996). This material was subsequently published as a book.

[169]. Gnedenko, A. M., and V. M. Gnedenko. *For One's Comrades, or Everything about the Cossacks.* Moscow, The Int'l Fund of Slavic Writing and Culture. ARP Int. Co., 1993.

[170]. The A. V. Shchusev Museum of Architecture, archive 1246/1-13.

[171]. Golenishchev-Kutuzov, I. N. *The Mediaeval Latin Literature of Italy.* Moscow, Nauka, 1972.

[172]. Golitsyn, N. S. *The Great Warlords of History.* Vol. 1. St. Petersburg, 1878.

[173]. Golovanov, Y. *Etudes on Scientists.* Moscow, Molodaya Gvardiya, 1976.

[174]. Golovin, B. N. *Language and Statistics.* Moscow, 1971.

[175]. Goloubovsky, P. V. *The Pechenegs, the Torks, and the Polovtsy before the Tartar Invasion.* Kiev, 1884.

[176]. Goloubtsov, A. P. *Selected Readings on Ecclesial Archaeology and Liturgy.* St. Petersburg, Statis, 1995.

[177]. Goloubtsova, E. S., and V. M. Smirin. *"On the Attempts of Using the 'New Methods' of Statistical Analysis to Ancient Historical Material."* The Courier of Ancient History, 1982, No. 1: 171-195.

[178]. Goloubtsova, E. S., and G. A. Koshelenko. *Ancient History and the "New Methods."* Historical Issues, No. 8 (1982).

[179]. Goloubtsova, E. S., and Y. A. Zavenyagin. *Another Account of the New Methods and the Chronology of Antiquity.* Historical Issues, No. 12 (1983): 68-83.

[180]. Homer. *Iliad.* Translated by N. I. Gnedich. Moscow, Khudozhestvennaya Literatura, 1969. See also: Homer, *The Iliad of Homer.* Chicago University Press, London, 1962.

[180:1]. Homer. *The Odyssey of Homer.* New York, Harper & Row, 1967.

[181]. Goneim, M. *The Lost Pyramid.* Moscow, Geographiz, 1959. English edition: Goneim, M. *The Lost Pyramid.* New York, Rinehart, 1956.

[182]. Gorbachevsky, B. *Crosses, Fires, and Books.* Moscow, Sovetskaya Rossiya, 1965.

[183]. Gordeyev, A. A. *History of the Cossacks.* Vol. 1-4. Moscow, Strastnoi Boulevard, 1992.

[184]. Gordeyev, N. V. *The Czar Cannon.* Moscow, Moskovskiy Rabochiy, 1969.

[185]. *The Towns and Cities of Russia. An Encyclopaedia.* Moscow, The Great Russian Encyclopaedia Publications, 1994.

[186]. Gorsey, Gerome. *Notes on Russia. XVI – Early XVII century.* Moscow, MSU Press, 1990.

[187]. *The State Armoury.* Album. Moscow, Sovetskiy Khudozhnik, 1988. A new edition by Galart Press, Moscow, 1990.

[188]. *The A. S. Pushkin Museum of Fine Arts.* Catalogue of paintings. Moscow, 1995, Mazzotta. Printed in Italy.

[189]. *The Ruler is a Friend of his Subjects, or Political Court Hortatives and Moralistic Speculations of Kan-Shi, Khan of Manchuria and China. Collected by his son, Khan Yun-Jin.* St. Petersburg, 1795.

[190]. Goulianitsky, N. F., ed. *The Urbanism of the Muscovite State of the XVI-XVII centuries.* Moscow, The Russian Academy of Architecture. Stroyizdat, 1994.

[191]. *The Faceted Chamber in the Moscow Kremlin.* Leningrad, Aurora, 1982.

[192]. Granovsky, T. N. *Lectures on Mediaeval History.* Moscow, Nauka, 1986.

[193]. Grebelsky, Peter K., and Alexander B. Mirvis. *The House of the Romanovs. Biographical Information about the Members of the Reigning House, their Predecessors and Relations.* St. Petersburg, LIO Redaktor, 1992.

[194]. Mina, Gregory. *Uffizi and Pitti. The Art of the Florentine Galleries.* Album. From the *Great Museums of the World* series. Moscow, Slovo, 1999. A translation of the Italian edition by Magnus Edizioni, Udine, Italy, 1994, 1996.

[195]. Gregorovius, F. *Mediaeval History of Athens.* St. Petersburg, 1900. German edition: Gregorovius, F. *Geschichte der Stadt Athen im Mittelalter.* Stuttgart, 1889.

[196]. Gregorovius, F. *Mediaeval History of Rome. The V-XVI century.* Vols. 1-5. St. Petersburg, 1902-1912. English edition: Gregorovius, F. *History of the City of Rome in the Middle Ages.* London, G. Bell & Sons, 1900-1909.

[197]. Grekov, B. D., and A. Y. Yakubovsky. *The Golden Horde and its Decline.* Moscow-Leningrad, USSR Academy of Sciences, 1950.

[198]. *Greece: Temples, Sepulchres and Treasures.* The *Lost Civilizations* Encyclopaedia. Translated from English by N. Belov. Moscow, Terra Publishing Centre, 1997. Original edition, Time-Life Books BV, 1994.

[199]. Gribanov, E. D., and D. A. Balalykin. *Medicine of Moscow on the Medals of Imperial Russia*. Moscow, Triada-X, 1999.

[200]. Nicephor, Gregoras. *Roman History, beginning from the Conquest of Constantinople by the Latins*. St. Petersburg, 1862.

[201]. Grigorovich, V. *An Account of Travelling through European Russia*. Moscow, 1877.

[202]. Grigoriev, V. V. *Saray: The Capital of the Golden Horde, and the Issue of its Location*. St. Petersburg, 1845.

[203]. Grigoriev, G. L. *Who was Ivan the Terrible Really Afraid of? On the Origins of the Oprichnina*. Moscow, Intergraph Service, 1998.

[204]. Grigoulevich, I. R. *The History of the Inquisition*. Moscow, Nauka, 1970.

[205]. Grigoulevich, I. R. *The Inquisition*. Moscow, Politizdat, 1985.

[206]. Grishin, Yakov. *The Tartars of Poland and Lithuania (the Heirs of the Golden Horde)*. Kazan, The Tartar Publishing House, 1995.

[207]. Groslie, B. *Borobudur. The Greatest Collection of Buddhist Sculpture in the World is being Destroyed by Erosion*. The *UNESCO Courier*, No. 6 (1968): 23-27.

[208]. Gudzy, N. K. *History of Early Russian Literature*. Moscow, Uchpedgiz, 1938. English edition: New York, Macmillan & Co, 1949.

[209]. Gouliaev, V. I. *Pre-Columbian Voyages to America. Myths and Reality*. Moscow, Mezhdunarodnye Otnoshenia, 1991.

[210]. Gouliaev, V. I. *America and the Old World in the Pre-Columbian Epoch*. Moscow, Nauka, 1968.

[210:1]. Gouliaev, V. I. *Following the Conquistadors*. Moscow, The USSR Academy of Sciences, Nauka, 1976.

[211]. Gumilev, L. N. *Ancient Russia and the Great Steppe*. Moscow, Mysl, 1992.

[212]. Gumilev, L. N. *In Search of the Figmental Kingdom (the Legend of the Kingdom of Presbyter Johannes*. Moscow, Tanais, 1994.

[213]. Gumilev, L. N. *Hunnu*. St. Petersburg: Time-Out-Compass, 1993.

[214]. Gumilev, L. N. *The Black Legend*. Moscow, Ekopros, 1994.

[215]. Gumilev L. N. *The Huns in China*. Moscow, Nauka, 1974.

[216]. Gumilev, L. N. *From Rus' to Russia*. Moscow, Ekopros, 1992.

[217]. Gourevich, A. Y. *The Mediaeval Cultural Categories*. Moscow, Kultura, 1972.

[218]. Gourevich, V. B. *An Introduction into Spherical Astronomy*. Moscow, Nauka, 1978.

[219]. Gouter, R. S., and Y. L. Polounov. *Girolamo Cardano*. From the *Founding Fathers of Science and Technology* series. Moscow, Znaniye, 1980.

[220]. Goutz, Alexander K. *The True History of Russia*. Omsk, Omsk State University Press, 1999.

[221]. D. *The Stirrup of Quiet Don: the Enigmas of the Novel*. Paris, YMCA Press, 1974.

[222]. Davidenko, I. V. *The Word Was, The Word Is, The Word Shall Always Be... A Philological Fantasy*. Moscow, Russkiy Dvor Press, 1999.

[223]. Dal, V. *An Explanatory Dictionary of the Living Russian Language*. St. Petersburg-Moscow, The M. O. Wolf Society Press, 1912.

[224]. Dal, V. *An Explanatory Dictionary of the Living Russian Language*. St. Petersburg-Moscow, The M. O. Wolf Society Press, 1914. Reprinted Moscow, Citadel, 1998.

[225]. Dal, Vladimir. *An Explanatory Dictionary of the Living Russian Language*. Moscow, State National and Foreign Dictionary Publishing House, 1956.

[226]. Damascene, John. *Dialectic.* Moscow, 1862. See also: John of Damascus. *Dialectica.* New York, St. Bonaventure Franciscan Institute, 1953.

[227]. Damascene, John. *Three Apologies against the Detractors of the Holy Icons or Effigies.* St. Petersburg, 1893. English edition: Baker, T. *John Damascene on Holy Images Followed by Three Sermons of the Assumption.* London, 1898.

[228]. Dantas, G. *Parthenon in Peril.* The *UNESCO Courier,* No. 6 (1968): 16-18, 34.

[229]. Dante, Alighieri. *Minor Œuvres.* Moscow, Nauka, 1968. Also see: Dante, Alighieri. *Opere Minori.* Florence, 1856.

[230]. Dante, Alighieri. *The Divine Comedy.* Translated from the Italian by A. A. Ilushin. Moscow, Philological Department of the M. V. Lomonosov Moscow State University, 1995.

[231]. Darethes of Phrygia. *The History of the Destruction of Troy.* St. Petersburg, Aleteya, 1997.

[232]. Darkevich, V. P. *The Secular Art of Byzantium. Works of Byzantine Art in the Eastern Europe of the X-XIII century.* Moscow, Iskusstvo, 1975.

[233]. Darkevich, V. P. *The Argonauts of the Middle Ages.* Moscow, Nauka, 1976.

[233:1]. *The Gifts of the Magi – a Source of Bliss until Our Day.* Translated from modern Greek by M. Klimenko. The Holy Mount Athon, the Monastery of St. Paul the Apostle. Information about this book was obtained from the *Holy Lamp* newspaper published by the Preobrazhensky Temple in the Bolshie Vyazyomy village, No. 1 (1996).

[234]. *The Gifts Made by the Imperial House of Russia to the Museum of History.* Catalogue of an exhibition. Moscow, The State Museum of History, Publishing Department. 1993.

[235]. Dowley, Tim. *The Biblical Atlas.* Three's Company & Angus Hudson Ltd., 1989. Russian translation: Moscow, The Russian Biblical Society, 1994.

[236]. Cameniata, Johannes. *Two Byzantine Chronicles of the X century. The Psamathian Chronicle; The Conquest of Thessalonica.* Moscow, Oriental Literature Publications, 1962. Also see: Cameniata, Joannes. *De Exicidio Thessalonicae.* In: Clugnet, L. *Bibliothèque hagiographique orientale.* Paris, 1901-1905.

[237]. Dvoretsky, I. K. *Latin-Russian Dictionary.* 50,000 words. Moscow, Russkiy Yazyk, 1976.

[237:1]. Deveuze, Lily. *Carcassonne.* The *Golden Book* series (in Russian). Florence, Bonechi, Central Typography, 2000.

[238]. Dementyeva, V. V. *"The Roman History of Charles Rollen" as Read by a Russian Nobleman.* The *Ancient History Courier,* No. 4 (1991): 117-122.

[239]. Denisov, L. I. *The Orthodox Monasteries of the Russian Empire.* Moscow, 1908. 389-393.

[240]. Jalal, Assad. *Constantinople. From Byzantium to Istanbul.* Moscow, M. & S. Sabashnikov, 1919. French edition: Jalâl, A. *Constantinople de Byzance à Stamboul.* Paris, 1909.

[241]. Jivelegov, A. K. *Dante Alighieri.* From the *Celebrity Biographies* series. Moscow, OGIZ, The Magazine and Newspaper Trust, 1933.

[242]. Jivelegov, A. K. *Leonardo da Vinci.* From the *Celebrity Biographies* series. Moscow, OGIZ, The Magazine and Newspaper Trust, 1935.

[243]. Giovanni, Villani. *The New Chronicle, or the History of Florence.* Moscow, Nauka, 1997. Italian edition: *Cronica di Giovanni Villani a miglior lezione redotta coll'aiuto detesti a penna.* Florence, Magheri, 1823; Rome, Multigrafica, 1980. Vols. 1-8.

[244]. Giovanni, Novelli. *The Shroud of Turin: The Issue Remains Open.* Translated from Italian. Moscow, Franciscan Press, 1998.

[245]. Giua, Michele. *The History of Chemistry.* Moscow, Mir, 1975. Italian original: Giua, Michele. *Storia della chimica, dell'alchimia alle dottrine moderne.* Chiantore, Turin, 1946; Union Tipografiko-Editrice Torinese, 1962.

[246]. Digests of Justinian. Selected fragments translated by I. S. Peretersky. Moscow, Nauka, 1984.

[247]. Diehl, Ch. *History of the Byzantine Empire.* Moscow, IL, 1948. English edition: Princeton, NJ, Princeton University Press, 1925.

[248]. Diehl, Ch. *Chief Problems of the Byzantine History.* Moscow, 1947. French edition: Diehl, Ch. *Les Grands Problèmes de l'Histoire Byzantine.* Paris, Armand Diehl Library, A. Colin, 1947.

[249]. Diels, H. *Ancient Technology.* Moscow-Leningrad, ONTI-GTTI, 1934.

[250]. Diophantes. *Arithmetics.* Moscow, Nauka, 1974. See also: Diophantus, Alexandrinus. *Diophanti Alexandrini Opera Omnia, cum graecis commentaries.* Lipsiae: in aedibus B. G. Teubner, 1893-1895.

[251]. Diringer, D. *The Alphabet.* Moscow, IL, 1963. English edition: London, Hutchinson & Co., 1968.

[252]. Dietmar, A. B. *Ancient Geography.* Moscow, Nauka, 1980.

[253]. Yankov, V. P., comp. *Following the Roads of the Millennia.* A collection of historical articles and essays. Book four. Moscow, Molodaya Gvardia, 1991.

[254]. Drboglav, D. A. *Mysteries of Ancient Latin Hallmarks of IX-XIV century Swords.* Moscow, MSU Press, 1984.

[255]. *Ancient Russian Icon Art.* Moscow, Kedr, 1993. From the collection of the Tretyakovskaya Gallery.

[256]. *Ancient Russian Literature. Depictions of Society.* Moscow, Nauka, 1991.

[257]. Bonhard-Levin, G. M., ed. *Ancient Civilizations.* Moscow, Mysl, 1989.

[258]. Struve, V. V., and D. P. Kallistov., eds. *Ancient Greece.* Moscow, USSR Academy of Sciences, 1956.

[259]. Drews, Arthur. *The Christ Myth.* Vol. 2. Moscow, Krasnaya Nov', 1924. English edition by T. Fisher Unwin. London and Leipzig, 1910.

[260]. Drews, Arthur. *Did St. Peter the Apostle Really Exist?* Moscow, Atheist, 1924. See also: A. Drews. *Die Petrus-le-gende.* Jena, E. Diederichs, 1924.

[261]. Drümel, Johann Heinrich. *An Attempt of Proving the Ararat Origins of the Russians Historically as those of the First Nation after the Deluge.* St. Petersburg, 1785. A Russian translation of a German book published in Nuremberg in 1744.

[262]. Douboshin, G. N. *A Reference Book for Celestial Mechanics and Astrodynamics.* Moscow, Nauka, 1976.

[263]. Doubrovsky, A. S., N. N. Nepeyvoda, and Y. A. Chikanov. *On the Chronology of Ptolemy's Almagest. A Secondary Mathematical and Methodological Analysis.* The *Samoobrazovanie (Self-Education)* magazine (Moscow), No. 1, 1999.

[263:1]. Duby, Georges. *The Middle Ages (987-1460). From Hugo Capet to Joan of Arc.* Moscow, Mezhdunarodnye Otnosheniya, 2000. French original: Duby, Georges. *Le Moyen Âge. De Hugues Capet à Jeanne d'Arc (987-1460).* Collection *Pluriel.* Hachette, 1987.

[264]. Dupuy, R. Ernest, and Trevor N. Dupuy. *The Harper Encyclopaedia of Military History. From 3500 BC to the Present.* Commentary by the Polygon Press. Vol. 1: 3500 bc-1400 ad. Vol. 2: 1400–1800. St. Petersburg-Moscow, Polygon-AST, 1997. English original published by Harper Collins.

[265]. Dürer, Albrecht. *Tractates. Diaries. Letters.* St. Petersburg, Azbuka, 2000.

[265:1]. [Dürer] *Albrecht Dürer. Engravings.* Moscow, Magma Ltd., 2001. First published in 1980 by Hubschmidt et Bouret.

[265:2]. *The Jewish Encyclopaedia.* Vols. 1-16. A reprint of the Brockhaus-Efron edition for the Society for Scientific Judaic Publications, St. Petersburg. Moscow, Terra-Terra, 1991.

[266]. *The Hebraic Text of the Old Testament (The Tanach).* London, the British and Foreign Bible Society, 1977.

[267]. Eusebius Pamphilus. *Ecclesial History.* St. Petersburg, 1848. English edition: Eusebius Pamphilus. *History of the Church.* London, 1890.

[268]. Eusebius Pamphilus. *Eusebius Pamphilus, Bischop of the Palestinian Caesarea, on the Toponymy of the Holy Writ. St. Jerome of Strydon on the Hebraic Locations and Names.* Translated by I. Pomyalovsky. St. Petersburg, 1894. Latin edition: Eusebius Pamphilus. *Eusebii Pamphili Episcopi Caesariensis Onomasticon Urbium et Locorum Sacrae Scripturae.* Berolini, 1862.

[269]. Eutropius. *A Concise History Starting with the City's Creation.* From the *Roman Historians of the IV century* series. Moscow, Russian Political Encyclopaedia, 1997.

[270]. Yegorov, D. N. *An Introduction into the Mediaeval Studies. The Historiography and the Source Studies.* Vols. 1-2. Moscow, High Courses of Female Education, Department of History and Philosophy, Publishing Society.

[271]. Yermolayev, G. *Mystery of the "Quiet flows the Don."* Slavic and European Journal, 18, 3 (1974).

[272]. Yermolayev, G. *The True Authorship of the "Quiet flows the Don."* Slavic and European Journal, 20, 3 (1976).

[273]. Yefremov, Y. N., and E. D. Pavlovskaya. *Dating the "Almagest" by the Actual Stellar Movements.* The USSR Academy of Sciences Archive, Vol. 294, No. 2: 310-313.

[274]. Yefremov, Y. N., and E. D. Pavlovskaya. *Determining the Epoch of the Almagest Star Catalogue's Creation by the Analysis of the Actual Stellar Movements. (On the Problem of Ptolemy's Star Catalogue Authorship). The Historical and Astronomical Research.* Moscow, Nauka, 1989. 175-192.

[275]. Jambus, M. *The Hierarchical Cluster Analysis and Related Correspondences.* Moscow, Finances and Statistics, 1988. Also see: Kendall, M., and A. Stewart. *The Advanced Theory of Statistics* (4th edition). London, C. Griffin, 1977.

[275:1]. *Living History of the Orient.* Collected works. Moscow, Znanie, 1998.

[276]. Zivkovic, Branislav. *Les monuments de la Peinture Serbe Médiévale.* Zivkovic, Branislav. *Zica. Les dessins des fresques.* Belgrade, Institut pour la protection des monuments historiques de la Republique de Serbie, 1985.

[277]. *The Art of Ancient Russia. XI – early XIII century. Inlays, Frescoes, Icons.* Leningrad, Khudozhnik RSFSR, 1982.

[278]. Cellini, Benvenuto. *The Life of Benvenuto Cellini, the Son of Maestro Giovanni Cellini, a Florentine, Written in Florence by Himself.* Moscow, 1958. The English edition was published by Edito-Service in Geneva, 1968.

[278:1]. *The Hagiography of Reverend Sergiy (The Life and the Great Deeds of the Most Reverend and Blessed Father Sergiy the Thaumaturge, the Hegumen of Radonezh and the Entire Russia).* Compiled by Hieromonk Nikon (subsequently an Archimandrite). 5th edition. The Laura of Serge and The Holy Trinity. Own typography. 1904.

[279]. *The Life of Savva Storozhevsky.* Reprinted after an old XVII century edition. Published in the *Zvenigorod Region History Materials,* Issue 3. Moscow, The Archaeographical Centre, 1994.

[280]. Zhitomirsky, S. V. *The Astronomical Works of Archimedes.* Historical and Astronomical Research, Issue 13. Moscow, Nauka, 1977.

[281]. Zholkovsky, A. V. *Pasternak's Book of Books.* The *Zvezda (Star)* magazine, No. 12 (1997).

[282]. Zabelin, I. E. *Quotidian Life of Russian Czarinas in the XVI and XVII centuries.* Novosibirsk, Nauka, 1992.

[283]. Zabelin, I. E. *The History of Moscow.* Moscow, Svarog, 1996.

[284]. Zabelin, I. E. *The History of Moscow.* Moscow, Stolitsa, 1990.

[285]. Zabelin, I. E. *The Historical Description of the Stauropigial Monastery of Moscow.* 2nd edition. Moscow, 1893.

[286]. Zaborov, M. A. *History of the Crusades in Documents and Materials.* Moscow, Vyshchaya Shkola, 1977.

[287]. Zaborov, M. A. *Crusaders in the East.* Moscow, Nauka, Chief Editing Board of Oriental Literature, 1980.

[288]. Zavelskiy, F. S. *Time and its Keeping.* Moscow, Nauka, 1987.

[289]. Porfiriev, G., ed. *The Mysteries and Conundrums of the "Quiet flows the Don."* Collected works. Samara, P.S., 1996.

[290]. *The Gospel Teachings.* Jordanville, the Rev. Job. Pogayevsky Typography, 1987.

[290:1]. Zaliznyak, A. A., and V. L. Yanin. *The XI century Psalm Book of Novgorod as the Oldest Book in Russia.* The *RAS Courier,* Vol. 71, No. 3 (2001): 202-209.

[291]. Zamarovsky, V. *Mysteries of the Hittites.* Moscow, Nauka, 1968. Also see: Zamarovsky, V. *Za tajemstvism rise Chetitu.* Prague, 1964.

[291:1]. Zamkova, M. V. *Louvre. (The Masterpieces of World Art in your Home).* Album. Moscow, Olma-Obrazovanie, 2002.

[292]. *Notes of the Russian and Slavic Archaeology Department of the Russian Archaeological Society.* Vol. XII. Petrograd, Typography of Y. Bashmakov & Co, 1918.

[293]. *Star Charts of the Norhern and the Southern Hemisphere.* Edition: *Maru severni a jizni hvezdne oblohy.* Czechoslovakia, Kartografie Praha, 1971.

[294]. Kondrashina, V. A., and L. A. Timoshina, eds. *Zvenigorod Over Six Centuries.* A collection of articles. To the 600th anniversary of the Savvi-no-Storozhevsky monastery. The Moscow Oblast Administration Culture Committee. The Zvenigorod Museum of History, Arts, and Architecture. The Federal Archive Service of Russia. Russian State Archive of Ancient Acts. Moscow, URSS Press, 1998.

[294:1]. Zgura, V. V. *Kolomenskoye. An Aperçu of its Cultural History and Monuments.* Moscow, O.I.R.U., 1928.

[295]. Zelinskiy, A. N. *Constructive Principles of the Ancient Russian Calendar.* The *Context 1978* collection. Moscow, Nauka, 1978.

[296]. Zelinskiy, F. *Selected Biographies of Ideas.* Vols. I-IV. St. Petersburg, 1905-1922.

[297]. Zenin, D. *The Ancient Artillery: Truth and Fiction.* The *Science and Technology* magazine, No. 5 (1982): 25-29.

[298]. Zenkovsky, S. A. *Old Ritualists of Russia. The XVII century Religious Movements.* Moscow, Tserkov, 1995.

[299]. Zima, D., and N. Zima. *Nostradamus Deciphered.* Moscow, Ripol Klassik, 1998.

[299:1]. *The Banner of Reverend Serge (Sergiy) of Radonezh.* Psaltyr, 1934. Re-printed by RIO Dennitsa, Moscow, 1991.

[300]. Zoubov, V. P. *Aristotle.* Moscow, The USSR Academy of Sciences Press, 1963.

[301]. *Ivan IV The Terrible.* Essays. St. Petersburg, Azbuka, 2000.

[301:1]. Ivanov, O. *The Zamoskvorechye: Chronicle Pages.* Moscow, V. Shevchouk Publications, Inc., 2000.

[302]. Idelson, N. *History of the Calendar.* Leningrad, Scientific Publications, 1925.

[303]. Idries, Shah. *Sufism.* Moscow, 1993.

[304]. Ieger, Oscar. *Global History.* Vols. 1-4. St. Petersburg, A. F. Marx, 1894-1904.

[304:1]. Ieger, Oscar. *Global History.* Vols. 1-4. St. Petersburg, A. F. Marx, 1904. Amended and expanded. Faximile reprint: Moscow, AST, 2000.

[304:2]. Ieger, Oscar. *Global History.* Vols. 1-4. St. Petersburg, A. F. Marx, 1904. 3rd ed., amended and expanded. Faximile reprint: Moscow, AST, 2001; St Petersburg, Polygon, 2001.

[305]. *Jerusalem in Russian Culture.* Collected essays. Moscow, Nauka, 1994.

[306]. *Selected Letters of A. N. Roudnev to V. N. Leonova.* Frankfurt-am-Main, Nadezhda, 1981.

[306:1]. *A Representation of the Terrestrial Globe.* Russian map from the *Rarities of Russian Cartography* series. (There is no compilation date anywhere on the map. The publishers date it to mid-XVIII century, q.v. in the annotation). Moscow, the Kartair Cartographical Association, 1996.

[307]. Derevenskiy, B. G., comp. *Jesus Christ in Historical Documents.* From the *Ancient Christianity* series, *Sources* section. St. Petersburg, Aleteya, 1998.

[308]. Ouspensky, L. A. *Icon Art of Ancient Russia.* Album. Foreword by S. S. Averintsev, compiled by N. I. Bednik. St. Petersburg, Khudozhnik Rossii, 1993.

[309]. Ilyin, A. A. *The Classification of Russian Provincial Coins.* Issue 1. Leningrad, The State Hermitage, 1940.

[310]. Ilyin, M., and T. Moiseyeva. *Moscow and its Environs.* Moscow, 1979.

[311]. Ilyin, M. *The Ways and the Quests of an Arts Historian.* Moscow, Iskusstvo Publications, 1970.

[312]. Illarion. *On the Law and the Bliss.* Moscow, Stolitsa and Skriptoriy, 1994.

[312:1]. *The Names of Moscow Streets* (multiple authors). Under the general editorship of A. M. Pegov. Moscow, Moskovskiy Rabochiy, 1972.

[313]. de la Vega, Inca Garcilazo. *History of the State of the Incas.* Leningrad, Nauka, 1974.

[314]. *Foreigners on Ancient Moscow. Moscow of the XV-XVII centuries.* Collected texts. Moscow, Stolitsa, 1991.

[315]. of Hildesheim, Johann. *A Legend of the Three Holy Kings.* Translated from German. Moscow, Enigma-Aleteya, 1998. German edition: von Hildesheim, Johan. *Die Legende von den Heiligen Drei Königen.* Berlin, 1925.

[316]. *The Art of the Countries and the Peoples of the World. A Brief Scientific Encyclopaedia.* Vol. 1. Moscow, Soviet Encyclopaedia Publications, 1962.

[317]. *Islam: an Encyclopaedic Dictionary.* Moscow, Nauka, General Editing Board for Oriental Literature, 1991.

[318]. Martzyshevskaya, K. A., B. J. Sordo-Peña, and S. Mariñero. *Spanish-Russian and Russian-Spanish Dictionary.* Moscow, Russkiy Yazyk, 1990.

[319]. *Historical and Astronomical Research.* Moscow, Fizmatgiz, 1955.

[320]. *Historical and Astronomical Research.* Issue 8. Moscow, Fizmatgiz, 1962.

[321]. *Historical and Astronomical Research.* Issue 1. Moscow-Leningrad, 1948.

[322]. *Historical Notes of Nicephorus Vriennius.* St. Petersburg, 1858.

[323]. *History of Byzantium.* Vol. 1. Moscow, Nauka, 1967.

[324]. *History of Byzantium.* Vols. 2-3. Moscow, Nauka, 1967.

[325]. *History of the Orient. Vol. 2. Mediaeval Orient.* Russian Academy of Sciences, the Department of Oriental Sciences. Moscow, Vostochnaya Literatura, RAS, 1995.

[326]. Kouzishchin, V. I., ed. *History of the Ancient Orient.* Moscow, 1979.

[327]. Kouzishchin, V. I., and A. G. Bokshchanin., eds. *History of the Ancient Rome.* Moscow, 1971.

[328]. *History of Europe.* Published in Europe as an initiative of Frederic Delouche. A Collective of 12 European Historians. Minsk, Vysheyshaya Shkola; Moscow, Prosveshchenie, 1996. Translated from *Histoire de l'Europe.* Hachette, 1992.

[328:1]. *History of Europe. The Renaissance.* Moscow, Minsk, Harvest, AST, Inc., 2000.

[329]. Melnik, A. G., ed. *History and Culture of the Land of Rostov. 1998.* Collected essays. Rostov, The Rostov Kremlin State Museum and Reserve, 1999.

[330]. *History of the Inquisition in Three Volumes.* Vols. 1 and 2: Lee, Henry Charles. *History of the Inquisition in the Middle Ages.* A reprint of the F. A. Efron, I. A. Brockhaus edition. 1911-1912. Vol. 3: Lozinsky, S. G. *History of the Spanish Inquisition.* A reprint of the F. A. Efron, I. A. Brockhaus edition. 1914. Moscow, The Ladomir Scientific and Publishing Centre, 1994.

[330:1]. *History of Moscow in the Documents of the XII-XVIII century from the Russian State Archive of Ancient Acts.* The Russian State Archive of Ancient Acts, Moscow Municipal Archive Association. Moscow, Mosgorarkhiv, 1997.

[331]. Sakharov, A. N., ed. *History of Moscow. From the Earliest Days until Our Time.* Three volumes. Moscow, the RAS Institute of Russian History, the Moscow Municipal Association, Mosgorarkhiv Press. Vol. 1: XII-XVII century. Vol. 2: XIX century. 1997.

[332]. *Russian History. From the Ancient Slavs to Peter the Great. Encyclopaedia for Children.* Vol. 5. Moscow, Avanta, 1995.

[333]. Udaltsov, A. D., E. A. Kosminsky, O. L. Weinstein, eds. *Mediaeval History.* Moscow, OGIZ, 1941.

[334]. Skazkin, S. D., ed. *Mediaeval History.* Volumes 1-2. Moscow, 1977.

[335]. *History of French Literature.* Collected essays. St. Petersburg, 1887. English edition: Demogeot, J., *History of French Literature.* London, Rivingstons, 1884 (1883).

[336]. Helmolt, H., ed. *The History of Humanity. Global History.* Vols. 1-9. Translated from German. St. Petersburg: Prosveshchenie, 1896.

[337]. Istrin, V. M. *I-IV Editions of the Explanatory Paleya.* St. Petersburg, The Imperial Academic Typography, 1907.

[338]. Istrin, V. M. *The Chronicle of John Malalas in Slavic Translation.* A reprint of V. M. Istrin's materials. Moscow, John Wiley & Sons, 1994.

[339]. Pouchkov, P. I., ed. *Extinct Nations.* Collected essays. Moscow, Nauka, 1988.

[340]. *Itogi (The Resume).* Weekly magazine. No. 37 (223) (12 September 2000). Moscow, Sem Dney Press.

[341]. Duchich, Jovan. *Duke Sava Vladislavich. The First Serbian Diplomat at the court of Peter the Great and Catherine I.* Belgrade, Dereta, 1999.

[342]. Kazhdan, A. P. *The Origins and the Purport of Christianity.* Moscow, 1962.

[343]. Kazhdan, A. P. *The Social Compound of the Byzantine Ruling Class of the XI-XII century.* Moscow, Nauka, 1974.

[344]. Kazakova, N. A. *Western Europe in Russian Written Sources of the XV-XVI century.* Leningrad, Nauka, 1980.

[345]. Kazamanova, A. N. *An Introduction to Ancient Numismatics.* Moscow, Moscow University Press, 1969.

[346]. *The Cossack Circle.* Quiet flows the Don. Special edition 1. Moscow, Russkoye Slovo, 1991.

[347]. Skrylov, A. I., and G. V. Gubarev. *The Cossack Dictionary and Handbook.* Cleveland, 1966. Reprinted Moscow, Sozidanie Ltd., 1992.

[348]. Fomenko, A. T., V. V. Kalashnikov, and G. V. Nosovskiy. *The Geometry of Mobile Star Configurations and the Dating of the Almagest.* Problems of stochastic model stability. Seminar works. The National System Research Institute, 1988. 59-78.

[349]. Fomenko, A. T., V. V. Kalashnikov, and G. V. Nosovskiy. *The Statistical Analysis and Dating of the Observations that the Almagest Star Catalogue is Based upon.* Report theses of the 5th Int'l Probability Theory Conference in Vilnius, the Lithuanian Academy of Sciences Institute of Mathematics and Cybernetics, Vol. 3 (1989): 271-272.

[350]. Fomenko, A. T., V. V. Kalashnikov, and G. V. Nosovskiy. *Dating the Almagest by Variable Star Configurations.* The USSR AS Reports, Vol. 307, No. 4 (1989): 829-832. English translation published in Soviet Phys. Dokl., Vol. 34, No. 8 (1989): 666-668.

[351]. Fomenko, A. T., V. V. Kalashnikov, and G. V. Nosovskiy. *A Retrospective Analysis of the Almagest Star Catalogue and the Problem of its Dating.* Preprint. Moscow, National System Research Institute, 1990. 60 p.

[352]. Fomenko, A. T., V. V. Kalashnikov, and G. V. Nosovskiy. *A Quantitative Analysis of the Almagest Star Catalogue.* Pre-print. Moscow, National System Research Institute, 1990. 62 p.

[353]. Fomenko, A. T., V. V. Kalashnikov, and G. V. Nosovskiy. *Dating the Almagest Star Catalogue.* Preprint. Moscow, National System Research Institute, 1990. 58 p.

[354]. Fomenko, A. T., V. V. Kalashnikov, and G. V. Nosovskiy. *Ptolemy's Star Catalogue Dated by Mathematicians. Hypotheses, Predictions, and the Future of Science.* The Int'l Annual Journal. No. 23 (1990): 78-92. Moscow, Znaniye.

[355]. Fomenko, A. T., V. V. Kalashnikov, and G. V. Nosovskiy. *A Statistical Analysis of the Almagest Star Catalogue.* The USSR AS Reports. Vol. 313, No. 6 (1990): 1315-1320.

[356]. Fomenko, A. T., V. V. Kalashnikov, and G. V. Nosovskiy. *Dating the Almagest Star Catalogue. A Statistical and Geometric Analysis.* Moscow, Faktorial, 1995.

[356:1]. Fomenko, A. T., V. V. Kalashnikov, and G. V. Nosovskiy. *An Astronomical Analysis of Chronology. The Almagest. Zodiacs.* Moscow, The Delovoi Express Financial, 2000.

[357]. Fomenko, A. T., V. V. Kalashnikov, and S. T. Rachev. *New Methods of Comparing Volume Functions of Historical Texts.* Seminar works. Moscow, National System Research Institute, 1986. 33-45.

[358]. Kaleda, G. *The Shroud of Our Lord Jesus Christ. To the Centenary of the Manifestation of the Holiest of Relics, 1898-1998.* 4th edition. Moscow, Zakatyevsky Monastery Press, 1998.

[358:1]. *Russia and the World on Russian Maps.* Moscow, published by Vneshtorgbank and the State Museum of History in 2001. Compiled by B. Sergeyev and A. Zaitsev. Maps from the collection of the State Museum of History, 16, Kuznetskiy Most, 103301, Moscow.

[359]. *The Stonework Chronicle of the old Moscow.* Moscow, Sovremennnik, 1985.

[360]. Kamensky, A. B. *The Life and the Fate of the Empress Catherine the Great.* Moscow, Znanie, 1997.

[361]. Kaneva, Katerina, Alessandro Cechi, and Antonio Natali. *Uffizi. A Guide and a Catalogue of the Art Gallery.* Scala/ Becocci, 1997. Moscow, Izobrazitelnoye Iskusstvo, 1997.

[362]. Karamzin, N. M. *History of the State of Russia.* St. Petersburg, 1842. A reprint of the fifth edition that came out as 3 books with P. M. Stroyev's *Key* attached. Books I, II, III, IV. Moscow, Kniga, 1988, 1989.

[363]. Karamzin, N. M. *History of the State of Russia* (Academic edition). Moscow, Nauka. Vol. 1: 1989. Vols. 2-3: 1991. Vol. 4: 1992. Vol. 5: 1993.

[364]. Karger, M. K. *Ancient Kiev. Essays on the History of the Material Culture of this Ancient Russian City.* Vol. 1. Moscow-Leningrad, The USSR AS Press, 1958.

[365]. Karger, M. *Novgorod the Great.* Moscow, The USSR Academy of Architecture. The Architectural History and Theory Institute. 1946.

[366]. *Karelin Andrei Osipovich. Legacy of an Artist.* Nizhni Novgorod, Arnika, 1994.

[367]. Karnovich, E. P. *Patrimonial Names and Titles in Russia.* St. Petersburg, 1886. Reprinted in Moscow, Bimpa Press, 1991.

[368]. Valcanover, Francesco. *Carpaccio.* Album. Moscow, Slovo, 1996. The Italian edition was published in the *Great Masters of Italian Art* series. Florence, Scala, Istituto Fotografico Editoriale, Antella, 1989.

[369]. Karpenko. V. V. *The Names on the Sky at Night.* Moscow, Nauka, 1981.

[370]. Carpiceci, Alberto Carlo. *The Art and History of Egypt. 5000 Years of Civilization.* Russian edition. Florence, Casa Editrice Bonechi, 1997.

[371]. Carpiceci, Alberto Carlo. *The Art and History of Egypt. 5000 Years of Civilization.* Florence, Bonechi, 1999.

[372]. Kartashev, A. V. *Essays on the History of Russian Church.* Vols. 1, 2. Moscow, Nauka, 1991.

[373]. Kartashev, A. V. *Essays on the History of Russian Church.* Moscow, Terra, 1992.

[374]. Carter, H. *The Tomb of Tutankhamen.* Moscow, Oriental Literature, 1959.

[375]. Quintus Curtius Rufus. *The Story of Alexander the Great.* Moscow, MSU Press, 1993.

[376]. Denisenko, D. V., and N. S. Kellin. *When Were the Famous Dendera Zodiacs Really Created?* An appendix to Fomenko, A. T. *Criticism of Traditional Chronology of Antiquity and the Middle Ages (What Century is it Now?).* Moscow, MSU Publications, the MSU Department of Mechanical Mathematics, 1993. 156-166.

[377]. Fomenko, A. T., N. S. Kellin, and G. V. Nosovskiy. *The Issue of the Veracity of the "Ancient" History of Russia by M. V. Lomonosov. Lomonosov or Miller?* The Moscow University Courier, Series 9: Philology, No. 1 (1991): 116-125.

[378]. Kenderova, Stoyanka, and Beshevliev, Boyan. *The Balkan Peninsula on AlIdrisi's Map. Palaeographic, Historical and Geographical Research.* Part 1. Sofia, 1990.

[379]. Ceram, C. *Gods, Graves and Scholars.* Moscow, Inostrannaya Literatura, 1960. English original: London, Victor Gollancz in association with Sidgwick & Jackson, 1971.

[380]. Ceram, C. *Gods, Graves and Scholars.* St. Petersburg, Nizhegorodskaya Yarmarka, KEM, 1994.

[381]. Kibalova, L., O. Gerbenova, and M. Lamarova. *An Illustrated Encyclopaedia of Fashion.* Prague, Artia, 1966.

[382]. Kinnam, Johann. *A Brief Review of the Reigns of John and Manuel Comneni.* St. Petersburg, 1859.

[383]. Kinzhalov, R. V. *The Ancient Mayan Culture.* Leningrad, Nauka, 1971.

[384]. Kiriaku, Georgios P. *Cyprus in Colours.* Limassol, Cyprus, K. P. Kiriaku (Books & Office Requisites) Ltd., 1987.

[385]. Kirpichnikov, A. N. *The Pages of the "Iron Book."* Nauka I Zhizn *(Science and Life)* magazine, No. 6 (1966): 49-55.

[385:1]. Kiselyova L. I. *What do the Mediaeval Chronicles Tell Us?* Leningrad, Nauka, 1978.

[386]. Kyetsaa, H. *The Battle for the "Quiet flows the Don."* Seanado-Statica, 22, 1976.

[387]. Kyetsaa, H. *The Battle for the "Quiet flows the Don."* USA, Pergamon Press, 1977.

[388]. Klassen, E. I. *New Materials for the Studies of the Historical Dawn of Slavs in General, and pre-Ryurik Russo-Slavs in Particular, with an Aperçu of the BC History of Russia.* Issues 1-3. With the *Descriptions of the Monuments Explaining the History of the Slavs and the Russians Compiled by Fadey Volansky and Translated by E. Klassen.* Moscow University Press, 1854. Reprinted by Andreyev i Soglasie, St. Petersburg, 1995.

[389]. Klassovsky, V. *A Systematic Description of Pompeii and the Artefacts Discovered There.* St. Petersburg, 1848.

[390]. Klein, L. S. *Archaeology Controverts Physics*. The *Priroda (Nature)* magazine, No. 2 (1966): 51-62.

[391]. Klein, L. S. *Archaeology Controverts Physics (continued)*. The *Priroda (Nature)* magazine, No. 3 (1966): 94-107.

[391:1]. Klengel-Brandt, E. *A Journey into the Old Babylon*. Moscow, Nauka, General Editing Board for Oriental Literature, the USSR AS, Institute of Oriental Studies, 1979. Translated from German: Klengel-Brandt, E. *Reise in das alte Babylon*. Leipzig, 1971.

[392]. Kligene N., and L. Telxnis. *Methods of Determining Change Points in Random Processes*. Avtomatika i Telemekhanika (Automatics and Telemechanics), No. 10 (1983): 5-56.

[393]. Klimishin, I. A. *Chronology and the Calendar*. Moscow, Nauka, 2nd edition, 1985.

[394]. Klimishin, I. A. *Chronology and the Calendar*. Moscow, Nauka, 3rd edition, 1990.

[395]. Klimishin, I. A. *The Discovery of the Universe*. Moscow, Nauka, 1987.

[396]. Klyuchevsky, V. O. *Unreleased Works*. Moscow, Nauka, 1983.

[397]. *The Book of the Mormon. Another Testament of Jesus Christ*. Translated by Joseph Smith, Jun. Salt Lake City, The Church of Jesus Christ of the Latter Day Saints, 1991. (Quoting the Russian translation of 1988).

[398]. *The Book of Cosmas Indicopleustes*. Published by V. S. Golyshenko and V. F. Doubrovina. RAS, the V. V. Vinogradov Institute of the Russian Language. Moscow, Indrik, 1997.

[399]. Loparev, H. M., ed. *The Book of the Pilgrim. Holy Places in Czar-Grad Described by Anthony, the Archbishop of Novgorod in 1200*. "The Orthodox Palestinian Collection," Vol. 17, 3rd edition. St. Petersburg, 1899.

[400]. *Literary Centres of the Ancient Russia in the XI-XVI century*. St. Petersburg, Nauka, 1991.

[401]. Knorina, L. V. *Linguistic Aspects of the Hebraic Commentary Tradition*. *Voprosy Yazykoznania (Linguistic Issues)*, No. 1 (1997): 97-108.

[402]. Kowalski, Jan Wierusz. *Papacy and the Popes*. Moscow, Political Literature Publications, 1991. A translation of the Polish book *Poczet Papiezy*. Warsaw, 1985.

[403]. Kovalchenko, I. D. *The Use of Quantitative Methods and Computers in Historical Research*. The *Voprosy Istorii (Historical Issues)* journal, No. 9 (1984): 61-73.

[404]. Kogan, V. M. *The History of the House of Ryurikovichi*. St. Petersburg, Belvedere, 1993.

[405]. Kozlov, V. *A Case of Church Robbery*. The *Moskovskiy Zhurnal (Moscow Magazine)*, No. 7 (1991).

[406]. Kozlov, V. *Under the Flag of Nihilism*. The *Moskovskiy Zhurnal (Moscow Magazine)*, No. 6 (1991).

[407]. Kozlov, V. P. *Falsification Mysteries. An Analysis of Historical Source Forgeries of the XVIII-XIX centuries*. Moscow, Aspekt, 1996.

[407:1]. Kozlov, V. T. *The 30-Year War. European Splendour. The Renaissance. Humanism. The Enlightenment.* Moscow, The V. T. Kozlov Regional Public Fund for the Support and Development of Arts and Culture, 2001. 44.

[408]. Kozlov, P. *Yaroslavl.* Yaroslavl, The Upper Volga Publishing House, 1972.

[409]. Kozlov, P. I., and V. F. Marov. *Yaroslavl. A Guide and a Reference Book.* Yaroslavl, The Upper Volga, 1988.

[410]. Kokkinoftas, Kostis and Theocharidis, Ioannis. *"Enkolpion." A Brief Description of St. Kykkos Monastery.* Nicosia, The St. Kykkos Monastery Research Centre, 1995.

[411]. Kolodny, L. "Turbulence over the 'Quiet flows the Don.' Fragments of the Past: the Sources used for a Certain XX century Animad version. *Moskovskaya Pravda* (5 and 7 March, 1989).

[412]. Rauschenbach, B .V., ed. *Bells. History and Contemporaneity.* Compiled by Y. V. Pukhnachev. The Scientific Counsel for World Culture History, the USSR AS. Moscow, Nauka, 1985.

[413]. Kolosov, Vassily. *Perambulations in the Environs of the Simonov Monastery.* Moscow, 1806.

[414]. Kolchin, B. A., and Y. A. Sher. *Absolute Archaeological Datings and their Problems.* Moscow, Nauka, 1972.

[415]. Kohlrausch, F. *History of Germany.* Vols. I, II. Moscow, 1860. English edition: Kohlrausch, F. *A History of Germany, from the Earliest Period to the Present Time.* New York, D. Appelton & Co, 1896.

[415:1]. Kolyazin, V. F. *From The Passion Play Mystery to the Carnival. The Histrionics of the German Religious and Popular Stage of the Early and the Late Middle Ages.* Moscow, Nauka, 2002.

[416]. *Archimandrite Palladius Kafarov Commentary on Marco Polo's Voyage through Northern China.* St. Petersburg, 1902.

[417]. Comnena, Anna. *The Alexiad.* Moscow, Nauka, 1965. English edition: Harmondsworth, Penguin, 1969.

[418]. Comnena, Anna. *The Alexiad.* St. Petersburg. Aleteya, 1996.

[419]. Comnena, Anna. *A Brief Account of the Deeds of King Alexis Comnenus.* St. Petersburg, 1859.

[420]. Kondakov, N. P. *The Iconography of Our Lady.* 3 volumes. Moscow, Palomnik. Vols. 1 and 2, 1998. Vol. 3, 1999.

[420:1]. Kondratov, Alexander. *The Mysteries of the Three Oceans.* Leningrad, Gidrometeoizdat, 1971.

[421]. Kondratyev, I. K. *The Ancient Moscow. A Historical Review and a Full List of the City's Monuments.* Moscow, Voyenizdat, 1996.

[422]. Kondrashina, V. A. *The Savvino-Storozhevsky Monastery. 600 Years since the Foundation of the Coenoby of Rev. Savva.* An album of photographs. Moscow, Leto, 1998.

[423]. Koniskiy, G. (The Archbishop of Byelorussia). *The History of Russians, or the Lesser Russia.* The Moscow University Typography, 1846.

[424]. *Konstantin Mikhailovich from Ostrovitsa. The Notes of a Janissary.* In-

troduction, translation, and commentary by A. I. Rogov. Published in the *Monuments of Mediaeval History of the Nations of Central and Eastern Europe* series. The USSR AS, Institute of Slavic and Balkan Studies. Moscow, Nauka, 1978.

[425]. Konstantinov, N. *The Secret Alphabet of Stolnik Baryatinsky.* The *Nauka i Zhizn (Science and Life)* magazine, No. 10 (1972): 118-119.

[426]. *Context 1978.* Collected works. Moscow, Nauka, 1978.

[427]. *The Koran.* Moscow, Oriental Literature, 1963.

[428]. *The Koran.* Translated by I. Y. Krachkovsky. Moscow, Raritet, 1990.

[429]. Al Rosha, Dr. Mohammed Said., ed. *The Koran.* 2nd edition, revised and enlarged by Valeria Prokhorova. Damascus-Moscow, The Al-Furkan Centre and Mikhar Corp., 2553, 10.2.95, 1996.

[430]. *The Ecclesial Law Book (Kormchaya) of 1620.* 256/238, The Manuscript Fund of the Russian National Library (Moscow).

[430:1]. Kornilov N. I., Solodova Y. P. *Jewels and gems.* Moscow, Nedra, 1983.

[431]. Korkh, A. S. *Mikhail Illarionovich Koutouzov.* The Moscow State Museum of History. n.d.

[432]. Korsh, M. *A Brief Dictionary of Mythology and Antiquities.* St. Petersburg, A. S. Souvorin, 1894. Reprinted: Kaluga, Amata, Golden Alley, 1993.

[433]. Kosambi, D. *The Culture and Civilization of Ancient India.* Moscow, Progress, 1968. English edition: Kosambi D. *The Culture and Civilization of Ancient India in Historical Outline.* London, Routledge & Kegan Paul, 1965.

[434]. Kosidowski, Z. *When the Sun was God.* Moscow, Nauka, 1968. Polish edition: Kosidowsky Z. *Gdy Slonce Bylo Bogiem.* Warsaw, 1962.

[435]. Kostomarov, N. I. *The Reign of the House of St. Vladimir.* Moscow, Voyenizdat, 1993.

[436]. Kostomarov, N. I. *The Age of Turmoil in Early XVII century Moscovia (1604-1613).* Moscow, Charli, 1994.

[437]. Kostomarov, N. I. *Bogdan Khmelnitsky.* Moscow, Charlie, 1994.

[437:1]. Kochergina, V. A. *Sanskrit-Russian Dictionary.* About 30.000 words. Moscow, Filologia, 1996.

[438]. Golubev, A. A., comp. *The Kostroma Region.* Moscow, Planeta, 1988.

[439]. Cramer, C. *Mathematical Methods of Statistics.* Moscow, Mir, 1975. English original: Princeton, NJ, Princeton University Press, 1958.

[440]. *The Concise Geographical Encyclopaedia.* Vol. 1, Moscow, State Academic Soviet Encyclopaedia Publications, 1960.

[440:1]. Krekshin, P. N. *A Criticism of the Freshly-Printed Book of 1761 about the Origins of Rome and the Actions of its People and Monarchs.* The reverse of the last sheet says: "Criticism by the Nobleman of the Great New Town Peter of Nicephor, son of Kreksha, in 1762, on the 30th day of September, St. Petersburg." The manuscript is kept in the State Archive of the Yaroslavl Oblast as Manuscript #43 (431).

[441]. *The Peasant War in Russia Led by Stepan Razin.* Collected documents. Vols. 1-4. Moscow, Academy of Sciences, 1954-1970.

[442]. Luchinat, Christina Acidini. *Benozzo Gozzoli*. Published in the *Great Masters of Italian Art* series. Moscow, Slovo, 1996. Italian edition: Scala, Istituto Fotografico Editoriale, 1995.

[443]. Kriesh, Elli G. *The Treasure of Troy and its History*. Moscow, Raduga, 1996. German original: Kriesh, Elli G. *Der Schatz von Troja und seine Geschichte*. Carlsen, 1994.

[444]. Kryvelev, I. A. *The Excavations in the "Biblical" Countries*. Moscow, Sovietskaya Rossia, 1965.

[445]. Kryvelev, I. A. *A Book about the Bible*. Moscow, Sotsekgiz, 1958.

[446]. Krylov, A. N. *Newton and his Role in Global Science. 1643-1943*. The USSR Academy of Sciences. Moscow-Leningrad, USSR AS Publications, 1943.

[447]. Xenophon. *History of the Hellenes*. Leningrad, Ogiz, 1935. English edition: Xenophon. *Hellenica*. In: W. Briggs, Tutorial Series, Books III, IV. London, 1894.

[448]. Koublanov, M. M. *The New Testament. Research and Discoveries*. Moscow, Nauka, 1968.

[449]. Koudriavtsev, M. P. *Moscow the Third Rome. A Historical and Urbanistic Research*. Moscow, Sol System, 1994.

[450]. Koudriavtsev, O. F., comp. *Russia in the First Half of the XVI century. A European View*. The Russian AS, Global History Institute. Moscow, Russkiy Mir, 1997.

[451]. Kouznetsov, V. G. *Newton*. Moscow, Mysl, 1982.

[452]. Koulakovsky, Y. A. *Byzantine History*. Vols. 1, 2. St. Petersburg, Aleteya, 1996.

[453]. Koulikovsky, P. G. *Stellar Astronomy*. Moscow, Nauka, 1978.

[454]. Koun, N. A. *The Predecessors of Christianity*. Moscow, 1922.

[455]. Kourbatov, L. G. *Byzantine History*. Moscow, Vyshaya Shkola, 1984.

[456]. *The UNESCO Courier* magazine, No. 12 (1968).

[457]. Koutouzov, B. *The Church Reform of the XVII century*. The *Tserkov (Church)* magazine (Moscow), Issue 1 (1992).

[457:1]. Koutsenko, G., and Y. Novikov. *Make Yourself A Present of Health*. Moscow, Moskovskiy Rabochiy, 1988.

[458]. Cimpan, F. *The History of the Pi Number*. Moscow, Nauka, 1971 (1984). Romanian original: Cipman, F. *Istoria Numarului pi*. Bucharest, Tineret Press, 1965.

[458:1]. Cumont, Franz. *The Mysteries of Mithras. Magicum*. St. Petersburg, Eurasia, 2000. Original edition: Franz Cumont. *Les Mystères de Mithra. Magicum*. Brussels, H. Lamertin, 1913.

[459]. Lavisse, E., and A. Rambaud. *History of the Crusades*. Vols. I and II. Moscow, 1914. French original: *Histoire générale du IVe siècle à nos jours. L'Europe féodale, les croisades, 1095-1270*. Paris, A. Colin & Cie, 1893-1901.

[460]. *The Lavrenty Chronicle*. (A complete compilation of Russian chronicles). V. 1. Moscow, Yazyki Russkoi Kulturi, 1997.

[461]. Lavrov, N. F. *A Guide to the Churches of Uglich*. Uglich, the Municipal Mu-

seum of Arts and History, 1994. A re-print from an 1869 original, Yaroslavl, the Province Typography.

[462]. Lazarev, V. N. *The Icon Art of Novgorod.* Moscow, Iskusstvo, 1969.

[462:1]. Lombroso. C. *Genius and Madness.* Moscow, Respublika, 1995.

[463]. Lann, E. *A Literary Mystification.* Moscow, 1930.

[464]. Lauer, Jean-Philippe. *The Mystery of the Egyptian Pyramids.* Moscow, Nauka, 1966. French edition: *Le Mystère des Pyramides.* Paris, Presses de la Cité, 1974.

[465]. Deacon, Leon. *History.* Moscow, Nauka, 1988. See also: *Leonis Diaconi Caloensis Historiae libri decem.* E recensione C. B. Hasii. Bonnae, 1828.

[466]. Levandovsky, A. P. *Charlemagne. From the Empire towards Europe.* Moscow, Soratnik, 1995.

[467]. Levitan, E., and N. Mamouna. *The Star of Bethlehem.* The *Nauka i Zhizn (Science and Life)* magazine, No. 11 (1989).

[468]. Levchenko, M. V. *Byzantine History.* Moscow-Leningrad, Ogiz, Sotsekgiz, 1940.

[469]. *The Legend of Dr. Faustus.* Moscow, Nauka, 1978. Also see: *The History of the Damnable Life and Deserved Death of Doctor John Faustus.* London, G. Routledge; New York, E. P. Duttom, 1925.

[470]. Lehmann. *An Illustrated History of Superstition and Sorcery from the Antiquity to Our Days.* Moscow, Knizhnoe Delo, 1900. Also see: Lehmann, A. *Overto og trolddom fra de aeldste til vore dage.* Copenhagen, J. Frimodt, 1893-1896.

[471]. Lentsman, Y. A. *The Origins of Christianity.* Moscow, USSR AS Press, 1958.

[471:1]. *The Life and Art of Leonardo.* Moscow, Byely Gorod, 2001. Giunti Gruppo Editoriale, Florence, 2000.

[472]. Leonid. *A Systematic Description of A. S. Ouvarov's Russo-Slavic Manuscripts.* Moscow, 1894.

[473]. Leontyeva, G. A., Shorin, P. A. and Kobrin, V. B. *The Keys to the Mysteries of Clio. Palaeography, Metrology, Chronology, Heraldic Studies, Numismatics, Onomatology and Genealogy.* Moscow, Prosveshchenie, 1994.

[473:1]. Leskov, A. M. *Burial Mounds: Findings and Problems.* Leningrad, Nauka, 1981.

[474]. Lesna, Ivan. *On the Ails of the Great.* Prague, Grafit, 1990.

[475]. Lesnoy, Sergei. *History of the Slavs Revised.* Melbourne, 1956.

[476]. Lesnoy, Sergei. *A Non-Distorted History of the Russians.* Vols. 1-10. Paris, 1957.

[477]. Lesnoy, Sergei. *Russia, where are you from?* Winnipeg, 1964.

[477:0]. Lesnoy, Sergei. *The Book of Veles.* Moscow, Zakharov, 2002.

[477:1]. *A Chronicler of Hellas and Rome.* Vol. 1. The RAS Institute of Russian Literature (The House of Pushkin). St. Petersburg, Dmitry Boulanin, 1999.

[478]. Libby, W. F. *Carbon-14: a Nuclear Chronometer of Archaeology.* The *UNESCO Courier,* No. 7 (No. 139)(1968).

[479]. Libby, W. F. *The Radiocarbon Dating Method.* The International Peaceful Nuclear Energy Conference materials (Geneva), Vol. 16 (1987): 41-64.

[480]. Libby, W. F. *Radiocarbon: an Atomic Clock.* The annual *Nauka i Chelovechestvo (Science and Humanity)* journal (1962): 190-200. Moscow, Znaniye.

[481]. Libman, M., and G. Ostrovskiy. *Counterfeit Masterpieces.* Moscow, Sovetskiy Khudozhnik, 1966.

[482]. Livy, Titus. *Roman History since the Foundation of the City.* 6 volumes. Translation and general editorship by P. Adrianov. Moscow, E. Herbeck Typography, 1897-1899.

[483]. Livy, Titus. *Roman History since the Foundation of the City.* Vols. 1, 2 and 3. Moscow, Nauka, Vol. 1 (1989), Vol. 2 (1991), Vol. 3 (1993). English edition: Livy, Titus. *Works.* Cambridge, Mass; London, Heinemann, 1914.

[484]. Livraga, Jorge A. *Thebe.* Moscow, New Acropolis, 1995.

[485]. *Linguistic Encyclopedic Dictionary.* Moscow, Soviet Encyclopedia Publications, 1990.

[486]. Lipinskaya, Y., and M. Martsinyak. *Ancient Egyptian Mythology.* Moscow, Iskusstvo, 1983.

[487]. Lituanus, Michalonis. *On the Customs of the Tartars, the Lithuanians and the Muscovites.* Moscow, MSU Publications, 1994. See also: Michalonis Lituani. *De moribus tartarorum, lituanorum et moschorum fragmina X, multiplici historia referta et Johannis Lascii poloni De diis samagitarum, caeterorumque sarmatarum et falsorum christianorum. Item de religione armeniorum et de initio regiminus Stephani Batori.* Nunc primum per J. Jac. Grasserum, C. P. ex manuscriptio authentico edita. Basileae, apud Conradum Waldkirchium, MDCXV, 1-41.

[488]. *Literary legacy. V. I. Lenin and A. V. Lunacharsky. Correspondence, Reports, Documents.* Moscow, Nauka, 1971.

[489]. Lifshitz, G. M. *Essays on Early Christianity and Biblical Historiography.* Minsk: Vysheyshaya Shkola, 1970.

[490]. Likhachev, N. P. *The Artistic Manner of Andrei Rublev.* St. Petersburg, 1907.

[490:1]. Likhacheva, E. A. *The Seven Hills of Moscow.* Moscow, Nauka, 1990.

[491]. Lozinsky, S. G. *History of the Spanish Inquisition.* St. Petersburg, Brockhaus and Efron, 1914.

[492]. Lozinsky, S. G. *History of the Papacy.* Vols. I and II. Moscow, The Central TsS SWB Publications of USSR, 1934.

[493]. Lomonosov, M. V. *Selected Works.* Vol. 2. History, philology, poetry. Moscow, Nauka, 1986.

[493:1]. Gowing, Sir Lawrence. *Paintings in the Louvre.* Introduction by Michel Laclotte. Russian Translation by MK-Import, Ltd., Moscow, Mezhdunarodnaya Kniga, 1987. English edition: Stewart, Tabori & Chang, Inc., 1987.

[493:2]. Loades, D. *Henry VIII and his Queens.* The *Mark in History* series. Moscow, Feniks.

[494]. Pardi, J., comp. *The Pilot Chart of the Gibraltar and the Mediterranean.* Translated by I. Shestakov. Moscow, 1846.

[495]. Lourie, F. M. *Russian and Global History in Tables. Synchrony tables (XXX century BC – XIX Century). World Governors. Genealogical Tables. Glossary.* St. Petersburg, Karavella, 1995.

[496]. Louchin, A. A. *The Slavs and History.* An appendix to the *Molodaya Gvardia (Young Guard)* magazine, No. 9 (1997): 260-351.

[497]. Lyzlov, Andrei. *History of the Scythians.* Moscow, Nauka, 1990.

[497:1]. Liozzi, Mario. *History of Physics.* Moscow, Mir, 1970.

[498]. Lewis, G. C. *A Research of Ancient Roman History and its Veracity.* Hannover, 1852. German edition: *Untersuchungen über die Glaubwürdigkeit der altrömischen Geschichte,* Hannover, 1858.

[499]. Magi, Giovanna. *Luxor. The Valleys of the Kings, Queens, Noblemen and Craftsmen. Memnon's colossi. Deir-el-Bakhari – Medinet-Abu – Ramesseum.* Florence, Casa Editrice Bonechi via Cairoli, 1999.

[500]. Makariy (Boulgakov), the Metropolitan of Moscow and Kolomna. *History of the Russian Church.* Books 1-7. Moscow, The Spaso-Preobrazhensky Monastery of Valaam Publications, 1994-1996.

[500:1]. Makariy, Archimandrite. *Ancient Ecclesial Monuments. History of the Hierarchy of Nizhniy Novgorod.* The *True Tales of Nizhniy Novgorod* series. Nizhniy Novgorod, Nizhegorodskaya Yarmarka, 1999.

[501]. Makarov, A. G., and S. E. Makarova. *The Scotch Thistle Blossom. Towards the Sources of the "Quiet flows the Don."* Moscow, Photocopied by the General Research Institute of Gas Industry, 1991.

[502]. Makarov, A. G., and S. E. Makarova. *Around the "Quiet flows the Don." From Myth Creation to a Search for Truth.* Moscow, Probel, 2000.

[502:1]. Machiavelli, Niccolo. *The Prince. Ruminations in re the First Decade of Titus Livy.* – St. Petersburg, Azbuka, 2002.

[502:2]. Machiavelli, Niccolo. *The History of Florence.* – Leningrad, Nauka, 1973.

[503]. Malalas, John. *The Chronicle.* Published by O. V. Tvorogov according to *The Chronographer of Sofia* in the *Works of the Ancient Russian Literature Department,* Vol. 37, pp. 192-221. Moscow, Nauka. English edition: *The Chronicle of John Malalas.* Chicago, Chicago University Press, 1940.

[504]. Kantor, A. M., ed. *A Concise History of Fine Arts.* Moscow, Iskusstvo, 1981; Dresden, VEB Verlag der Kunst, 1981.

[504:1]. *The Compact Soviet Encyclopaedia.* Vols. 1-10. Moscow, Sovetskaya Encyclopaedia, Inc., 1928.

[505]. Malinovskaya, L. N. *The Graveyard of the Khans (Mezarlyk).* Bakhchisaray, the State Historical and Cultural Reserve, 1991.

[506]. Malinovskiy, A. F. *A Review of Moscow.* Moscow, Moskovskiy Rabochiy, 1992.

[507]. *A Concise Atlas of the World.* Moscow, General Department of Geodetics and Cartography of the USSR Council of Ministers. 1979.

[508]. Malver, A. *Science and Religion.* Russian translation by L. and E. Kroukovsky. N.p., 1925.

[509]. Marijnissen, R. H., and P. Ruyffelaere. *Hieronymus Bosch.* Commentated album. Antwerp, Mercatorfonds, 1987, 1995. Russian translation by Mezhdunarodnaya Kniga. Moscow, 1998.

[510]. Marco Polo. *A Book on the Diversity of the World.* The Personal Library of Borges. St. Petersburg, Amphora, 1999.

[511]. Markov, A. A. *One of the Uses of the Statistical Method. The Academy of Sciences News,* Series 6, Vol. X, Issue 4 (1916).

[512]. Martynov, G. *On the Origins of Roman Chronicles.* Moscow University Press, 1903.

[513]. Massa, Isaac. *A Brief Report of the Beginning and the Origins of Modern Muscovite Wars and Unrest that Occurred Before 1610 in the Brief Time when Several Rulers Reigned.* Moscow, The Sergei Doubnov Fund, Rita-Print, 1997.

[514]. Massa, Isaac. *A Brief Report on Moscovia.* Moscow, 1937.

[514:1]. Matveyenko, V. A., and L. I. Shchegoleva. *The Chronicle of George the Coenobite.* Russian text, comments, indications. Moscow, Bogorodskiy Pechatnik, 2000.

[515]. Matvievskaya, G. P. *Albrecht Dürer the Scientist. 1471-1528.* A series of scientist biographies. Moscow, The USSR AS, Nauka, 1987.

[516]. Matvievskaya, G. P. *As-Sufi.* In *Historical and Astronomical Research* (Moscow, Nauka), Issue 16 (1983): 93-138.

[517]. Matuzova, V. I. *Mediaeval English Sources.* Moscow, Nauka, 1979.

[518]. Vlastar, Matthew. *Collection of Rules Devised by Holy Fathers.* Balakhna, P. A. Ovchinnikov, The F. P. Volkov typography, 1908.

[519]. Smirnov B. L., editor and translator. *The Mahabharata.* Vols. 1-8. Tashkent, the Turkmenian SSR Academy of Sciences, 1955-1972. Vol. 1: two poems from the III book – *Nala* and *Savitri* (*The Greatness of Marital Virtue*) (2nd edition 1959); Vol. 2 – *The Bhagavad Gita* (1956); Vol. 3: *The Highlander* (1957); Vol. 4: *The Conversation of Markandhea* (1958); Vol. 5: *Mokshadharma* (1961); Vol. 6: *A Journey Through the Treasuries* (1962); Vol. 7: *The Book of Bheeshma and the Book of the Battle of Maces* (1963); Vol. 8: *Attacking the Sleeping Ones* (1972). English edition: Chicago-London, Chicago University Press, 1973. Also see the edition by the Jaico Publishing House, Bombay, 1976.

[519:1]. *The Mahabharata. Narayana.* Issue V, book 2. 2nd edition. Translated and edited by Academician B. L. Smirnov of the Turkmenian SSR Academy of Sciences. The TSSR AS, Ashkhabad, Ylym, 1984.

[519:2]. *The Mahabharata. The Four Tales.* Translated from Sanskrit by S. Lipkin. Interlineary by O. Volkova. Moscow, Khudozhestvennaya Literatura, 1969.

[520]. *The Mahabharata. The Ramayana.* Moscow, Khudozhestvennaya Literatura, 1974. Also see: *The Ramayana.* Madras, Periyar Self-Respect Propaganda Institution, 1972.

[520:1]. *The Mahabharata. Book 2. Sabhaparva, or the Book of the Congregation.* Translated from Sanskrit by V. I. Kalyanov. The *Literary Monuments* series. Moscow-Leningrad, Nauka, 1962.

[520:2]. *The Mahabharata. Book 4. Virataparva, or the Book of Virata.* Translated from Sanskrit by V. I. Kalyanov. The *Literary Monuments* series. Leningrad, Nauka, 1967.

[520:3]. *The Mahabharata. Book 5. Udhiyogaparva, or the Book of Diligence.* Translated from Sanskrit by V. I. Kalyanov. The *Literary Monuments* series. Leningrad, Nauka, 1976.

[520:4]. *The Bhagavad Gita as it is.* Complete edition with authentic Sanskrit texts, Russian transliteration, word-for-word and literary translation, and extensive commentaries. The Bhaktivedanta Book Trust. Moscow-Leningrad-Calcutta-Bombay-New Delhi, 1984. The first English edition of the Bhagavad Gita: Wilkins. *The Bhagavad Gita, or dialogs of Kreeshna and Arjoon.* London, 1785. See also: Etgerton, F. *Bhagavad Gita,* Vols. 1-2. Harvard University Press, 1946 (with transcr. of the text).

[520:5]. *The Mahabharata. Book 7. Dronaparva, or the Book of Drona.* Translated from Sanskrit by V. I. Kalyanov. The *Literary Monuments* series. St. Petersburg, Nauka, 1993.

[520:6]. *The Mahabharata. Book 3. The Book of the Woods (Aryanyakaparva).* Translated from Sanskrit by A. V. Vasilkov and S. L. Neveleva. The *Monuments of Oriental Literature* series. LXXX, 1987.

[520:7]. *The Burning of the Snakes. A Tale from the Indian Epic, the Mahabharata.* Translated by V. I. Kalyanov. Moscow, Goslitizdat, 1958.

[521]. Mezentsev, M. T. *The Fate of Novels (Concerning the Discussion on the "Quiet flows the Don" Authorship Problem).* Samara, P. S. Press, 1994.

[522]. Medvedev, R. *Who Wrote the "Quiet flows the Don"?* Paris, Christian Bourg, 1975.

[522:1]. Meyer, M. S., A. F. Deribas, and N. B. Shuvalova. *Turkey. The Book of Wanderings.* A historical guidebook. Project author S. M. Bourygin. Moscow, Veche, Khartia, 2000.

[523]. Melnikova, E. A. *Ancient Scandinavian Geographical Works.* Moscow, Nauka, 1986.

[524]. *Memoirs of Margaret de Valois.* Translated by I. V. Shevlyagina. Introduction and comments by S. L. Pleshkova. French original: *Mémoires de Marguerite de Valois.* Paris, The Library of P. Jannet, MDCCCLVIII. Moscow University Press, 1995.

[525]. *Methods of Studying the Oldest Sources on the History of the USSR Nations.* Collected articles. Moscow, Nauka, 1978.

[526]. *Methodical Research of Absolute Geochronology. Report Theses of the 3rd Methodical Symposium of 1976.* Moscow, USSR AS Press, 1976.

[527]. Meshchersky, N. A. *History of the Literary Russian Language.* Leningrad, 1981.

[528]. Miceletti, Emma. *Domenico Ghirlandio.* Moscow, Slovo, 1996. Italian original: Italy, Scala, Istituto Fotografico Editoriale, 1995.

[529]. Miller, G. F. *Selected Oeuvres on Russian History.* The *Monuments of Historical Thought* series. Moscow, Nauka, RAS, 1996.

[530]. *The World of the Bible*. Magazine. 1993/1(1). Published by the Russian Society of Bible Studies.

[531]. *The World of Geography. Geography and the Geographers. The Environment*. Moscow, Mysl, 1984.

[532]. Meletinsky, E. M., ed. *Dictionary of Mythology*. Moscow, Sovetskaya Encyclopaedia, 1991.

[533]. *Myths of the World. An Encyclopaedia*. Vols. 1 and 2. Moscow, Sovetskaya Encyclopaedia, 1980 (Vol. 1) and 1981 (Vol. 2).

[534]. Mikhailov, A. A. *The Eclipse Theory*. Moscow, Gostekhteoretizdat, 1954.

[535]. Mikhailov, A. A. *This Peculiar Radiocarbon Method*. In *Science and Technology*, No. 8 (1983): 31-32.

[536]. Mokeyev, G. A. *Mozhaysk – A Holy Town for the Russians*. Moscow, Kedr, 1992.

[537]. Mokretsova, I. P., and V. L. Romanova. *French Miniature Illustrations of the XIII century in Soviet Publications. 1270-1300*. Moscow, Iskusstvo, 1984.

[537:1]. Moleva, N. M. *True Muscovite Stories. A Hundred Addresses of Russian History and Culture*. To the 850-year anniversary of Moscow. Moscow, Znaniye, 1997.

[538]. Mommsen, T. *The History of Rome*. Moscow, 1936.

[539]. Mommsen, T. *The History of Rome*. Vol. 3. Moscow, Ogiz, 1941. English edition: London, Macmillan & Co, 1913.

[540]. Mongayt, A. L. *The Writing upon the Stone*. Moscow, Znanie, 1969.

[541]. *Mongolian Sources Related to Dayan-Khan*. A compilation. Moscow, Nauka, 1986

[541:1]. Mordovtsev, D. L. *Collected works*. Vols. 1-14. Moscow, Terra, 1995.

[542]. Morozov, N. A. *The Revelation in Thunder and Storm. History of the Apocalypse*. Moscow, 1907. 2nd edition Moscow, 1910. English translation: Northfield, Minnesota, 1941.

[543]. Morozov, N. A. *The History of the Biblical Prophecies and their Literary Characteristics. The Prophets*. Moscow, the I. D. Sytin Society Typography, 1914.

[544]. Morozov, N. A. *Christ. History of Humanity in the Light of Natural Scientific Studies*. Vols. 1-7. Moscow-Leningrad, Gosizdat, 1924-1932. Vol. 1: 1924 (2nd edition 1927), Vol. 2: 1926, Vol. 3: 1927, Vol. 4: 1928, Vol. 5: 1929, Vol. 6: 1930, Vol. 7: 1932. The first volume was published twice: in 1924 and 1927. Kraft Publications in Moscow made a reprint of all seven volumes in 1998.

[545]. Morozov, N. A. *An Astronomical Revolution in Historical Science*. The *Novy Mir (New World)* magazine, No. 4 (1925): 133-143. In reference to the article by Prof. N. M. Nikolsky.

[546]. Morozov, N. A. *Linguistic Ranges*. The AS Newsletter, Department of Russian Language and Literature. Books 1-4, Vol. XX, 1915.

[547]. Morozov, N. A. *On Russian History*. The manuscript of the 8th volume of the work *Christ*. Moscow, the RAS Archive. Published in Moscow by Kraft and Lean in the end of the year 2000, as *A New Point of View on Russian History*.

[547:1]. Morozov, N.A. *The Asian Christs. (History of Humanity in the Light of Natural Scientific Studies).* Vol. 9 of the work titled *Christ.* Moscow, Kraft+ Ltd., 2003.

[547:2]. Morozov, N.A. *The Mirages of Historical Wastelands between Tigris and Euphrates. (History of Humanity in the Light of Natural Scientific Studies).* Vol. 10 of the work titled *Christ.* Moscow, Kraft+ Ltd., 2002.

[548]. Fomenko A. T., and L. E. Morozova. *Quantitative Methods in Macro-Textology (with Artefacts of the XVI-XVII "Age of Troubles" Used as Examples).* Complex methods in the study of historical processes. Moscow, the USSR Institute of History, Academy of Sciences, 1987. 163-181.

[549]. *Moscow.* An album. Moscow, Avrora Press; St. Petersburg, 1996.

[550]. *Illustrated History of Moscow.* Vol. 1. From the dawn of time until 1917. Moscow, Mysl, 1985.

[551]. *Moscow and the Moscow Oblast. City Plan. Topographical Map. 1:200000.* 3rd edition. Moscow, The Military Typography Headquarters Department, 1998.

[552]. *The Moscow Kremlin. Arkhangelsky Cathedral.* Moscow, The Moscow Kremlin State Museum and Reserve for History and Culture, 1995.

[553]. *The Moscow Kremlin. Ouspensky Cathedral.* Moscow, The Moscow Kremlin State Museum and Reserve for History and Culture, 1995.

[554]. *The Moscow Chronicler.* Compilation. Issue 1. Moscow, Moskovskiy Rabochiy, 1988.

[555]. *The Moscow Oblast Museum of History in Istra. A Guide-book.* Moscow, Moskovskiy Rabochiy, 1989.

[556]. *The Andrei Rublev Museum.* A brochure. Published by the Central Andrei Rublev Museum of Ancient Russian Culture and Art in Moscow, 10, Andronyevskaya Square. n.d.

[557]. Mouravyev, M. V. *Novgorod the Great. A Historical Account and Guide-book.* Leningrad: The State Historical Material Culture Academy Art Edition Popularization Committee, n.d.

[558]. Mouravyev, S. *History of the First Four Centuries of Christianity.* St. Petersburg, 1866.

[559]. Murad, Aji. *The Polovtsy Field Wormwood.* Moscow, Pik-Kontekst, 1994

[560]. Murad, Aji. *Europe, the Turkomans and the Great Steppe.* Moscow, Mysl, 1998

[561]. Mouratov, K. I. *Peasant War Led by E. I. Pougachev.* Moscow, Prosveshchenie, 1980.

[562]. Mylnikov, A. S. *A Picture of a Slavic World as Viewed from the Eastern Europe. Ethnogenetic Legends, Conjectures, and Proto-Hypotheses of the XVI – Early XVIII century.* St. Petersburg, The Petersburg Oriental Studies Centre, 1996.

[563]. Mylnikov, A. S. *The Legend of the Russian Prince (Russo-Slavic Relations of the XVIII century in the World of Folk Culture).* Leningrad, Nauka, 1987.

[564]. Malory, Thomas. *Le Morte d'Arthure.* Moscow, Nauka, 1974. English

original taken from *The Works of Sir Thomas Malory* edited by E. Vinaver, Oxford, 1947.

[565]. Najip, E. N. *A Comparative Historical Dictionary of the XIV century Turkic Languages.* Book I. Moscow, 1979.

[566]. *The Land of Smolensk.* Moscow, Moskovskiy Rabochiy, 1971.

[567]. Takeshi, Nagata. *The Magnetic Field of the Earth in the Past.* In *Nauka i Chelovechestvo (Science and Humanity).* 1965 annual edition. Moscow, Znaniye. 169-175.

[568]. Nazarevskiy, V. V. *Selected Fragments of Muscovite History. 1147-1913.* Moscow, Svarog, 1996.

[569]. Vyacheslav (Savinykh). *Concise History of the Andronicus Monastery.* Moscow, The Sudarium Temple of the Andronicus Monastery, 1999.

[570]. *The Scientific Research Museum of Architecture.* Moscow, 1962.

[571]. Neugebauer, O. *The Exact Sciences in Antiquity.* Moscow, Nauka, 1968. English edition in the series *Acta Historica Scientiarum Naturalism et Medicinalium.* Vol. 9. Copenhagen, 1957. New York, Harper & Bros., 1962.

[572]. Neuhardt, A. A., and I. A. Shishova. *The Seven Wonders of the Ancient World.* The USSR AS, the Leningrad Department of the History Institute. Moscow-Leningrad, Nauka, 1966.

[573]. Leping, A. A., and N. P. Strakhova, eds. *German-Russian Dictionary.* 80,000 words. Moscow, The State National and International Dictionary Publications, 1958.

[574]. Nemirovskiy, A. I. *The Etruscans. From Myth to History.* Moscow, Nauka, 1983.

[575]. Nemirovskiy, E. L. *The Literary World from the Dawn of History until the Early XX century.* Moscow, Kniga, 1986.

[576]. Nemoyevskiy, Andrei. *Jesus the God.* Petersburg, State Publishing House, 1920.

[577]. Nennius. *History of the Brits.* From: Geoffrey of Monmouth. *History of the Brits. The Life of Merlin.* Moscow, Nauka, 1984. English edition: Nennius. *Historia Brittonum.* Galfridus Monemutensis (Geoffrey of Monmouth). *Historia Britonum. Vita Merlini. Six old English Chronicles.* Edited by J.A.Giles. London, 1848.

[577:1]. Nersesyan, L. V. *Dionysius the Icon Master and the Murals of the Feropontov Monastery.* Moscow, Severniy Palomnik, 2002.

[578]. Nechvolodov, A. *Tales of the Russian Land.* Books 1 and 2. Moscow, Svarog, 1997. A new edition of the books published by the State Typography of St. Petersburg in 1913.

[579]. Niese, B. *A Description of the Roman History and Source Studies.* German edition: *Grundriss der römischen Geschichte nebst Quellenkunde.* St. Petersburg, 1908. German edition: Munich, 1923.

[579:1]. Nikerov, V. A. *History as an Exact Science.* (Based on the materials of A. T. Fomenko and G. V. Nosovskiy. *The New Chronology*). Moscow, Ecmo-Press, Yauza, 2002.

[580]. Nikolayev, D. *The Weapon that Failed to Save Byzantium.* In *Tekhnika i Nauka (Science and Technology),* No. 9 (1983): 29-36.

[581]. Nikolayeva, T. V. *The Ancient Zvenigorod.* Moscow, Iskusstvo, 1978.

[582]. *Nikolai Aleksandrovich Morozov.* In *Bibliography of the Scientists of the USSR.* Moscow, Nauka, 1981.

[583]. *Nikolai Aleksandrovich Morozov, the Encyclopaedist Scientist.* A collection of articles. Moscow, Nauka, 1982.

[584]. *Nikolai Aleksandrovich Morozov. Biographical Stages and Activities.* The *USSR AS Courier,* Nos. 7 and 8 (1944).

[585]. Nikolskiy, N. M. *An Astronomical Revolution in Historical Science.* The *Novy Mir (New World)* magazine, Vol. 1 (1925): 157-175. (In re. N. Morozov's œuvre *Christ.* Leningrad, 1924.)

[586]. Nikonov, V. A. *Name and Society.* Moscow, Nauka, 1974.

[586:1]. *A Collection of Chronicles titled the Patriarchal, or the Nikon Chronicle.* The Complete Collection of Russian Chronicles (CCRC), Vols. IX-XIV. Moscow, Yazyki Russkoi Kultury, 2000.

[587]. *Novellino.* Literary monuments. Moscow, Nauka, 1984.

[588]. Novozhilov, N. I. *The Meteorological Works of N. A. Morozov.* The *Priroda (Nature)* magazine, No. 10 (1954).

[589]. *The New Testament of Our Lord Jesus Christ.* Brussels, Life with God, 1965.

[590]. Nosovskiy, G. V. *Certain Statistical Methods of Researching Historical Sources, and Examples of their Application.* Source study methods of Russian social thinking; historical studies of the feudal epoch. A collection of academic publications. Moscow, The USSR History Institute, AS, 1989. 181-196.

[591]. Nosovskiy, G. V. *The Beginning of Our Era and the Julian Calendar.* Information processes and systems. Scientific and technological information, Series 2. Moscow, the National Science and Technology Information Institute, No. 5 (1992): 7-18.

[592]. Nosovskiy, G. V. *The True Dating of the Famous First Oecumenical Counsel and the Real Beginning of the AD Era.* An appendix of A. T. Fomenko's *Global Chronology.* Moscow, The MSU Mathematical Mechanics Department, 1993. 288-394.

[593]. Fomenko, A. T., and G. V. Nosovskiy. *The Determination of Original Structures in Intermixed Sequences.* Works of a vector and tensor analysis seminar. Moscow, MSU Press, Issue 22 (1985): 119-131.

[594]. Fomenko, A. T., and G. V. Nosovskiy. *Some Methods and Results of Intermixed Sequence Analysis.* Works of a vector and tensor analysis seminar. Moscow, MSU Press, Issue 23 (1988): 104-121.

[595]. Fomenko, A. T., and G. V. Nosovskiy. *Determining the Propinquity Quotient and Duplicate Identification in Chronological Lists.* Report theses of the 5th International Probability Theory and Mathematical Statistics Conference. Vilnius, The Lithuanian AS Institute of Mathematics and Cybernetics, Vol. 4 (1989): 111-112.

[596]. Fomenko, A. T., and G. V. Nosovskiy. *Statistical Duplicates in Ordered Lists with Subdivisions. Cybernetic Issues.* Semiotic research. Moscow, Scientific Counsel for the Study of the General Problem of Cybernetics. The USSR AS, 1989. 138-148.

[597]. Fomenko, A. T., and G. V. Nosovskiy. *Duplicate Identification in Chronological Lists (The Histogram Method of Related Name Distribution Frequencies).* Problems of stochastic model stability. Seminar works. Moscow, The National System Research Institute, 1989. 112-125.

[598]. Fomenko, A. T., and G. V. Nosovskiy. *Statistical Research of Parallel Occurrences and Biographies in British Chronological and Historical Materials.* Semiotics and Informatics. Moscow, The National System Research Institute, Issue 34 (1994): 205-233.

[599]. Fomenko, A. T., and G. V. Nosovskiy. *The New Chronology and the Concept of the Ancient History of Russia, Britain and Rome. (Facts. Statistics. Hypotheses.)* Vol. 1: *Russia.* Vol. 2: *England, Rome.* Moscow, the MSU Centre of Research and Pre-University Education, 1995. 2nd edition: 1996.

[600]. Fomenko, A. T., and G. V. Nosovskiy. *Mathematical and Statistical Models of Information Distribution in Historical Chronicles.* The Mathematical Issues of Cybernetics. Physical and Mathematical Literature (Moscow, Nauka), Issue 6 (1996): 71-116.

[601]. Fomenko, A. T., and G. V. Nosovskiy. *The Empire (Russia, Turkey, China, Europe and Egypt. New Mathematical Chronology of Antiquity).* Moscow, Faktorial, 1996. Re-editions: 1997, 1998 and 1999.

[602]. Fomenko, A. T., and G. V. Nosovskiy. *Russia and Rome. The Correctness of Our Understanding of Eurasian History.* Vols. 1 and 2. Moscow, Olimp, 1997. 2nd edition: 1999.

[603]. Fomenko, A. T., and G. V. Nosovskiy. *The New Chronology of Russia.* Moscow, Faktorial, 1997. Re-editions: 1998 and 1999.

[604]. Fomenko, A. T., and G. V. Nosovskiy. *The Mathematical Chronology of Biblical Events.* Moscow, Nauka, 1997.

[605]. Fomenko, A. T., and G. V. Nosovskiy. *The Biblical Russia.* Vols. 1 and 2. Moscow, Faktorial, 1998.

[606]. Fomenko, A. T., and G. V. Nosovskiy. *Horde-Russia as Reflected in Biblical Books.* Moscow, Anvik, 1998.

[607]. Fomenko, A. T., and G. V. Nosovskiy. *An Introduction to the New Chronology (Which Century is it Now?).* Moscow, Kraft and Lean, 1999.

[608]. Fomenko, A. T., and G. V. Nosovskiy. *The New Chronology of Russia, Britain and Rome.* Moscow, Anvik, 1999. A substantially revised and enlarged single-volume edition.

[608:1]. Fomenko, A. T., and G. V. Nosovskiy. *The New Chronology of Russia, Britain and Rome.* Moscow, Delovoi Express Financial, 2001.

[609]. Fomenko, A. T., and G. V. Nosovskiy. *The Biblical Russia. Selected Chapters I. (The Empire of Horde-Russia and the Bible. The New Mathematical Chronology of Antiquity. A History of Biblical Editions and Manuscripts. XI-*

XII century Events in the New Testament. The Pentateuch). Moscow, Faktorial, 1999.

[610]. Fomenko, A. T., and G. V. Nosovskiy. *A Reconstruction of Global History (The New Chronology).* Moscow, Delovoi Express Financial, 1999.

[611]. Fomenko, A. T., and G. V. Nosovskiy. *Old Criticisms and the New Chronology.* The *Neva* magazine (St. Petersburg), No. 2 (1999): 143158.

[612]. Fomenko, A. T., and G. V. Nosovskiy. *The Biblical Russia. Selected Chapters II. (The Empire of Horde-Russia and the Bible. History of the XIV-XVI century in the Final Chapters of the Books of Kings. XV-XVI century History of the Pages of the Books of Esther and Judith. Reformation Epoch of the XVI-XVII century).* Moscow, Faktorial, 2000.

[613]. Fomenko, A. T., and G. V. Nosovskiy. *A Reconstruction of Global History. The Research of 1999-2000 (The New Chronology).* Moscow, Delovoi Express Financial, 2000.

[613:1]. Fomenko, A. T., and G. V. Nosovskiy. *The New Chronology of Egypt. The Astronomical Dating of the Ancient Egyptian Monuments. The Research of 2000-2002.* Moscow, Veche, 2002.

[613:2]. Fomenko, A. T., and Nosovskiy, G. V. *The New Chronology of Egypt. The Astronomical Dating of the Ancient Egyptian Monuments.* 2nd edition, re-worked and expanded. Moscow, Veche, 2003.

[614]. Newton, Robert. *The Crime of Claudius Ptolemy.* Moscow, Nauka, 1985. English original: Baltimore-London, John Hopkins University Press, 1977.

[615]. Olearius, Adam. *A Detailed Account of the Moscovian and Persian Journey of the Holstein Ambassadors in 1633, 1636 and 1639.* Translated from German by P. Barsov. Moscow, 1870.

[616]. Oleynikov, A. *The Geological Clock.* Leningrad, Nedra, 1975.

[617]. Orbini, Mavro. *A Historiographical Book on the Origins of the Names, the Glory and the Expansion of the Slavs. Compiled from many Historical Books through the Office of Marourbin, the Archimandrite of Raguzha.* Translated into Russian from Italian. Typography of St. Petersburg, 1722.

[618]. Orbini, Mavro. *Kingdom of the Slavs.* Sofia, Nauka i Izkustvo, 1983.

[618:1]. Oreshnikov, A. V. *Pre-1547 Russian Coins.* A reprint of the 1896 edition by the State Museum of History. Russian State Archive of Ancient Acts. Moscow, The Archaeographical Centre, 1996.

[619]. Orlenko, M. I. *Sir Isaac Newton. A Biographical Aperçu.* Donetsk, 1927.

[620]. Orlov, A. S. *Certain Style Characteristics of Russian History Fiction of the XVI-XVII century.* In *Russian Philological News,* Vol. 13, Book 4 (1908): 344-379.

[621]. *The Ostrog Bible (The Bible, or the Books of the Old and the New Covenant, in the Language of the Slavs).* Ostrog, 1581. Reprinted as *The Ostrog Bible.* The Soviet Culture Fund Commission for the Publication of Literary Artefacts. Moscow-Leningrad, Slovo-Art, 1988. "The phototypic copy of the 1581 text was supervised by I. V. Dergacheva with references to the copies from the Scientific Library of A. M. Gorky Moscow State University."

[622]. *National History from the Earliest Days and until 1917.* Encyclopaedia, Vol. 1. Moscow, The Great Russian Encyclopaedia Publications, 1994.

[623]. Bavin, S. P., and G. V. Popov. *The Revelation of St. John as Reflected in the Global Literary Tradition.* The catalogue of an exhibition organized in Moscow by the Greek Embassy in 1994. A joint publication of the Greek Embassy and the State Library of Russia. Moscow, Indrik, 1995.

[623:1]. A postcard with an Egyptian zodiac. *The Creation Scene.* Egypt, El-Faraana Advertising & Printing, 2000.

[624]. *Historical and Folk Tale Aperçus. From Cheops to Christ.* A compilation. Translated from German. Moscow, 1890. Reprinted by the Moscow Int'l Translator School in 1993.

[625]. Pausanius. *A Description of Hellas, or a Voyage through Greece in II century AD.* Moscow, 1880. English edition: Pausanius. *Guide to Greece.* Harmondsworth, Penguin, 1979.

[626]. Makarevich, G. V., ed. *The Architectural Monuments of Moscow. The Earthenware Town.* Moscow, Iskusstvo, 1989-1990.

[627]. Posokhin, M. V., ed. *The Architectural Monuments of Moscow. KitaiGorod.* Moscow, Iskusstvo, 1982.

[628]. Makarevich, G. V., ed. *The Architectural Monuments of Moscow. White Town.* Moscow, Iskusstvo, 1989.

[629]. Makarevich, G. V., ed. *The Architectural Monuments of Moscow. Zamoskvorechye.* Moscow, Iskusstvo, 1994.

[630]. *Artefacts of Diplomatic Relations with the Roman Empire.* Vol. 1. St Petersburg, 1851.

[631]. Rybakov, B. A., ed. *Artefacts of the Kulikovo Cycle.* St. Petersburg, RAS, The Institute of Russian History. Blitz, the Russo-Baltic Information Centre, 1998.

[632]. *Literary Artefacts of Ancient Russia. The XI – Early XII century.* Moscow, Khudozhestvennaya Literatura, 1978.

[633]. *Literary Artefacts of Ancient Russia. The XII century.* Moscow, Khudozhestvennaya Literatura, 1980.

[634]. *Literary Artefacts of Ancient Russia. The XIII century.* Moscow, Khudozhestvennaya Literatura, 1981.

[635]. *Literary Artefacts of Ancient Russia. The XIV – mid-XV century.* Moscow, Khudozhestvennaya Literatura, 1981.

[636]. *Literary Artefacts of Ancient Russia. Second Half of the XV century.* Moscow, Khudozhestvennaya Literatura, 1982.

[637]. *Literary Artefacts of Ancient Russia. Late XV – Early XVI century.* Moscow, Khudozhestvennaya Literatura, 1984.

[638]. *Literary Artefacts of Ancient Russia. Mid-XVI century.* Moscow, Khudozhestvennaya Literatura, 1985.

[639]. *Literary Artefacts of Ancient Russia. Second Half of the XVI century.* Moscow, Khudozhestvennaya Literatura, 1986.

[640]. *Literary Artefacts of Ancient Russia. Late XVI – Early XVII century.* Moscow, Khudozhestvennaya Literatura, 1987.

[641]. *Significant Works in Russian Law*. Issue 2. Moscow, 1954.

[642]. *Significant Works in Russian Law*. Issue 3. Moscow, 1955.

[643]. Pannekuk, A. *The History of Astronomy*. Moscow, Nauka, 1966.

[644]. Parandowski, J. *Petrarch*. The *Inostrannaya Literatura (Foreign Literature)* magazine, No. 6 (1974). Also see: Parandowski, J. *Petrarca*. Warsaw, 1957.

[645]. Paradisis, Alexander. *The Life and Labours of Balthazar Cossas (Pope John XXIII)*. Minsk, Belarus, 1980.

[646]. Pasek. *A Historical Description of Simon's Monastery in Moscow*. Moscow, 1843.

[647]. Romanenko, A. *The Patriarch Chambers of the Moscow Kremlin*. Moscow, The Moscow Kremlin State Museum and Reserve for History and Culture, 1994.

[648]. Pahimer, George. *The Story of Michael and Andronicus Palaeologi. The Reign of Michael Palaiologos*. St. Petersburg, 1862.

[648:1]. Pashkov, B. G. *Holy Russia – Russia – The Russian Empire. The Genealogical Tree of the Principal Russian Clans (862-1917)*. Moscow, TsentrKom, 1996.

[649]. *The First Muscovite Princes*. In *Historical Portraits* series. Moscow, Ganna, 1992.

[650]. Perepyolkin, Y. A. *The Coup of Amenkhotep IV*. Part 1. Books 1 and 2. Moscow, Nauka, 1967.

[651]. *The Correspondence of Ivan the Terrible and Andrei Kurbskiy*. In *Literary Landmarks* series. Leningrad, Nauka, 1979. 2nd edition: Moscow, Nauka, 1993.

[652]. *The Song of Roland*. International Literature Collection. Moscow, Khudozhestvennaya Literatura, 1976. English edition by J. M. Dent & Sons, 1972.

[653]. Petrov, A. M. *The Great Silk Route. The Simplest, but Largely Unknown Facts*. Moscow, Vostochnaya Literatura, RAS, 1995.

[654]. Petruchenko, O. *Latin-Russian Dictionary*. Moscow, published by the V. V. Dumnov and the Heirs of Silayev Brothers, 1914. Reprinted by the Graeco-Latin Department of Y. A. Shichalin, 1994.

[654:1]. *The Maritime Voyage of St. Brendan (Navigation Sancti Brendani Abbatis saec X AD)*. St. Petersburg, Azbuka-Klassika, 2002. English translation: *Navigatio Sancti Brendani Abbatis from Early Latin Manuscripts*. Ed., introd. and notes: C. Selmer, Notre Dame, 1959.

[655]. *Plan of the Imperial Capital City of Moscow, Created under the Supervision of Ivan Michurin, the Architect, in 1739. The First Geodetic Plan of Moscow*. The General Council of Ministers, Department of Geodetics and Cartography (the Cartographer Cooperative). Published together with a calendar for 1989.

[656]. Plano Carpini, G. del. *History of the Mongols*. William of Rubruck. *The Journey to the Oriental Countries. The Book of Marco Polo*. Moscow, Mysl, 1997. See also: *The Journey of William of Rubruck to the Eastern Parts of the World, 1253-55*. Prepared by W. W. Rockhill. 1900.

221

[657]. Plato. *Collected Works.* Vol. 3. Moscow, Mysl, 1972. English edition: *The Works of Plato.* Bohn's Classical Library, 1848.

[658]. Pletnyova, S. A. *The Khazars.* Moscow, Nauka, 1976.

[659]. Pleshkova, S. L. *Catherine of Medici. The Black Queen.* Moscow, Moscow University Press, 1994.

[660]. Plutarch. *Comparative Biographies.* Vol. 1: Moscow, USSR AN Press, 1961; Vol. 2: Moscow, USSR AN Press, 1963; Vol. 3: Moscow, Nauka, 1964. English edition: Plutarch. *The Lives of the Noble Graecians and Romans.* In *Great Books of the Western World* series. Vol. 13. Encyclopaedia Britannica, Inc. Chicago, University of Chicago, 1952 (2nd edition 1990). See also: Plutarch. *Plutarch's Lives.* London, Dilly, 1792.

[661]. Plyukhanova, M. B. *Subjects and Symbols of the Muscovite Kingdom.* St. Petersburg, Akropol, 1995.

[662]. *Kremlin. A Brief Guide.* Moscow, Moskovskiy Rabochiy, 1960.

[663]. *The Yearly Chronicle.* Part 1. Text and translation. Moscow-Leningrad, The USSR AN Press, 1950.

[664]. *The Yearly Chronicle.* Published in the *Dawn of the Russian Literature* series (XI – early XII century). Moscow, Khudozhestvennaya Literatura, 1978. 23-277.

[665]. *The Tale of Varlaam and Ioasaph.* Leningrad, Nauka, 1985.

[666]. Likhachev, D. S., ed. *The Tale of the Kulikovo Battle. The Text and the Miniatures of the Authorized Compilation of the XVI century.* Published by the XVI century manuscript kept in the USSR Academy of Sciences Library (The Authorized Compilation of Chronicles, Osterman's Vol. II, sheet 3 – 126 reverse). Leningrad, Aurora, 1984.

[666:1]. Podosinov, A. V., and A. M. Belov. *Lingua Latina. Latin-Russian Dictionary.* About 15,000 words. Moscow, Flinta, Nauka, 2000.

[667]. Pokrovskiy, N. N. *A Voyage in Search of Rare Books.* Moscow, Kniga. 2nd edition, 1988.

[668]. Polak, I. F. *A Course of General Astronomy.* Moscow, Gonti, 1938.

[669]. Polybius. *History in 40 Volumes.* Moscow, 1899.

[670]. *The Complete Symphony of the Canonical Books of the Holy Writ.* St. Petersburg, The Bible For Everybody, 1996.

[671]. *The Complete Collection of Russian Chonicles.* Vol. 33. Leningrad, Nauka, 1977.

[672]. *The Complete Collection of Russian Chonicles.* Vol. 35. Moscow, Nauka, 1980.

[673]. Polo, M. *The Journey.* Translated from French. Leningrad, 1940.

[674]. Poluboyarinova, M. D. *Russians in the Golden Horde.* Moscow, Nauka, 1978.

[674:1]. [*Pompeii*]. *Pompeii.* Album. Authors: Filippo Coarelli, Emilio de Albentiis, Maria Paola Guidobaldi, Fabricio Pesando, and Antonio Varone. Moscow, Slovo, 2002. Printed in Italy.

[674:2]. [*Pompeii*]. Nappo, Salvatore. *Pompeii.* Album. From the *World Wonder*

Atlas series. Moscow, Bertelsmann Media Moskau, 2001. English original: Salvatore Ciro Nappo. *Pompeii.* White Star, 1998, Vercelli, Italy.

[675]. Popovskiy, M. A. *Time Conquered. A Tale of Nikolai Morozov.* Moscow, Political Literature, 1975.

[676]. *The Portuguese-Russian and Russian-Portuguese Dictionary.* Kiev, Perun, 1999.

[677]. *The Successors of Marco Polo. Voyages of the Westerners into the Countries of the Three Indias.* Moscow, Nauka, 1968.

[678]. Pospelov, M. *The Benediction of Reverend Sergei. Moskva* magazine, 1990

[679]. Postnikov, A. V. *Maps of the Russian Lands: A Brief Review of the History of Geographical Studies and Cartography of Our Fatherland.* Moscow, Nash Dom – L'Age d'Homme, 1996.

[680]. Postnikov, M. M. *A Critical Research of the Chronology of the Ancient World.* Vols. 1-3. Moscow, Kraft and Lean, 2000. [A. T. Fomenko's remark: This book is a publication of a manuscript of more than 1000 pages written by Doctors of Physics and Mathematics A. S. Mishchenko and A. T. Fomenko. It was edited by M. M. Postnikov, and came out signed with his name. He acknowledges this fact in the preface to Vol. 1, on page 6, albeit cagily.]

[681]. Fomenko A. T., and M. M. Postnikov. *New Methods of Statistical Analysis of the Narrative and Digital Material of Ancient History.* Moscow, Scientific Counsel for the Study of the General Problem of Cybernetics, USSR AS, 1980. 1-36.

[682]. Fomenko A. T., and M. M. Postnikov. *New Methods of Statistical Analysis of the Narrative and Digital Material of Ancient History.* Scientific note of the Tartu University, works related to sign symbols. XV, Cultural Typology, Cultural Influence Feedback. Tartu University Press, Release 576 (1982): 24-43.

[683]. Postnikov, M. M. *The Greatest Mystification in the World?* In *Tekhnika i Nauka (Science & Technology),* 1982, No. 7, pp. 28-33.

[684]. Potin, V. M. *Coins. Treasures. Collections. Numismatic essays.* St. Petersburg, Iskusstvo-SPb, 1993.

[685]. Potin, V. M. *Ancient Russia and the European States of the X-XIII century.* Leningrad, Sovetskiy Khudozhnik, 1968.

[685:1]. Pope-Hennessy, John. *Fra Angelico.* Album. Moscow, Slovo, 1996. Scala, 1995, Istituto Fotografico Editoriale.

[686]. Pokhlyobkin, V. V. *The Foreign Affairs of the Holy Russia, Russia and the USSR over the 1000 Years in Names, Dates and Facts. A Reference Book.* Moscow, Mezhdunarodnye Otnoshenya, 1992.

[687]. *Merited Academician N. A. Morozov. Memoirs.* Vols. 1 and 2. The USSR Academy of Sciences. Moscow, USSR AS Press, 1962.

[688]. *Orthodox Art and the Savvino-Storozhevsky Monastery.* Materials of scientific conferences dedicated to the 600th anniversary of the Savvino-Storozhevsky Monastery, 17 December 1997 and 22 September 1998. The Zvenigorod Museum of Architecture, History, and Arts. Zvenigorod, Savva Plus M, 1998.

[689]. Malinovskaya, N., ed. *Prado. Paintings.* Album. Translated from Spanish. Lunwerg Editores. Barcelona-Madrid, 1994. Russian translation: Moscow, MK-Import, 1999.

[690]. *Reverend Joseph Volotsky. The Illuminator.* Published by the Spaso-Preobrazhensky Monastery of Valaam. Blessed by the Holiest Patriarch of Moscow and the Entire Russia, Alexiy II. Moscow, 1993.

[691]. Priester, E. *A Brief History of Austria.* Moscow, IL, 1952. German edition: *Kurze Geschichte Österreichs.* Vienna, Globus, 1946.

[692]. Prishchepenko, V. N. *The Pages of Russian History.* Vol. 1: 1988. Vol. 2: 2000. Moscow, Profizdat.

[693]. *Problems of Museum Collection Formation and Studies of the State Museum of Religious History.* Leningrad, The RSFSR Ministry of Culture, publised by the State Museum of History of Religions, 1990.

[694]. Procopius of Caesarea. *On the Buildings.* The *Vestnik Drevnei Istorii (Courier of Ancient History)* magazine, No. 4 (1939): 201-298. See also: Procopius of Caesarea. *On the Buildings of Justinian.* London, Palestine Piligrim Society, 1888.

[695]. Procopius. *The Gothic War.* Moscow, The USSR AS Press, 1950.

[696]. Procopius. *The Gothic War. On the Buildings.* Moscow, Arktos, Vika-Press, 1996. See also: Procopius of Caesarea. *Procopius.* Vol. 7. London, William Heinemann; New York, Macmillan & Co. 1914-1940.

[697]. Procopius of Caesarea. *The Persian War. The War with the Vandals. Arcane History.* St. Petersburg, Aleteya, 1998.

[698]. Proskouriakov, V. M. *Johannes Gutenberg.* The *Celebrity Biographies* series. Moscow, the Literary Magazine Union, 1933.

[699]. Prokhorov, G. M. *The Tale of Batu-Khan's Invasion in Lavrenty's Chronicle.* Published as part of *The Russian Literary History Research. XI-XVII centuries.* Leningrad, Nauka, 1974.

[700]. *Book of Psalms.* Moscow, 1657. (Private collection.)

[701]. *The book of Psalms with Appendices.* Published in the *Great City of Moscow in the Year 7160 [1652 AD], in the Month of October, on the 1st Day.* New edition: Moscow, The Vvedenskaya Church of St. Trinity Coreligionist Typography, 1867.

[702]. Psellus, Michael. *Chronography.* Moscow, Nauka, 1978. English edition: *The Chronographia of Michael Psellus.* London, Routledge & Kegan Paul, 1953.

[703]. Pskovskiy, Y. P. *Novae and Supernovae.* Moscow, Nauka, 1974.

[704]. Ptolemy, Claudius. *Almagest, or the Mathematical Tractate in Thirteen Volumes.* Translated by I. N. Veselovskiy. Moscow, Nauka, Fizmatlit, 1998.

[705]. Poisson, A., N. A. Morozov, F. Schwarz, M. Eliade, and K. G. Jung. *The Theory and Symbols of Alchemy. The Great Work.* Kiev, Novy Akropol, Bront Ltd., 1995.

[706]. Mashkov, I. P., ed. *A Guide to Moscow.* Moscow, Muscovite Architectural Society for the Members of the V Convention of Architects in Moscow, 1913.

[707]. *The Voyage of Columbus. Diaries, Letters, Documents.* Moscow, The State Geographical Literature Press, 1952.

[708]. Putilov, Boris. *Ancient Russia in Personae. Gods, Heroes, People.* St. Petersburg, Azbuka, 1999.

[709]. Pushkin, A. *Collected Works.* Leningrad, The State Fiction Publishers, 1935.

[710]. *Pushkin A. in the Recollections of Contemporaries.* Two volumes. Moscow, Khudozhestvennaya Literatura, 1974.

[711]. *Pushkin's Memorial Places in Russia. A Guidebook.* Moscow, Profizdat, 1894.

[711:1]. Pylyaev, M. I. *The Old Petersburg. Accounts of the Capital's Past.* A reprint of A. S. Souvorov's 1889 St. Petersburg edition. Moscow, IKPA, 1990.

[712]. Lukovich-Pyanovich, Olga. *The Serbs . . . The Oldest of Nations.* Vols. 1-3. Belgrade, Miroslav, 1993-1994.

[713]. Pietrangeli, Carlo. *Vatican.* From the *Great Museums of the World* series. Moscow, Slovo, 1998. A translation of the Italian edition by Magnus Editioni, Udine, 1996.

[714]. *Five Centuries of European Drawings.* The drawings of old masters from the former collection of Franz König. The 1.10.1995-21.01.1996 exhibition catalogue. The Russian Federation Ministry of Culture, The State A. S. Pushkin Museum of Fine Art. Moscow-Milan, Leonardo Arte (versions in Russian and in English).

[715]. *The Radzivillovskaya Chronicle.* The text. The research. A description of the miniatures. St. Petersburg, Glagol; Moscow, Iskusstvo, 1994.

[716]. *The Radzivillovskaya Chronicle.* The Complete Collection of Russian Chronicles, Vol. 38. Leningrad, Nauka, 1989.

[717]. *Radiocarbon.* Collected articles. Vilnius, 1971.

[718]. *The Imprecision of Radiocarbon Datings.* The *Priroda (Nature)* magazine, No. 3 (1990): 117. (*New Scientist,* Vol. 123, No. 1684 (1989): 26).

[719]. Radzig, N. *The Origins of Roman Chronicles.* Moscow University Press, 1903.

[720]. *The Book of Rank. 1457-1598.* Moscow, Nauka, 1966.

[721]. Razoumov, G. A., and M. F. Khasin. *The Drowning cities.* Moscow, Nauka, 1978.

[722]. Wright, J. K. *The Geographical Lore of the Time of the Crusades. A Study in the History of Medieval Science and Tradition in Western Europe.* Moscow, Nauka, 1988. English original published in New York in 1925.

[722:1]. Reizer, V. I. *The Process of Joan of Arc.* Moscow-Leningrad, Nauka, 1964.

[723]. Fomenko, A. T., and S. T. Rachev. *Volume Functions of Historical Texts and the Amplitude Correlation Principle.* Source study methods of Russian social thinking historical studies of the feudal epoch. A collection of academic publications. Moscow, The USSR History Institute, AS, 1989. 161-180.

[724]. Rashid ad-Din. *History of the Mongols.* St. Petersburg, 1858.

[725]. Renan, J. *The Antichrist.* St. Petersburg, 1907. English edition: *Renan's Antichrist.* The Scott Library, 1899.

[726]. *Rome: Echoes of the Imperial Glory.* Translated from English by T. Azarkovich. The *Extinct Civilizations* series. Moscow, Terra, 1997. Original by Time-Life Books, 1994.

[727]. Rich, V. *Was there a Dark Age?* The *Khimia i Zhizn (Chemistry and Life)* magazine, No. 9 (1983): 84.

[728]. Riesterer, Peter P., and Roswitha Lambelet. *The Egyptian Museum in Cairo.* Cairo, Lehnert & Landrock, Orient Art Publishers, 1980. Russian edition, 1996.

[729]. Robert of Clari. *The Conquest of Constantinople.* Moscow, Nauka, 1986. English edition: McNeal, E. H. *The Conquest of Constantinople of Robert of Clari.* Translated with introduction and notes by E. Holmes McNeal. New York, 1936. Records of Civilization: Sources and Studies. Vol. XXIII. Reprint: New York, 1964, 1969.

[730]. Rogozina, Z. A. *The Earliest Days of Egyptian History.* Issue 2. Petrograd, A. F. Marx Typography, n.d.

[731]. Rozhdestvenskaya, L. A. *The Novgorod Kremlin. A Guide-book.* Lenizdat, 1980.

[732]. Rozhitsyn, V. S., and M. P. Zhakov. *The Origins of the Holy Books.* Leningrad, 1925.

[733]. Rozhkov, M. *N. A. Morozov – The Founding Father of the Dimension Number Analysis. The Successes of the Physical Sciences,* Vol. 49, Issue 1 (1953).

[734]. Rozanov, N. *History of the Temple of Our Lady's Birth in Staroye Simonovo, Moscow, Dedicated to its 500th Anniversary (1370-1870).* Moscow, Synodal Typography on Nikolskaya Street, 1870.

[735]. Romanyuk, S. *From the History of Small Muscovite Streets.* Moscow, 1988.

[735:1]. Romanyuk, S. *From the History of Small Muscovite Streets.* Moscow, Svarog, 2000.

[735:2]. Romanyuk, S. *The Lands of the Muscovite Villages.* Part I. Moscow, Svarog, 2001.

[735:3]. Romanyuk, S. *The Lands of the Muscovite Villages.* Part II. Moscow, Svarog, 1999.

[736]. *The Russian Academy of Sciences. Personae.* Three books. Book 1: 1724-1917. Book 2: 1918-1973. Book 3: 1974-1999. Moscow, Nauka, 1999.

[737]. Rossovskaya, V. A. *The Calendarian Distance of Ages.* Moscow, Ogiz, 1930.

[738]. *A Guide to the Paschalia for the Seminary Schools.* Moscow, The V. Gautier Typography, 1853. Reprinted in Moscow by Grad Kitezh in 1991.

[739]. Bleskina, O. N., comp. *An Illustrated book of Manuscripts of the USSR AS Library.* Catalogue for an exhibition of illustrated chronicles of the XI-XIX century written with roman letters. Leningrad, The USSR AS Library, 1991.

[740]. *Handwritten and Typeset Books. Collected Articles.* Moscow, Nauka, 1975.

[741]. *Manuscripts of the Late XV – early XVI century.* The Kirillo-Belozersk Collection, 275/532. The M. E. Saltykov-Shchedrin Public Library, St. Petersburg.

[742]. Roumyantsev, A. A. *Methods of Historical Analysis in the Works of Nikolai Aleksandrovich Morozov.* The Scientific Institute of P. F. Lesgaft Notes, Vol. 10. Leningrad, 1924.

[743]. Roumyantsev, A. A. *The Death and the Resurrection of the Saviour.* Moscow, Atheist, 1930.

[744]. Roumyantsev, N. V. *Orthodox Feasts.* Moscow, Ogiz, 1936.

[745]. *The Russian Bible. The Bible of 1499 and the Synodal Translation of the Bible.* Illustrated. 10 Vols. The Biblical Museum, 1992. Publishing department of the Muscovite Patriarchy, Moscow, 1992 (The Gennadievskaya Bible). Only the following volumes came out before the beginning of 2002: Vol. 4 (Book of Psalms), Vols. 7 and 8 (The New Testament), and Vol. 9 (Appendices, scientific descriptions). Vols. 7 and 8 were published by the Moscow Patriarchy in 1992; Vols. 4 and 9 published by the Novospassky Monastery, Moscow, 1997 (Vol. 4), 1998 (Vol. 9).

[746]. *The Pioneer of Russian Printing. A Brief Biography. Ivan Fedorov's "Alphabet" Published in 1578.* In collaboration with Translesizdat Ltd. Blessed by the Editing Board of the Muscovite Patriarchy. Moscow, Spolokhi, 2000.

[747]. *Russian Chronographer of 1512.* The Complete Collection of Russian Chronicles, Vol. 22. St. Petersburg, 1911.

[748]. Knyazevskaya, T. B., comp. *Russian Spiritual Chivalry.* Collected articles. Moscow, Nauka, 1996.

[749]. Leyn, K., ed. *Russian-German Dictionary.* 11th stereotype edition. Moscow, Russkiy Yazyk, 1991.

[750]. Dmitriev, N. K., ed. *Russian-Tartarian Dictionary.* The USSR AS, Kazan Affiliate of the Language, Literature and History Institute. Kazan, Tatknigoizdat, 1955.

[750:1]. Mustaioki, A., and E. Nikkilä. *Russian-Finnish Didactic Dictionary.* Abt. 12,500 words. Moscow, Russkiy Yazyk, 1982.

[751]. Shcherba, L. V., and M. R. Matousevich. *Russian-French Dictionary.* 9th stereotype edition. Moscow, Sovetskaya Encyclopaedia, 1969.

[752]. Rybakov, B. A. *From the History of Ancient Russia and Its Culture.* Moscow, MSU Press, 1984.

[753]. Rybakov, B. A. *The Kiev Russia and Russian Principalities. The XII-XIII century.* Moscow, Nauka, 1982, 1988.

[754]. Rybakov, B. A. *The Kiev Russia and Russian Principalities.* Moscow, Nauka, 1986.

[755]. Rybnikov, K. A. *History of Mathematics.* Moscow, MSU Press, 1974.

[756]. Ryabtsevitch, V. N. *What the Coins Tell Us.* Minsk, Narodnaya Asveta, 1977.

[757]. Savelyev, E. P. *Cossacks and their History.* Vols. 1 and 2. Vladikavkaz, 1991. A reprint of E. Savelyev's *Ancient History of the Cossacks.* Novocherkassk, 1915.

[758]. Savelyeva, E. A. *Olaus Magnus and his "History of the Northern Peoples."* Leningrad, Nauka, 1983. [Olaus Magnus. *Historia de gentibus septentrionalibus,* 1555].

[759]. *Prince Obolensky's Almanach.* Part 1, Sections 1-7. N.p., 1866.

[760]. Suetonius Caius Tranquillius. *History of the Twelve Caesars.* Moscow, Nau-

ka, 1966. See also the English edition: New York, AMS Press, 1967; as well as the one titled *The Twelve Caesars.* London, Folio Society, 1964.

[760:1]. *Collected Historical and Cultural Monuments of the Tatarstan Republic. Vol. 1. Administrative regions.* Kazan, Master Line, 1999.

[761]. *The General Catalogue of Slavic and Russian Handwritten Books Kept in USSR: The XI-XIII century.* Moscow, 1984.

[762]. *St. Stephen of Perm.* The *Old Russian Tales of Famous People, Places and Events* series. Article, text, translation from Old Russian, commentary. St. Petersburg, Glagol, 1995.

[763]. *Holy Relics of Old Moscow.* Russian National Art Library. Moscow, Nikos, Kontakt, 1993.

[763:1]. Stogov, Ilya, comp. *Holy Writings of the Mayans: Popol-Vukh, Rabinal-Achi.* Translated by R. V. Kinzhalov. With *The Report of Yucatan Affairs* by Brother Diego de Landa attached, translated by Y. V. Knorozov. The *Alexandrian Library* series. St. Petersburg, Amphora, 2000.

[764]. Semashko, I. I. *100 Great Women.* Moscow, Veche, 1999.

[765]. Sunderland, I. T. *Holy Books as Regarded by Science.* Gomel, Gomelskiy Rabochiy Western Regional, 1925.

[766]. Sergeyev, V. S. *The History of Ancient Greece.* Moscow-Leningrad, Ogiz, 1934.

[767]. Sergeyev, V. S. *Essays on the History of the Ancient Rome.* Vols. 1 and 2. Moscow, Ogiz, 1938.

[768]. Sizov, S. *Another Account of the Three "Unidentified" Sepulchres of the Arkhangelsky Cathedral of the Moscow Kremlin. Materials and Research.* Iskusstvo (Moscow), No. 1 (1973).

[768:1]. Shevchenko, V. F., ed. *Simbirsk and its Past. An Anthology of Texts on Local History.* Oulianovsk, Culture Studies Lab, 1993. The compilation includes the book by M. F. Superanskiy titled *Simbirsk and its Past (1648-1898). A Historical Account,* among others. Simbirsk, The Simbirsk Regional Scientific Archive Commission, The O. V. Mourakhovskaya Typography, 1899.

[769]. Sinelnikov, Vyacheslav (Rev. V. Sinelnikov). *The Shroud of Turin at Dawn of the New Era.* Moscow, Sretensky Friary, 2000.

[769:1]. Sinha, N. K., Banerjee, A. C. *History of India.* Moscow, Inostrannaya Literatura, 1954. English original: Calcutta, 1952.

[770]. Sipovskiy, V. D. *Native Antiquity: History of Russia in Accounts and Pictures.* Vol. 1: IX-XVI century. St. Petersburg, The V. F. Demakov Typography, 1879, 1888. Vol. 2: XIV-XVII century. St. Petersburg, D. D. Poluboyarinov Publishing House, 1904. Reprinted: Moscow, Sovremennik, 1993.

[771]. *The Tale of the Mamay Battle.* Facsimile edition. Moscow, Sovetskaya Rossiya, 1980.

[772]. *A Tale of the Lord's Passion.* Part of the Russian handwritten collection of Christian works in Church Slavonic. Private collection. The XVIII-XIX century.

[772:1]. *The Scythians, the Khazars and the Slavs. Ancient Russia. To the Centen-*

nary since the Birth of M. I. Artamonov. Report theses for the international scientific conference. St. Petersburg, State Hermitage, the State University of St. Petersburg, the RAS Institute of Material Culture History.

[773]. Skornyakova, Natalya. *Old Moscow. Engravings and Lithographs of the XVI-XIX Century from the Collection of the State Museum of History.* Moscow, Galart, 1996.

[774]. Skromnenko, S. (Stroev, S. M.) *The Inveracity of the Ancient Russian History and the Error of the Opinions Deeming Russian Chronicles Ancient.* St. Petersburg, 1834.

[775]. Skrynnikov, R. G. *The Reign of Terror.* St. Petersburg, Nauka, 1992.

[776]. Skrynnikov, R. G. *Ivan the Terrible.* Moscow, Nauka, 1975. The 2nd edition came out in 1983.

[777]. Skrynnikov, R. G. *Boris Godunov.* Moscow, Nauka, 1983.

[778]. Skrynnikov, R. G. *The State and the Church in Russia. The XIV-XVI Century. Eminent Figures in the Russian Church.* Novosibirsk, Nauka, Siberian Affiliate, 1991.

[779]. Skrynnikov, R. G. *The Tragedy of Novgorod.* Moscow, Sabashnikov, 1994.

[780]. Skrynnikov, R. G. *Russia before the "Age of Turmoil."* Moscow, Mysl, 1981.

[781]. *The Slavic Mythology. An Encyclopaedic Dictionary.* Moscow, Ellis Luck, 1995.

[781:0]. Tsepkov, A., comp. *The Slavic Chronicles.* St. Petersburg, Glagol,1996.

[781:1]. *A Dictionary of Russian Don Dialects,* Vols. 1 and 2. Rostov-on-Don, Rostov University Press, 1991.

[782]. *Dictionary of the Russian Language in the XI-XVII centuries.* Edition 1. Moscow, Nauka, 1975.

[783]. *Dictionary of the Russian Language in the XI-XVII centuries.* Edition 2. Moscow, Nauka.

[784]. *Dictionary of the Russian Language in the XI-XVII centuries.* Edition 3. Moscow, Nauka.

[785]. *Dictionary of the Russian Language in the XI-XVII centuries.* Edition 5. Moscow, Nauka.

[786]. *Dictionary of the Russian Language in the XI-XVII centuries.* Edition 6. Moscow, Nauka, 1979.

[787]. *Dictionary of the Russian Language in the XI-XVII centuries.* Edition 7. Moscow, Nauka, 1980.

[788]. *Dictionary of the Russian Language in the XI-XVII centuries.* Edition 8. Moscow, Nauka.

[789]. *Dictionary of the Russian Language in the XI-XVII centuries.* Edition 11. Moscow, Nauka, 1986.

[790]. *Dictionary of the Russian Language in the XI-XVII centuries.* Edition 13. Moscow, Nauka, 1987.

[791]. *Dictionary of the Russian Language in the XI-XVII centuries.* Edition 19. Moscow, Nauka.

[792]. Smirnov, A. P. *The Scythians.* The USSR AS Institute of Archaeology. Moscow, Nauka, 1966.

[793]. Smirnov, F. *Christian Liturgy in the First Three Centuries.* Kiev, 1874.

[794]. Soboleva, N. A. *Russian Seals.* Moscow, Nauka, 1991.

[795]. *A Collection of State Edicts and Covenants.* Moscow, 1894.

[796]. *The Soviet Encyclopaedic Dictionary.* Moscow, Sovetskaya Encyclopaedia, 1979.

[797]. *The Soviet Encyclopaedic Dictionary.* Moscow, Sovetskaya Encyclopaedia, 1984.

[797:1]. *The Great Treasures of the World.* Gianni Guadalupi, ed. Moscow, Astrel, AST, 2001. Italian original: *I grandi tresori – l'arte orafa dall' antico egitto all XX secolo.* Edizioni White Star, 1998.

[798]. Solovyov, V. *Collected Works.* Vol. 6. St. Petersburg, 1898.

[799]. Solovyov, S. M. *Collected Works.* Book 4, Vols. 7-8. Moscow, Mysl, 1989.

[800]. Solovyov, S. M. *Collected Works.* Book 6. Moscow, Mysl, 1991.

[800:1]. Solovyov, S. M. *The History of the Ancient Russia.* Moscow, Prosveshchenie, 1992.

[801]. Solonar, P. *Most Probably Fiction...* The *Tekhnika i Nauka* magazine, No. 4 (1983): 28-32.

[802]. *The Reports of the Imperial Orthodox Society of Palestine.* April 1894. St. Petersburg, 1894.

[803]. Palamarchuk, Pyotr, comp. *Fourty Times Fourty. A Concise Illustrated History of All the Churches in Moscow.* 4 volumes. Moscow, Kniga i Biznes Ltd., Krom Ltd., 1995.

[804]. Sotnikova, M. P. *The Oldest Russian Coins of the X-XI century. Catalogue and Study.* Moscow, Banki i Birzhi, 1995.

[805]. *The Spaso-Andronikov Monastery. A scheme. The Central Andrey Roublyov Museum of Ancient Russian Culture and Art.* Moscow, MO Sintez, 1989.

[806]. Spasskiy, I. G. *The Russian Monetary System.* Leningrad, Avrora, 1970.

[807]. Spasskiy, I. G. *The Russian "Yefimki." A Study and a Catalogue.* Novosibirsk, Nauka, Siberian Affiliation, 1988.

[808]. Speranskiy, M. N. *Cryptography in Southern Slavic and Russian Literary Artefacts.* Published in the *Encyclopaedia of Slavic Philology* series. Leningrad, 1929.

[808:1]. Spiridonov, A. M., and O. A. Yarovoy. *The Valaam Monastery: from Apostle Andrew to Hegumen Innocent (Historical Essays of the Valaam Monastery).* Moscow, Prometei, 1991.

[809]. Spirina, L. M. *The Treasures of the Sergiev Posad State Reserve Museum of Art and History. Ancient Russian Arts and Crafts.* Nizhny Novgorod, Nizhpoligraf, n.d.

[810]. *Contentious Issues of Native History of the XI-XVIII century.* Report theses and speeches of the first readings dedicated to the memory of A. A. Zimin. 13-18 May, 1990. Moscow, The USSR AS, Moscow State Institute of Historical and Archival Science, 1990.

[811]. Brouyevich, N. G., ed. *220 Years of the USSR Academy of Sciences. 1725-1945.* Moscow-Leningrad, The USSR AS Press, 1945.

[812]. *Mediaeval Decorative Stitching. Byzantium, the Balkans, Russia.* Catalogue of an exhibition. The XVIII Int'l Congress of Byzantine Scholars. Moscow, 8-15 August, 1991. Moscow, The USSR Ministry of Culture. State Museums of the Moscow Kremlin, 1991.

[813]. Sobolev, N. N., ed. *The Old Moscow.* Published by the Commission for the Studies of Old Moscow of the Imperial Archaeological Society of Russia. Issues 1, 2. Moscow, 1914 (Reprinted: Moscow, Stolitsa, 1993).

[814]. *A Dictionary of Old Slavic (by the X-XI century Manuscripts).* Moscow, Russkiy Yazyk, 1994.

[815]. Starostin, E. V. *Russian History in Foreign Archives.* Moscow, Vysshaya Shkola, 1994.

[815:1]. Stelletsky, I. Y. *In Search of the Library of Ivan the Terrible.* The *Mysteries of Russian History* series. Moscow, Sampo, 1999.

[816]. Stepanov, N. V. *The New Style and the Orthodox Paschalia.* Moscow, 1907.

[817]. Stepanov, N. V. *The Calendarian and Chronological Reference Book (for the Solution of Chronographical Time Problems).* Moscow, Synodal typography, 1915.

[817:1]. Pletneva, S. A., volume ed. *The Eurasian Steppes in the Middle Ages.* Collected works. In the *USSR Archaeology* series. B. A. Rybakov, general ed. Moscow, Nauka, 1981.

[818]. Stingl, Miloslav. *Mysteries of the Indian Pyramids.* Transl. from Czech by I. O. Malevich. Moscow, Progress, 1982.

[819]. Strabo. *Geography.* Moscow, Ladomir, 1994. English edition: Jones, H.L. *The Geography of Strabo. With an English translation. I-VIII.* London, 1917-1932.

[820]. *Builders of the Burial Mounds and Dwellers of the Caves.* The *Extinct Civilizations* encyclopaedia. Moscow, Terra, 1998. Translated from English by E. Krasoulin. Original edition: Time-Life Books BV, 1992.

[821]. Struyck, D. J. *A Brief Account of the History of Mathematics.* Moscow, Nauka, 1969.

[821:1]. Suzdalev, V. E. *Kolomenskoye – "Memory for Ages."* Moscow, Praktik-A, 1993.

[822]. Sukina, L. B. *History of Esther in the Russian Cultrure of the Second Half of the XVII century.* Part of the compilation: Melnik, A. G., ed. *History and Culture of the land of Rostov.* 1998. Collected essays. Rostov, The Rostov Kremlin State Museum and Reserve, 1999.

[823]. Suleimanov, Olzhas. *Az and Ya.* Alma-Ata, Zhazushy, 1975.

[823:1]. Sukhoroukov, Alexander. *From the History of Cards. The Cards Don't Lie!* The *Bridge in Russia* magazine, No. 1 (18) (2002), pp. 78-80. Moscow, Minuvsheye.

[824]. Sytin, P. V. *From the History of Russian Streets.* Moscow, Moskovskiy Rabochiy, 1958.

[825]. Sytin, P. V. *The Toponymy of Russian Streets.* Moscow, 1959.

[826]. Samuels, Ruth. *Following the Paths of Hebraic History.* Moscow, Art-Business-Centre, 1993.

[827]. Tabov, Jordan. *The Decline of Old Bulgaria.* Sofia, Morang, 1997. Russian transl.: Moscow, Kraft and Lean, 2000.

[828]. Tabov, Jordan. *The New Chronology of the Balkans. The Old Bulgaria.* Sofia, PCM-1, 2000.

[828:1]. Tabov, Jordan. *When did the Kiev Russia Become Baptized?* St. Petersburg, Neva. Moscow, Olma, 2003.

[829]. Rakhmanliev, R., comp. *Tamerlane. The Epoch. The Person. The Actions.* Collected works. Moscow, Gourash, 1992.

[830]. Tantlevskiy, I. R. *History and Ideology of the Qumran Community.* St. Petersburg, the RAS Institute of Oriental Studies, 1994.

[830:1]. Tate, Georges. *The Crusades.* Moscow, Olimp, Astrel, Ast, 2003.

[831]. *Tartarian-Russian Didactic Dictionary.* Moscow, Russkiy Yazyk, 1992.

[832]. Tatishchev, V. N. *Collected Works in Eight Volumes.* Moscow, Ladomir, 1994-1996.

[833]. Tacitus, Cornelius. *Collected Works.* Vols. I, II. Leningrad, Nauka, 1969. English ed.: *The Works of Tacitus.* London, Cornelii Taciti Historiarum libri qui supersunt. Published by Dr. Carl Heraeus. 4th ed.: Leipzig, G. Teubner, 1885.

[834]. *The Works of Maxim the Confessor.* The œuvres of the Holy Fathers in Russian translation. Vol. 69. The Moscow Seminary Academy, 1915.

[835]. *The Works of Nicephor, the Archbischop of Constantinople.* Moscow, 1904.

[836]. *The Works of Nile, the Holy Pilgrim of Sinai.* The œuvres of the Holy Fathers in Russian translation. Vols. 31-33. The Moscow Seminary Academy, 1858-1859.

[837]. *The Works of St. Isidore the Pelusiote.* The œuvres of the Holy Fathers in Russian translation. Vols. 34-36. The Moscow Seminary Academy, 1859-1860.

[838]. Tvorogov, O. V. *Ancient Russia: Events and People.* St. Petersburg, Nauka, 1994.

[839]. Tvorogov, O. V. *The Ryurikovichi Princes. Short Biographies.* Moscow, Russkiy Mir, 1992.

[840]. Tereshchenko, Alexander. *A Final Study of the Saray Region, with a Description of the Relics of the Desht-Kipchak Kingdom.* Scientific Notes of the Imperial Academy of Sciences, the 1st and 3rd Department. Vol. 2. St. Petersburg, 1854. 89-105.

[841]. Tikhomirov, M. N. *Old Moscow. The XII-XV century. Mediaeval Russia as the International Crossroads. XIV-XV century.* Moscow, Moskovskiy Rabochiy, 1992.

[842]. Tikhomirov, M. N. *Russian Culture of the X-XIII century.* Moscow, 1968.

[843]. Tikhomirov, M. N. *Mediaeval Moscow in the XIV-XV century.* Moscow, 1957.

[844]. Tokmakov, I. F. *A Historical and Archaeological Description of the Moscow Stauropigial Monastery of St. Simon.* Issues 1 and 2, Moscow, 1892-1896.

[845]. Lopukhin, A. P., ed. *Explanatory Bible, or the Commentary to all of the*

Books of the Holy Writ, from both the Old and the New Covenant. Vols. 1-12. Petersburg, published by the heirs of A. P. Lopukhin, 1904-1913. (2nd edition: Stockholm, the Bible Translation Institute, 1987).

[846]. Toll, N. P. *The Saviour's Icon from K. T. Soldatenkov's Collection.* Moscow, 1933.

[847]. Tolochko, P. P. *The Ancient Kiev.* Kiev, Naukova Dumka, 1976.

[848]. Tolstaya, Tatyana. *The River Okkerville. Short Stories.* Moscow, Podkova, 1999.

[849]. Troels-Lund, T. *The Sky and the Weltanschauung in the Flux of Time.* Odessa, 1912. German edition: Troels-Lund, T. *Himmelsbild und Weltanschauung im Wandel der Zeiten.* Leipzig, B. G. Teubner, 1929.

[850]. Tronskiy, I. M. *The History of Ancient Literature.* Leningrad, Uchpedgiz, 1947.

[850:1]. Trofimov, Zhores. *The N. M. Karamzin Memorial in Simbirsk. Known and Unknown Facts.* Moscow, Rossia Molodaya, 1992.

[851]. *Trojan Tales. Mediaeval Courteous Novels on the Trojan War by the Russian Chronicles of the XVI and XVII century.* Leningrad: Nauka, 1972.

[851:1]. Thulsi Das. *The Ramayana, or Ramacharitamanasa. The Multitude of Rama's Heroic Deeds.* Translated from Hindi by Academician A. P. Barannikov. Moscow-Leningrad, The USSR AS, Institute of Oriental Studies. Published by the USSR Academy of Sciences in 1948.

[852]. Tunmann. *The Khans of Crimea.* Simferopol, Tavria, 1991.

[853]. Turaev, B. A. *The History of the Ancient Orient.* Moscow, Ogiz, 1936.

[854]. Shcheka, Y. V. *The Turkish-Russian Dictionary.* Abt. 18,000 words. 3rd stereotype edition. Moscow, Citadel, 2000.

[855]. Turkhan, Gian. Istanbul. Gate to the Orient. Istanbul, Orient, 1996 (in Russian).

[855:1]. *Turkey. The Book of Wanderings. A Historical Guide-book.* Moscow, Veche, Khartia, 2000.

[856]. *A Millennium since the Baptism of Russia.* The materials of the International Ecclesian and Historical Conference (Kiev, 21-28 July, 1986). Moscow, Moscow Patriarchy, 1988.

[857]. Ouzdennikov, V. V. *Russian Coins. 1700-1917.* Moscow, Finances and Statistics, 1986.

[857:1]. *The Ukrainian Books Printed in Cyrillics in the XVI-XVII century.* A catalogue of editions kept in the V. I. Lenin State Library of USSR. Issue I. 1574 – 2nd half of the XVII century. Moscow, The State V. I. Lenin Library of the Lenin Order. Rare books department. 1976.

[858]. *The Streets of Moscow. A Reference Book.* Moscow, Moskovskiy Rabochiy, 1980.

[859]. *The Ural Meridian. Topical Itineraries. A Reference Guide-book.* Chelyabinsk, The Southern Ural Press, 1986.

[860]. Ousanovich, M. I. *The Scientific Foresight of N. A. Morozov. The Successes of Chemistry,* Vol. 16, Issue 3 (1947).

[861]. Ouspensky, D. N. *Modern Problems of Orthodox Theology.* The *Moscow Patriarchy* magazine, No. 9 (1962): 64-70.

[862]. *The Writ. The Pentateuch of Moses (from the Genesis to the Revelation).* Translation, introduction, and comments by I. S. Shifman. Moscow, Respublika, 1993.

[863]. Fyson, Nance. *The Greatest Treasures of the World. An Atlas of the World's Wonders.* Moscow, Bertelsmann Media Moskau, 1996. Mondruck Graphische Betriebe GmbH, Güntherslau (Germany), 1996. Translated from the English edition published by AA Publishing (a trading name of Automobile Association Development Limited, whose registred office is Norfolk House, Priestly Road, Basing-stoke, Hampshire RG24 9NY).

[864]. Falkovich, S. I. *Nikolai Alexandrovich Morozov, His Life and Works on Chemistry.* The *Priroda (Nature)* magazine, No. 11 (1947).

[865]. Falkovich, S. I. *Nikolai Alexandrovich Morozov as a Chemist (1854-1946).* The *USSR AS Courier,* Chemical Studies Department, No. 5 (1947).

[866]. Fasmer, M. *An Etymological Dictionary of the Russian Language.* Vols. 1-4. Translated from German. Moscow, Progress, 1986-1987.

[867]. [Fedorov]. *Ivan Fedorov [The Alphabet].* A facsimile edition. Moscow, Prosveshchenie, 1974.

[868]. Fedorov, V. V., and A. T. Fomenko. *Statistical Estimation of Chronological Nearness of Historical Texts.* A collection of articles for the *Problems of stochastic model stability* magazine. Seminar works. The National System Research Institute, 1983. 101-107. English translation published in the *Journal of Soviet Mathematics,* Vol. 32, No. 6 (1986): 668-675.

[869]. Fedorov-Davydov, G. A. *The Coins of the Muscovite Russia.* Moscow, MSU Press, 1981.

[870]. Fedorov-Davydov, G. A. *The Coins of the Nizhny Novgorod Principality.* Moscow, MSU Press, 1989.

[870:1]. Fedorov-Davydov, G. A. *Burial Mounds, Idols and Coins.* Moscow, Nauka, 1968.

[871]. Fedorov-Davydov, G. A. *Eight Centuries of Taciturnity.* The *Nauka i Zhizn (Science and Life)* magazine, No. 9 (1966): 74-76.

[872]. Fedorova, E. V. *Latin Epigraphics.* Moscow University Press, 1969.

[873]. Fedorova, E. V. *Latin Graffiti.* Moscow University Press, 1976.

[874]. Fedorova, E. V. *Imperial Rome in Faces.* Moscow University Press, 1979.

[875]. Fedorova, E. V. *Rome, Florence, Venice. Historical and Cultural Monuments.* Moscow University Press, 1985.

[876]. Theophilactus Simocattas. *History.* Moscow, Arktos, 1996.

[876:1]. Fersman, A. E. *Tales of Gemstones.* Moscow, Nauka, 1974.

[877]. Flavius, Joseph. *The Judean War.* Minsk, Belarus, 1991.

[878]. Flavius, Joseph. *Judean Antiquities.* Vols. 1, 2. Minsk, Belarus, 1994.

[879]. *Florentine Readings: The Life and Culture of Italy. Summer Lightnings.* Collected essays, translated by I. A. Mayevsky. Moscow, 1914.

[880]. Florinsky, V. M. *Primeval Slavs according to the Monuments of their Pre-Historic Life.* Tomsk, 1894.

[881]. Voigt, G. *The Renaissance of the Classical Literature.* Vols. I and II. Moscow, 1885. German edition: *Die Wiederbelebung des classischen Altertums oder das erste Jahrhundert des Humanismus.* Berlin, G. Reimer, 1893.

[882]. Foley, John. *The Guinness Encyclopaedia of Signs and Symbols.* Moscow, Veche, 1996. Original by Guinness Publishing Ltd., 1993.

[883]. Fomenko, A. T. "On the Calculations of the Second Derivative of Lunar Elongation." The problems of the mechanics of navigated movement. *Hierarchic systems.* The Inter-University Collection of Scientific Works. Perm, 1980. 161-166.

[884]. Fomenko, A. T. "Several Statistical Regularities of Information Density Disribution in Texts with Scales." *Semiotics and Informatics.* Moscow, The National Scientific and Technical Information Institute Publication, Issue 15 (1980): 99-124.

[885]. Fomenko, A. T. *Informative Functions and Related Statistical Regularities.* Report theses of the 3rd International Probability Theory and Mathematical Statistics Conference in Vilnius, the Lithuanian Academy of Sciences Institute of Mathematics and Cybernetics, 1981, Volume 2, pages 211-212.

[886]. Fomenko, A. T. *Duplicate Identification Methods and some of their Applications.* In *Doklady AN SSSR* (The USSR Academy of Sciences), Vol. 256, No. 6 (1981): 1326-1330.

[887]. Fomenko, A. T. *On the Qualities of the Second Derivative of Lunar Elongation and Related Statistical Regularities.* The Issues of Computational and Applied Mathematics. A collection of academic works. The Academy of Sciences of the Soviet Republic of Uzbekistan. Tashkent, Issue 63 (1981): 136-150.

[888]. Fomenko, A. T. *New Experimental Statistical Methods of Dating the Ancient Events and their Applications to the Global Chronology of the Ancient and Mediaeval World.* Pre-print. Order No. 3672, No. BO7201. Moscow, State Committee for Radio and TV Broadcasting, 1981. 1-100. English translation: Fomenko, A. T. *Some new empirical-statistical methods of dating and the analysis of present global chronology.* London, The British Library, Department of Printed Books. 1981. Cup. 918/87.

[889]. Fomenko, A. T. *Calculating the Second Derivative of Lunar Elongation and Related Statistical Regularities in the Distribution of Some Astronomical Data.* In *Operational and Automatic System Research,* Issue 20 (1982): 98-113. Kiev University Press.

[890]. Fomenko, A. T. *Concerning the Mystification Issue.* In *Science and Technology,* No. 11 (1982): 26-29.

[891]. Fomenko, A. T. *New Empirico-Statistical Method of Ordering Texts and Applications to Dating Problems.* In *Doklady AN SSSR* (The USSR Academy of Sciences Publications), Vol. 268, No. 6 (1983): 1322-1327.

[892]. Fomenko, A. T. *Distribution Geometry for Entire Points in Hyperregions.* The Vector and Tensor Analysis Seminar works (Moscow, MSU Press), Issue 21 (1983): 106-152.

[893]. Fomenko, A. T. *The Author's Invariant of Russian Literary Texts.* Methods

of Qualitative Analysis of Narrative Source Texts. Moscow, The USSR History Institute (The USSR Academy of Sciences), 1983. 86-109.

[894]. Fomenko, A. T. *The Global Chronological Map.* In *Chemistry and Life,* No. 11 (1983): 85-92.

[895]. Fomenko, A. T. *New Methods of the Chronologically Correct Ordering of Texts and their Applications to the Problems of Dating the Ancient Events.* Operational and Automatic System Research (Kiev University Press), Issue 21 (1983): 40-59.

[896]. Fomenko, A. T. *Methods of Statistical Processing of Parallels in Chronological Text and the Global Chronological Map.* Operational and Automatic System Research (Kiev University Press), Issue 22 (1983): 40-55.

[897]. Fomenko, A. T. *Statistical Frequency Damping Analysis of Chronological Texts and Global Chronological Applications.* Operational and Automatic System Research (Kiev University Press), Issue 24 (1984): 49-66.

[898]. Fomenko, A. T. *New Empirico-Statistical Method of Parallelism Determination and Duplicate Dating.* Problems of stochastic model stability. Seminar works. The National System Research Institute, Moscow, 1984. 154-177.

[899]. Fomenko, A. T. *Frequency Matrices and their Applications to Statistical Processing of Narrative Sources.* Report theses of the "Complex Methods of Historical Studies from Antiquity to Contemporaneity" conference. The Commission for Applying Natural Scientific Methods to Archaeology. Moscow, The USSR History Institute (The USSR Academy of Sciences), 1984. 135-136.

[900]. Fomenko, A. T. *Informative Functions and Related Statistical Regularities.* Statistics. Probability. Economics. The *Academic Statistical Notes* series. Vol. 49. Moscow, Nauka, 1985. 335-342.

[901]. Fomenko, A. T. *Duplicates in Mixed Sequences and the Frequency Damping Principle.* Report theses of the 4th Int'l Probability Theory and Mathematical Statistics Conference in Vilnius, the Lithuanian Academy of Sciences Institute of Mathematics and Cybernetics, Vol. 3. 1985. 246-248.

[902]. Fomenko, A. T., and L. E. Morozova. *Several Issues of Statistical Annual Account Source Processing Methods.* Mathematics in mediaeval narrative source studies. Moscow, Nauka, 1986. 107-129.

[903]. Fomenko, A. T. *Identifying Dependencies and Layered Structures in Narrative Texts.* Problems of stochastic model stability. Seminar works. The National System Research Institute, 1987. 33-45.

[904]. Fomenko, A. T. *Methods of Statistical Analysis of Narrative Texts and Chronological Applications. (The Identification and the Dating of Derivative Texts, Statistical Ancient Chronology, Statistics of the Ancient Astronomical Reports).* Moscow, Moscow University Press, 1990.

[905]. Fomenko, A. T. *Statistical Chronology.* New facts in life, science and technology. The *Mathematics and Cybernetics"* series, No. 7. Moscow, Znanie, 1990.

[906]. Fomenko, A. T. *Global Chronology. (A Research of Classical and Mediaeval*

History. Mathematical Methods of Source Analysis.) Moscow, MSU Department of Mathematics and Mechanics, 1993.

[907]. Fomenko, A. T. *A Criticism of the Traditional Chronology of Antiquity and the Middle Ages (What Century is it Now?).* A précis. Moscow, MSU Department of Mathematics and Mechanics, 1993.

[908]. Fomenko, A. T. *Methods of Mathematical Analysis of Historical Texts. Chronological Applications.* Moscow, Nauka, 1996.

[909]. Fomenko, A. T. *The New Chronology of Greece. Antiquity in the Middle Ages.* Vols. 1 and 2. Moscow, MSU Centre of Research and Pre-University Education, 1996.

[910]. Fomenko, A. T. *Statistical Chronology. A Mathematical View of History. What Century is it Now?* Belgrade, Margo-Art, 1997.

[911]. Fomenko, A. T. *Methods of Statistical Analysis of Historical Texts. Chronological Applications.* Vols. 1 and 2. Moscow, Kraft and Lean, 1999.

[912]. Fomenko, A. T. *New Methods of Statistical Analysis of Historical Texts. Applications to Chronology.* Vol. 1, Vol. 2. Vol. 3: Fomenko, A. T. *Antiquity in the Middle Ages. (Greek and Bible History).* Published in the series *Russian Studies in Mathematics and Sciences.* Scholary Monographs in Russian. Vol. 6-7. Lewiston-Queenston-Lampeter, The Edwin Mellen Press, 1999.

[912:1]. Fomenko, A. T., and G. V. Nosovskiy. *Demagogism instead of Scientific Analysis.* The RAS Courier, Vol. 9, No. 9 (2000): 797-800.

[912:2]. Fomenko, A. T., and G. V. Nosovskiy. *In Re the "Novgorod Datings" of A. A. Zaliznyak and V. L. Yanin.* The RAS Courier, Vol. 72, No. 2 (2002): 134-140.

[912:3]. Fomenko, T. N. *The Astronomical Datings of the "Ancient" Egyptian Zodiacs of Dendera and Esne (Latopolis).* In: Kalashnikov, V. V., G. V. Nosovskiy, and A. T. Fomenko. *The Astronomical Analysis of Chronology. The Almagest. Zodiacs.* Moscow, The Delovoi Express Financial, 2000. 635-810.

[913]. *The Epistle of Photius, the Holy Patriarch of Constantinople, to Michael, Prince of Bulgaria, on the Princely Incumbencies.* Moscow, 1779. See also: Photius. *Patriarch of Constantinople, Epistola ad Michaelem Bulgarorum Regem.* In: *Roman Spicilegium.* Rome, 1839-1844.

[914]. Cardini, Franco. *Origins of the Mediaeval Knightage.* A condensed translation from Italian by V. P. Gaiduk. La Nuova Italia, 1982. Moscow, Progress Publications, 1987.

[914:1]. France, Anatole. *Selected Short Stories.* Leningrad, Lenizdat, 1959.

[915]. Pototskaya, V. V., and N. P. Pototskaya. *French-Russian Dictionary.* 12th stereotype edition. Moscow, Sovetskaya Encyclopaedia. 1967.

[916]. Godfrey, Fr. O. F. M. *Following Christ.* Israel, Palphot Ltd., Millennium 2000, 2000.

[917]. Frazer, J. *Attis.* Moscow, Novaya Moskva, 1924. English ed.: *Adonis, Attis, Osiris.* London, Macmillan & Co, 1907.

[918]. Frazer, J. *Golden Bough.* Release 1. Moscow-Leningrad, Ogiz, 1931.

[919]. Frazer, J. *Golden Bough.* Releases 3, 4. Moscow, Atheist, 1928.

[920]. Frazer, J. *The Folklore in the Old Testament. Studies in Comparative Religion.* Moscow-Leningrad, Ogiz, The State Social Economics, 1931. English original: London, Macmillan & Co., 1918.

[921]. Fren, H. M. *Coins of the Khans of Juchiev Ulus of the Golden Horde.* St. Petersburg, 1832.

[922]. Frumkina, R. M. *Statistical Methods of Lexical Studies.* Moscow, 1964.

[923]. Thucydides. *The History of the Peloponnesian War.* Eight books. Translated by F. G. Mishchenko. Vols. 1, 2. Vol. 1: books 1-4. Vol. 2: books 5-8. Moscow, 1887-1888. English edition published in the series *"Great Books of the Western World.* Vol. 5. Encyclopaedia Britannica, Inc. Chicago, The University of Chicago, 1952 (2nd edition 1990). See also the Penguin Books edition. London, 1954.

[924]. Thucydides. *History.* Leningrad, Nauka, 1981.

[925]. von Senger, Harro. *Stratagems. On the Chinese Art of Life and Survival.* Moscow, Progress, 1995.

[926]. Herrmann, D. *The Pioneers of the Skies.* Translated from German by K. B. Shingareva and A. A. Konopikhin. Moscow, Mir, 1981. German edition: Herrmann, Dieter B. *Entdecker des Himmels.* Leipzig-Jena-Berlin, Urania-Verlag, 1979.

[927]. Chlodowski, R. I. *Francesco Petrarch.* Moscow, Nauka, 1974.

[928]. *The Pilgrimage of Hegumen Daniel.* Literary Monuments of Ancient Russia. XII Century. Moscow, Khudozhestvennaya Literatura, 1980. 25-115.

[929]. *Afanasy Nikitin's Voyage over the Three Seas. 1466-1472.* Moscow-Leningrad, the Academy of Sciences, Literary Masterpieces, The USSR AS Publications, 1948.

[930]. Hollingsworth, Mary. *Art in the History of Humanity.* Moscow, Iskusstvo, 1989. Russian translation of the edition titled *L'Arte Nella Storia Dell'Uomo.* Saggio introduttivo di Giulio Carlo Argan. Firenze, Giunti Gruppo Editoriale, 1989.

[931]. *The Kholmogory Chronicle. The Dvina Chronicler.* The Complete Collection of Russian Chronicles, Vol. 33. Leningrad, Nauka, 1977.

[932]. Khomyakov, A. S. *Collected Works in Two Volumes.* A supplement to the *Issues of Philosophy.* Vol. 1. Works on historiosophy. Moscow, the Moscow Fund of Philosophy, Medium Press, 1994.

[933]. Aconiatus, Nicetas. *History Beginning with the Reign of John Comnenus.* St. Petersburg, 1860. Also see the *Historia* by Nicetas Aconiatus in J. P. Migne's *Patrologiae cursus completes. Series graeca.* Vol. 140. Paris, 1857-1886.

[934]. Aconiatus, Nicetas. *History Beginning with the Reign of John Comnenus (1186-1206).* The *Byzantine Historians* series, Vol. 5. St. Petersburg, 1862. Also see the *Historia* by Nicetas Aconiatus in J. P. Migne's *Patrologiae cursus completes. Series graeca.* Vol. 140. Paris, 1857-1886

[935]. Hogue, John. *Nostradamus. The Complete Prophecies.* First published in Great Britain in 1996 by Element Books Ltd., Shaftesbury, Dorset. Moscow, Fair-Press, The Grand Publishing and Trading House, 1999.

[935:1]. Boutenev, Khreptovich. *Florence and Rome in Relation to Two XV-century Events in Russian History. A Concise Illustrated Account Compiled by Khreptovich Boutenev, Esq.* Moscow, 1909.

[936]. *Christianity. An Encyclopaedic Dictionary.* The Encyclopaedic Dictionary of Brockhaus and Efron. New Encyclopaedic Dictionary of Brockhaus and Efron. The Orthodox Encyclopaedia of Theology. Vols. 1-3. Moscow, The Great Russian Encyclopaedia, 1993.

[937]. Pokrovskiy, N. N., ed. *Christianity and the Russian Church of the Feudal Period (Materials).* Novosibirsk, Nauka, Siberian Affiliation, 1989.

[938]. Istrin, V. M., ed. *The Chronicle of John Malalas (A Slavic Translation).* St. Petersburg, 1911.

[939]. *The Chronographer.* Russian National Library, the Manuscript Section. Rumyantsevsky Fund, 457.

[940]. *The Lutheran Chronographer.* Private collection, 1680.

[941]. Rantsov, V. L., comp. *The Chronology of Global and Russian History.* St. Petersburg, Brockhaus-Efron, 1905. Reprinted in Kaliningrad: Argument, Yantarny Skaz, 1995.

[942]. *The Chronology of Russian History. An Encyclopaedic Reference Book.* Moscow, Mezhdunarodnye Otnosheniya, 1994.

[943]. Prakhov, Adrian, ed. *The Treasures of Russian Art.* A Monthly Almanac of the Imperial Society for Supporting Fine Arts. Year IV, No. 2-4, No. 5 (1904). Issue 5: The Relics of the Savvino-Storozhevsky monastery. Historical review by Alexander Ouspensky. Reprinted in Moscow, Severo-Print Typography, 1998. To the 600th anniversary of the Savvino-Storozhevsky stauropigial friary.

[944]. Khoudyakov, M. G. *Accounts of the History of the Kazan Khanate.* Kazan, State Publishing House, 1923. Reprinted in: *On the Junction of Continents and Civilizations.* Moscow, Insan, 1996. Published separately: Moscow, Insan, SFK, 1991.

[945]. Kjetsaa, G., S. Gustavsson, B. Beckman, and S. Gil. *The Problems of the "Quiet flows the Don's" Authorship. Who Wrote the "Quiet flows the Don"?* Moscow, Kniga, 1989. Translated from the Solum Forlag edition. Oslo-New Jersey, Humanities Press.

[946]. Zeitlin, Z. *Galileo.* The *Celebrity Biographies* series, Issue 5-6. The Literary Magazine Association, Moscow, 1935.

[947]. Petrov, Leonid, comp. *The Dictionary of Ecclesial History. (A Referential Theological Dictionary, Predominantly Oriented At Ecclesial History).* St. Petersburg, the Province Department Typography, 1889. Reprinted: the Sretenskiy Monastery, 1996.

[948]. Cicero, Marcus Tullius. *Dialogues. On the State. On the Laws.* Moscow, Nauka, 1966. English edition: Cicero, Marcus Tullius. *Works.* Cambridge, Mass; Harvard University Press; London, Heinemann, 1977.

[949]. Cicero, Marcus Tullius. *Three Tractates on the Art of Rhetoric.* Moscow, Nauka, 1972. English edition: Cicero, Marcus Tullius. *Works.* Cambridge, Mass; Harvard University Press; London, Heinemann, 1977.

[950]. Cicero, Marcus Tullius. *On the Old Age. On Friendship. On Responsibilities.* Moscow, Nauka, 1972. English edition: Cicero, Marcus Tullius. *Old Age and Friendship...* London, Cassel's National Library, 1889.

[951]. Cicero, Marcus Tullius. *Philosophical Tractates.* Moscow, Nauka, 1985. English edition: Cicero, Marcus Tullius. *Works.* Cambridge, Mass; Harvard University Press; London, Heinemann, 1977.

[952]. Chagin, G. N. *The Ancient Land of Perm.* Moscow, Iskusstvo, 1988.

[953]. Chekin, L. S. *The Cartography of the Christian Middle Ages in the VIII-XIII century.* Moscow, Oriental Literature, RAS, 1999.

[953:1]. Chernetsov, A. V. *The Gilded Doors of the XVI century. The Cathedrals of the Moscow Kremlin and the Trinity Cathedral of the Ipatyevsky Monastery in Kostroma.* Moscow, The RAS, Nauka, 1992.

[954]. Chernin, A. D. *The Physics of Time.* Moscow, Nauka, 1987.

[955]. Chernykh, P. Y. *A Historical and Etymological Dictionary of the Modern Russian Language.* Vols. 1, 2. Moscow, Russkiy Yazyk, 1993.

[955:1]. Chernyak, E. B. *The Mysteries of France. Conspiracy, Intrigue, Mystification.* Moscow, Ostozhye Press, 1996.

[955:2]. Chernyak, E. B. *The Time of the Conspiracies Long Forgotten.* Moscow, Mezhdunarodnye Otnosheniya, 1994.

[956]. Chertkov, A. D. *On the Language of the Pelasgians that used to Inhabit Italy, and its Comparison to Ancient Slavic.* The periodical edition of the Moscow Society for the Historical Studies of Russian Antiquities, Book 23. Moscow, 1855.

[957]. Chertkov, A. D. *A Description of Ancient Russian Coins.* Moscow, Selivanovsky Typography, 1834.

[958]. Cinzia, Valigi. *Rome and the Vatican.* Narni-Terni, Italy, Plurigraf, 1995.

[959]. Chistovich, I. *Textual Corrections of the Slavic Bible Before the 1751 Edition.* (Article 2). The Orthodox Review, Vol. 2 (May Book, 1860): 41-72.

[960]. Chistyakov, A. S. *The Story of Peter the Great.* Reprint. Moscow, Buklet, Dvoinaya Raduga, 1992.

[961]. Chistyakova, N. A., and N. V. Voulikh. *The History of Ancient Literature.* Moscow, Vyshaya Shkola, 1972.

[962]. *Imperial Society for History and Russian Antiquities Readings.* Book I, Part 5. 1858.

[963]. *The Miraculous Icons of Our Lady.* Sisterhood of the Holy Martyr Elizabeth, the Great Princess. 103287. Moscow, 40, 2nd Khutorskaya St., 1998.

[964]. [Champollion] *J. F. Champollion and Egyptian Hieroglyphs Deciphered.* Collected works under the general editorship of I. S. Katznelson. Moscow, Nauka, 1979.

[965]. Chantepie de la Saussaye, D. P. *Illustrated History of Religions.* Moscow, 1899. English edition: *Manual of the Science of Religion.* London-New York, Longmans, Green and Co., 1891.

[966]. Chantepie de la Saussaye, D. P. *Illustrated History of Religions.* Vols. 1 and 2. Moscow, Spaso-Preobrazhensky Stauropigial Monastery of Valaam, reprinted in 1992.

[967]. Shakhmatov, A. A. *Manuscript Description. The Radzivilovskaya Chronicle, or the Chronicle of Königsberg.* Vol. 2. Articles on the text and the miniatures of the manuscript. St. Petersburg, Imperial Antiquarian Bibliophile Society, CXVIII, 1902.

[968]. Shevchenko, M. Y. *The Star Catalogue of Claudius Ptolemy: Special Characteristics of Ancient Astronomical Observations.* Historico-Astronomical Research. Issue 17. Moscow, Nauka, 1988. 167-186.

[969]. *Masterpieces among the Paintings in the Museums of the USSR. The Art of Ancient Russia. The Renaissance Art.* Issue 1. Moscow, Goznak, 1974.

[970]. Sheynman, M. M. *Belief in the Devil in the History of Religion.* Moscow, Nauka, 1977.

[971]. Shakespeare. *Collected Works in Five Volumes.* From the *Library of Great Writers* series under the editorship of S. A. Vengerov. St. Petersburg, Brockhaus-Efron, 1902-1904.

[972]. Shakespeare, William. *The Complete Works in Eight Volumes.* Under the editorship of A. Smirnov and A. Anixt. Moscow, Iskusstvo, 1960.

[973]. Shakespeare, William. *King Richard III. Tragedy in Five Acts.* Translated by Georgy Ben. St. Petersburg, Zvezda, 1997.

[974]. *600th Anniversary of the Kulikovo Battle.* Brochure. Vneshtorgizdat, Moscow State Museum of History. 1980.

[975]. Shilov, Y. A. *The Proto-Homeland of the Aryans. History, Tradition, Mythology.* Kiev, Sinto, 1995.

[976]. Shiryaev, A. N. *Consecutive Statistical Analysis.* Moscow, Nauka, 1976.

[977]. Shiryaev, E. E. *Belarus: White Russia, Black Russia and Lithuania on the Maps.* Minsk, Science & Technology, 1991.

[978]. Shklovsky, I. S. *Supernovae.* Moscow, 1968 (1st edition). Moscow, Nauka, 1976 (2nd edition). English edition: London-New York, Wiley, 1968.

[979]. Schlezer, A. L. *Public and Private Life of Augustus Ludwig Schlezer as Related by Himself.* In the *Imperial Academy of Sciences, Russian Language and Literature Department* series, Vol. 13. St. Petersburg, 1875.

[980]. Shlyapkin I. A. *Description of the Manuscripts of the Spaso-Yefimiev Monastery in Suzdal.* The Masterpieces of Ancient Literature, Issue 4, No. 16. St. Petersburg, 1881.

[981]. Spilevskiy A. V. *The Almagest and Chronology.* The Ancient History Courier, No. 3 (1988): 134-160.

[982]. Schulmann, Eliezer. *The Sequence of Biblical Events.* Translated from Hebrew. Moscow, the Ministry of Defence Publications, 1990.

[983]. Shchepkin, V. N. *Russian Palaeography.* Moscow, Nauka, 1967.

[984]. Shcherbatov, M. M. *Russian History from the Dawn of Time.* St. Petersburg, 1901.

[985]. Eulia, Chelebi. *The Book of Travels. Campaigns of the Tatars and Voyages through the Crimea (1641-1667).* Simferopol, Tavria, 1996.

[985:1]. Eisler, Colin (Leman, Robert). *The Museums of Berlin.* Moscow, Colin Eisler and Little, Brown and Company, Inc. Compilation. Slovo, the *World's Greatest Museums* series, 2002 (1996).

[985:2]. Eisler, Colin. *The Art of the Hermitage.* Moscow, Biblion, 2001.

[986]. Aitken, M. J. *Physics and Archaeology.* Moscow, IL, 1964. English original: New York, Interscience Publishers, 1961.

[987]. Ehlebracht, Peter. *Tragedy of the Pyramids. Egyptian Shrines Plundered for 5000 Years.* Moscow, Progress, 1984. German original: *Haltet die Pyramiden Fest! 5000 Jahre Grabraub in Ägypten.* Düsseldorf-Vienna, Econ, 1980.

[987:1]. Englund, Peter. *Poltava. How an Army Perished.* Moscow, Novoye Literaturnoye Obozrenie, 1995. Original: Stockholm, Bokförgalet Atlantis, 1988.

[988]. *The Encyclopaedic Dictionary.* Vols. 1-82; supplementary volumes 1-4. St. Petersburg, Brockhaus and Efron, 1890-1907.

[988:0]. Brockhaus, F. A., and I. A. Efron. *The Encyclopaedic Dictionary.* St. Petersburg, 1898. Reprinted: St. Petersburg, Polradis, 1994.

[988:1]. *Encyclopaedia for Children.* Vol. 7: *Art.* Moscow, Avanta-plus, 1997.

[989]. *The Encyclopaedia of Elementary Mathematics. Book 1. Arithmetics.* Moscow-Leningrad, the State Publishing House of Theoretical Technical Literature, 1951.

[990]. Artamonov, M. I., ed. *The Hermitage.* Album. Leningrad, Sovetskiy Khudozhnik, 1964.

[991]. Ern, V. *The Revelation in Thunder and Storm. Anatomy of N. A. Morozov's Book.* Moscow, 1907.

[991:1]. *The Art of Goldsmithery in Russia.* Album. Moscow, Interbook-Business, Yural Ltd, 2002.

[992]. Yuvalova, E. P. *German Sculpture of 1200-1270.* Moscow, Iskusstvo, 1983.

[993]. Yanin, V. L. *I Sent You a Birch-Rind Epistle.* Moscow, MSU Press, 1965. A revised edition: Moscow, 1998.

[993:1]. Jannella, Cecilia. *Simone Martini.* Album. Moscow, Slovo, 1996. Scala, 1995, Istituto Forografico Editoriale.

[994]. Ponomaryov, A. M., ed. *Yaroslavl. History of the City in Documents and First-Hand Materials from First References to 1917.* Yaroslavl, Upper Volga Publications, 1990.

[995]. *Yaroslavl. Map 0-37 (1:1,000,000).* The General Council of Ministers, Department of Geodetics and Cartography, 1980.

[996]. *Yaroslavl. Monuments of Art and Architecture.* Yaroslavl: Upper Volga Publications, 1994.

Sources in foriegn languages

[997]. Chrysostomos, Abbot. *The Holy Royal Monastery of Kykko Founded with a Cross.* Limassol, Cyprus, Kykko Monastery, printed by D. Couvas & Sons, Ltd., 1969.

[998]. *ABC kulturnich pamatek Ceskoslovenska.* Prague, Panorama, 1985.

[999]. Abulafia, David. *Frederick II. A Medieval Emperor.* New York-Oxford, Oxford University Press, 1988.

[1000]. Abu Mashar. *De magnis coinctiombus.* Augsburg, Erhard Ratdolt (The Pulkovo Observatory Library), 1489.

[1001]. Adam, L. *North-West American Indian Art and its Early Chinese Parallels.* Man, Volume 36, No. 2-3 (1936): 45.

[1002]. Puech, Aime. *St. Jean Chrisostome et les mœurs de son temps.* Paris, 1891.

[1003]. Albright, W. F. *From the Stone Age to Christianity.* 7th edition. New York, 1957.

[1004]. Albumasar. *De Astrú Scientia.* 1515. (The Pulkovo Observatory Library.)

[1005]. Alibert, Louis. *Dictionnaire Occitan-Francais. Selon les parles languedociens.* Toulouse, Institut d'études Occitanes, 1996.

[1006]. *A List of Books on the History of Science.* 2nd supplement, Part 3. Astronomy. Chicago, The J. Crerar Library, 1944.

[1007]. Allen, Phillip. *L'Atlas des Atlas. Le monde vu par les cartographes.* Brepols, 1993.

[1008]. *Almagestu Cl. Ptolemaei Phelusiensis Alexandrini.* Anno Virginei Partus, 1515.

[1009]. *America. Das frühe Bild der Neuen Welt. Ausstellung der Bayerischen Staatsbibliothek München.* Munich, Prestel Verlag, 1992.

[1009:1]. Silverman, David P., ed. *Ancient Egypt.* New York, Oxford University Press, 1977.

[1010]. Thorpe, B., ed. *Ancient Laws and Institutes of England...* Volume 1. London, 1840. 198.

[1011]. Anke, Victor. *The Life of Charlemagne.* Aachen, Einhard Verlag, 1995.

[1012]. *Annales de la Société Royale d'Archéologie de Bruxelles. Fondée a Bruxelles en 1887. Mémoires, rapports et documents.* Publication périodique. Tome 41e. Secrétariat Général. Musée de la Porte de Hal Bruxelles. 1937.

[1013]. Apianus, P. *Cosmographicus Liber Petri Apiani mathematici studiose collectus.* (The Pulkovo Observatory Library). Landshutae, impensis P. Apiani, 1524.

[1013:1]. Arellano, Alexandra. *All Cuzco. Peru.* Fisa Escudo de Oro. Centre of Regional Studies of the Andes Bartolomé de las Casas, Lima, Peru. Instituto de Investigacion de la Facultad de Turismo y Hotelria, Universidad San Martin de Porres. 1999.

[1014]. Arnim, H. *Sprachliche Forschungen zur Chronologie der platonischen Dialoge.* Volume 269. Appendix 3. Sitzungen Wiener Akademie, 1912.

[1015]. Wolff, Arnold. *Cologne Cathedral. Its history – Its Works of Art.* Greven Verlag Köln GmbH, 1995.

[1016]. Wolff, Arnold, Rainer Gaertner, and Karl-Heinz Schmitz. *Cologne on the Rhine with City Map.* Cologne, Verlagsgesellschaft GmbH, 1995.

[1017]. Wolff, Arnold. *The Cologne Cathedral.* Cologne, Vista Point Verlag, 1990.

[1017:0]. Sachs, Abraham J. *Astronomical Diaries and Related Texts from Babylonia.* Compiled and edited by Hermann Hunger. Volume 1: Diaries from 652 BC to 262 BC. Volume 2: Diaries from 261 BC to 165 BC. Österreichische Akademie der Wissenschaften Philosophisch-Historische Klasse Denkschriften, 195. Bad. Verlag der Österreichischen Akademie der Wissenschaften. Vienna, 1988.

[1017:1]. Walker, Christopher, ed. *Astronomy before the Telescope*. Foreword by P. Moore. British Museum Press, 1996.

[1018]. Palairet, Jean. *Atlas Méthodique, Composé pour l'usage de son altesse sérénissime monseigneur le prince d'Orange et de Nassau stadhouder des sept provinces unies, etc. etc. etc.* Se trouve à Londres, chez Mess. J. Nourse & P. Vaillant dans le Strand; J. Neaulme à Amsterdam & à Berlin; & P. Gosse à La Haye. 1755.

[1019]. *Atlas Minor sive Geographia compendiosa in q.v. a Orbis Terrarum pavcis attamen novissimis Tabvlis ostenditvr. // Atlas Nouveau, contenant toutes les parties du monde, Où font Exactement Remarquees les Empires Monarchies, Royaumes, Etats, Republiques, &c, &c, &c. Receuillies des Meilleurs Auteurs.* Amsterdam: Regner & Josue Ottens, n.d.

[1020]. Auè, Michèlé. *Discover Cathar country. Le Pays Cathare.* Toulouse, MSM, 1992.

[1021]. Bacharach. *Astronomia.* (The Pulkovo Observatory Library), 1545.

[1022]. Bailly, J. S. *Histoire de l'astronomie ancienne depuis son origine jusqu'à l'établissement de l'école d'Alexandrie.* Paris, 1st edition 1775, 2nd edition 1781.

[1023]. Baily, F. *An account of the life of Sir John Flaemsteed.* London, 1835.

[1024]. Baily, F. *The Catalogues of Ptolemy, Ulugh Beigh, Tycho Brahe, Halley and Hevelins, deduced from the best authorities.* Royal Astr. Soc. Memoirs, XIII (1843): 1-248.

[1025]. Bakker, I., I. Vogel, and T. Wislanski. *TRB and other C-14 Dates from Poland. Helinium*, IX, 1969.

[1025:1]. Baldauf, Robert. *Historie und Kritik. (Einige kritische Bemerkungen.).* Basel: Friedrich Reinhardt, Universitäts-buchdruckerei, 1902.

[1026]. Bartholomaeus, Angicus. *De proprietatibus rerum.* lib. XV, cap. CXXXI. Apud A. Koburger. Nurenbergi, 1492,

[1027]. Barron, Roderick. *Decorative Maps. With Forty Full Colour Plates.* London, Bracken Books, 1989.

[1028]. Basilica, Sainte Cécile. *Albi. As de Cœur Collection. Guided Visit.* Albi, France: Apa-Poux S. A. Albi, 1992.

[1028:1]. Bély, Lucien. *Discovering the Cathars.* France, Éditions Sud Ouest, 2001.

[1029]. Bennet, J.A. *The Divided Circle. A History of Instruments for Astronomy Navigation and Surveying.* Christie's, Oxford, Phaidon, 1987.

[1030]. de Sainte-Maure, Benoit. *Chronique des ducs de Normandie par Benoit.* Publee... par C. Fahlin, t. I. In: Bibliotheca Ekmaniana universitatis regiae Upsaliensis, Uppsala, 1951. 8-11.

[1031]. del Castillo, Conquistador Bernal Días. *The Discovery and Conquest of Mexico.* New Introduction by Hugh Thomas. New York, Da Capo Press. 1996.

[1032]. Bernard, Lewis. *The Middle East. A brief History of the Last 2000 Years.* New York, Simon & Schuster, 1997.

[1033]. *Bibliography of books and papers published in 1963 on the History of Astronomy.* Moscow: Nauka, 1964.

[1034]. Binding, Rudolf G. *Der Goldene Schrein. Bilder deutschen Meister auf Goldgrund*. Leipzig, 1934.

[1035]. Blaeu, Joan. *Novus Atlas Sinensis*, 1655. Faksimiles nach der Prachtausgabe der Herzog von der August Bibliothek Wolfenbüttel. Herausgegeben von der Stiftung Volkswagenwerk Hannover. Mit Beiträgen von Hans Kauffmann und Yorck Alexander Haase, und einem Geleitwort von Gotthard Gambke. Verlag Müller und Schindler, 1973.

[1036]. *Le Grand Atlas de Blaeu*. Le Monde au XVIIe siècle. Introduction, descriptions et choix des cartes par John Goss. Ancient conseiller-expert cartographe chez Sotheby's. Avant-propos de Peter Clark. Conservateur à la Royal Geographical Society. Adaptation Française de Irmina Spinner. Publié avec le concours de la Royal Geographical Society. Paris: Gründ, 1992. Les cartes originales de *Grand Atlas de Blaeu. Le monde au XVIIe siècle* ont été publiées par Blaeu dans son *Atlas Major* publié à Amsterdam en 1662. L'édition originale 1990 par Studio Editions sous le titre original *Blaeu's Grand Atlas of the 17th Century World*. Première édition francaise 1992 par Librairie Gründ, Paris.

[1037]. Bloch, M. *La societe féodale*. Paris, 1968.

[1038]. Blöss, Christian, and Hans-Ulrich Niemitz. *C14-Crash. (Das Ende der Illusion mit Radiokarbonmethode und Dendrochronologie datieren zu können)*. Gräfelfing, Mantis Verlag, 1997.

[1039]. Blöss, Christian, and Hans-Ulrich Niemitz. *The Self-Deception of the C14 Method and Dendrochronology*. Zeitensprünge 8 (1996) 3 361-389. Mantis Verlag, January 1997.

[1040]. Bode, J.E. *Claudius Ptolemäeus, Astronom zu Alexandrien im zweyten Jahrhundert. Beobachtung und Beschreibung der Gestirne und der Bewegung. Vergleichnungen der neuern Beobachtungen von J.E.Bode*. With a historical review and commentary. Berlin und Stettin, 1795.

[1041]. Boll, F. *Studien über Claudius Ptolemäus*. Leipzig, 1894.

[1042]. Bonhoeffer, Dietrich. *Das Geheimnis der Heiligen Nacht*. Kiefel Verlag, Wuppertal/Gütersloh, Germany, 1995.

[1043]. Bonnet, C. *Geneva in Early Christian times*. Geneva, Foundation des Clefs de Saint-Pierre, 1986.

[1044]. Boquet, F. J. C. J. *Historie de l'Astronomie*. Paris, Payot, 1925.

[1045]. Borman, Z. *Astra*. (The Pulkovo Observatory Library). 1596.

[1045:1]. [Bosch] *Tout l'œuvre peint de Jerôme Bosch*. Introduction par Max J.Friedländer. Documentation par Mia Cinotti. Paris, Flammarion, 1967.

1045:2 [Bosch] Fraenger, Wilhelm. *Hieronymus Bosch*. VEB Verlag der Kunst Dresden, 1975.

[1046]. Boszkowska, Anna. *Tryumf Luni i Wenus. Pasja Hieronima Boscha*. Wydawnictwo Literacklie, Krakow, 1980.

[1047]. Bourbon, Fabio. *Lithographien von Frederick Catherwood. Die Mayas. Auf den Spuren einer versunkenen Kultur*. White Star, Via Candido Sassone, 22/24 13100, Vercelli, Italien, 1999. Deutschsprachige Ausgabe: Karl Mükker Verlag, Danziger Strasse 6, 91052 Erlangen.

[1048]. Brahe, T. *Tychonis Brahe Dani Opera omnia.* Ed. J. L. E. Dreyer. 15 Volumes. Copenhagen, 1913-1929.

[1049]. Brahe, T. *Equitis Dani Astronomorum Coryhaei Vita.* Authore Petro Gassendo. Regio ex Typographia Adriani Vlac. MDCLV.

[1049:1]. Lehane, Brendan (texte), Richard Novitz (photographies). *Irlande.* London, Flint River, 1997; Paris, Booking Int'l, 1997.

[1050]. Brenon, Anne. *Le vrai visage du Catharisme.* Toulouse, Ed. Loubatières, 1988.

[1050:1]. *British Museum. A Guide to the First, Second and Third Egyptian Rooms. Predynastic Human Remains, Mummies, Wooden Sarcophagi, Coffins and Cartonnage Mummy Cases, Chests and Coffers, and other Objects connected with the Funerary Rites of the Ancient Egyptians.* Third Edition, Revised and Enlarged. With 3 coloured and 32 half-tone plates. British Museum, 1924.

[1050:2]. *British Museum. A Guide to the Fourth, Fifth and Sixth Egyptian Rooms and the Coptic Room. A series of Collections of Small Egyptian Antiquities, which illustrate the Manners and Customs, the Arts and Crafts, the Religion and Literature, and the Funeral Rites and Ceremonies of the Ancient Egyptians and their Descendants, the Copts, from about B.C. 4500 to A.D. 1000.* With 7 plates and 157 illustrations in the text. British Museum, 1922.

[1050:3]. *British Museum. A Guide to the Egyptian Collections in the British Museum.* With 53 plates and 180 illustrations in the text. British Museum, 1909.

[1051]. Brodsky, B. E., and B. S. Darkhovsky. *Nonparametric Methods in Change-Point Problems.* The Netherlands, Kluwer Academic Publishers, 1993.

[1051:1]. Brodrick, M., and A. A. Morton. *A Concise Dictionary of Egyptian Archaeology. A handbook for students and travellers.* London, 1902. 2nd edition 1923, 3rd edition 1924. Reprint: Chicago, Aries, 1980.

[1052]. Brooke, Christopher. *From Alfred to Henry III. 871-1272.* The Norton Library History of England. New York, London, W. W. Norton & Company, 1961, 1968, 1969.

[1053]. Broughton, T. R. S. *The Magistrates of the Roman Republic.* Volumes 1, 2. London, 1951-1960.

[1053:1]. [Bruegel] Gerhard W. Menzel. *Pieter Bruegel der Ältere.* Leipzig, VEB E. A. Seemann, Buch- und Kunstverlag, 1966; 2 Auflage, 1974.

[1053:2]. Bovi, Arturo. *Bruegel. The life and work of the artist illustrated with 80 colour plates.* A Dolphin Art Book. London, Thames and Hudson, 1971. Reprinted 1974.

[1054]. Brugsch, H. *Recueil de Monuments Egyptiens, dessinés sur lieux.* Leipzig, 1862-1865.

[1055]. Buck, C. E., W. G. Gavanagh, and C. D. Litton. *Bayesian Approach to Interpreting Archaeological Data.* Series: Statistics in Practice. John Wiley & Sons, 1996.

[1056]. Bustos, Gerardo. *Yucatan and its Archaeological Sites.* Mexico, Monclem; Florence, Casa Editrice Bonechi, 1992.

[1057]. Cagnat, R. *Cours d'épigraphie latine*. 4e éd. Paris, 1914.

[1058]. Campbell, Tony. *Early Maps*. New York, Abbeville Press Publishers, 1981.

[1059]. Campos, José Guerra, and Jesús Precedo Lafuente. *Guide to the Cathedral of Santiago de Compostela*. Spain, Aldeasa, División Palacios y Museos, 1993.

[1060]. Cantacuzeny, Ioannis. *Opera Omnia. Patrologiae curcus completus. Series graeca*. T. CLIII, CLIV. J.-P. Migne, 1866.

[1060:1]. *Carcassonne (The City of Carcassonne. Cathar Castles)*. Production Leconte. Editions Estel-Blois. B. P. 45 - 41260 La Chaussée-Saint-Victor. Printed in E.E.C.

[1060:2]. *Cathares. Les ombres de l'Histoire. Carcassone: Histoire d'une Cité unique*. In: Pyrénées (Magazine). Une publication de Milan Presse. 2001. Éditions Milan et les auteurs. Ariège Pyrenées. (A special edition of the magazine dedicated to Cathar history).

[1061]. *Cathedral and Metropolitan Church of St. Stephen in Vienna*. Germany, Verlag Schnell & Steiner Regensburg, 1995.

[1061:1]. *Cathédrale de l'Annonciation. Le Kremlin de Moscou*. Les Musées d'Etat du Kremlin de Moscou, 1990.

[1062]. Cauville, S. *Le Zodiaque d'Osiris*. Peeters, Uitgeverij Peeters, Bondgenotenlaan 153, B-3000 Leuven.

[1062:1]. Cauville, S. *Dendara. Les chapelles osiriennes*. (5 vols.) Institut francais d'archeologie orientale du Caire, 1977.

[1063]. Chabas, F. *Mélanges égyptologiques. Deuxième série*. Ägyptolog. Zeitschrift. 1868. S. 49.

[1064]. Champfleury. *Historie de la Caricature au Moyen Age*. Paris, 1867-1871.

[1064:0]. Chapront-Touze, M., and J. Chapront. Lunar ephemere des computation software. (Program ELP2000-85, version 1.0, Fortran 77). Bureau des Longitudes, URA 707. 1988. Available online.

[1064:1]. *Château de Chillon*. Booklet. Château de Chillon, Veytaux (www.chillon.ch), 2000.

[1065]. Childress, David Hatcher. *Lost Cities of Atlantis, Ancient Europe & the Mediterranean*. Stelle, Illinois 60919 USA, Adventures Unlimited Press, 1996.

[1066]. Chirikov, B. V., and V. V. Vecheslavov. *Chaotic dynamics of comet Halley*. Astronomy and Astrophysics, Volume 221, No. 1 (1989): 146-154.

[1067]. Chmelarz, Eduard. *Die Ehrepforte des Kaisers Maximilian I*. Unterscheidheim 1972. Verlag Walter Uhl. Jahrbuch der Kunsthistorischen Sammlungen des Allerhöchsten Kaiserhauses. Herausgegeben unter Leitung des Oberstakämmerers seiner Kaiserlichen und Königlichen Apostolischen Majestät. Ferdinand Grafen zu Trauttmansdorff-Weinsberg vom K. K. Oberstkämmerer-Amte. Vierter Band. Mit 39 Kupfertafeln in Heliogravure und Radierung, 100 Holzschnittafeln und 56 Text-Illustrationen in Heliogravure, Holzschnitt und Zinkographie. Als Beilage: 16 Holzschnitte der Ehrenpforte des Kaisers Maximilian I. Wien, Druck und Verlag von Adolf Holzhausen, K. K. Hofbuchdrucker, 1886.

[1068]. Stubbs, W., ed. *Chronica magistri Rogeri de Houedone*. RS, N 51, Volume II. London, 1869, page 236. English translation: *The Annals of Roger de Hoveden, comprising the history of England and of other countries of Europe from A.D. 732 to A.D. 1201*. Tr. H. T. Riley, Volumes 1-2. London, Bohn's Antiquarian Library, 1853.

[1069]. Pestman, P.W. *Chronologie égyptienne d'après les textes démotiques*. Papyrologia Lugduno-Batava edidit Institutum Papyrologicum Universitatis Lugduno-Batavae Moderantibus M.David et B. A. von Groningen. Volume 15. Lugdunum Batavorum, 1967.

[1070]. Cipolla, Carlo M. *Money, Prices and Civilization in the Mediterranean World. 5-17 century*. Princeton University Press, 1956.

[1071]. *Claudii Ptolemaei Magnae Constructionis, id est perfectae coelestium motuum pertractationis. Lib. XIII. Theonis Alexanrini in eosdem Commentariorum Libri XI*; Basileal apud Ioannem Waledrum. C. priv. Caes. ad Quinquennium. 1538.

[1072]. *Claudii Ptolemaei Phelusiensis Alexandrini*. Anno Salutis, 1528.

[1073]. *Claudii Ptolemaei Pelusiensis Alexandrini omnia quac extant opera*. 1551.

[1074]. Clemens, Jöcle. *Speyer Cathedral*. Regensburg, Scgnell & Steiner, 1997.

[1075]. Clinton, H.F. *Fasti Hellenici, a Civil and Literary Chronology from the Earliest Times to the Death of Augustus*. Oxford, 1830-1841.

[1076]. Copernici, N. *Revolutionibus Orbium Caelestium*. Lib. VI. Ed. by G. Loachimi. Thoruni, 1873.

[1077]. Corbinianus. *Firmamentum Firmianum*. (Pulkovo Observatory Library). 1731.

[1078]. Cordier, H. *Marco Polo and His Book*. Introductory notices. In: *The Travels of Marco Polo*. The complete Yule-Cordier. Volumes 1 and 2. New York, Dover, 1993.

[1078:1]. Wytfliet, Cornelius. *Descriptionis Ptolemaicae Augmentum sive Occidentis notitia brevis commentario*. Louvain 1597. With an introduction by R. A. Skelton. Theatrvm Orbis Terrarvm. A Series of Atlases in Facsimile. 1st Series, Vol. V. Amsterdam, N. Israel, Meridian, 1964.

[1079]. Costard, G. *The History of Astronomy with its Application to Geography, History and Chronology*. London, J. Lister, 1967.

[1080]. Harmon, Craig. *The Natural Distribution of Radiocarbon and the Exchange Time of Carbon Dioxides between Atmosphere and Sea*. Volume 9. Tellus. 1957. 1-17.

[1081]. Harmon, Craig. *Carbon-13 in Plants and the Relationships between Carbon-13 and Carbon-14 Variations in Nature*. J. Geol., 62 (1954): 115-149.

[1081:1]. El Mahdy, Christine. *Mummies, Myths and Magic in Ancient Egypt*. Thames and Hudson, 1989.

[1082]. Crowe, C. *Carbon-14 activity during the past 5000 years*. Nature, Volume 182 (1958): 470.

[1083]. Danit Hadary-Salomon, ed. *2000 Years of Pilgrimage to the Holy Land*. Israel, AC Alfa Communication Ltd., 1999.

[1084]. *Das Münster zu Bonn. The Bonn Minster.* Former Collegiate Church of SS. Cassius and Florentius. Series: Kleine Kunstfürer. Achnell, Art Guide No. 593 (of 1954). Second English edition 1997. Regensburg, Germany, Verlag Schnell & Steiner GmbH Regensburg, 1997.

[1085]. David, Daniel. *Let There be Light. William Tyndale and the Making of the English Bible.* A British Library Exhibition at The Huntington. 19 November, 1996 – 7 February, 1997. London, The British Library, 1994.

[1086]. Davidovits, Joseph. *Alchemy and Pyramids. The Book of Stone.* Vol. 1. France-USA, Geopolymer Institute, 1983.

[1087]. Davidovits, Joseph. *Alchemy and Pyramids.* Translated from French by A. C. James and J. James. Rev. ed. *Que le Khnoum protège Khéops constructeur de pyramide.* Saint Quentin, France, 1983; Miami Shores, Fla., USA, Institute for Applied Archaeological Science, Barry University, 1984.

[1088]. Davidovits, Joseph. *Amenhotep, Joseph and Solomon.* 1st ed. Miami Shores, Fla., U.S.A., Geopolymer Institute, Institute for Applied Archaeological Science, Barry University, 1984.

[1089]. Davidovits, Joseph. *Que le dieu Khnoum protège Khéops constructeur de pyramide: histoire de la civilisation Égyptienne de 3500 é 1500 ans avant J.-C.* Saint-Quentin, 1978.

[1090]. Davidovits, Joseph. *Le calcaire des pierres des Grandes Pyramides d'Égypte serait un béton géopolyméré vieux de 4.600 ans.* Résumé des cours-conférences tenus en 1983 et 1984. *Revue des Questions Scientifiques,* Volume 156(2) (1986): 199-225.

[1091]. Davidovits, Joseph. *No more than 1,400 workers to build the Pyramid of Cheops with manmade stone.* 3rd Int. Congress of Egyptologists. Toronto, Canada: paper AA-126, publié dans Appendix 3 de Davidovits, 1983.

[1092]. Davidovits, Joseph, and Margie Morris. *The Pyramids: an Enigma Solved.* New York, Hippocrene Books, 1988. New York, Dorset Press, 1989, 1990.

[1093]. Davidovits J., J. Thodez, and Gaber M Hisham. *Pyramids of Egypt Made of Man-Made Stone, Myth or Fact?* Symposium on Archeometry 1984, Smithsonian Institution, abstract 26-27. Washington, D.C., USA, 1984.

[1094]. Davies, Nartin. *The Gutenberg Bible.* London, The British Library, 1996.

[1095]. Degrassi, A. *Fasti Capitolini.* 1954; I Fasti consolari dell'impero romano, 1952.

[1096]. Delambre, J. B. *Histoire de l'Astronomie.* 2 Volumes. Paris, 1817.

[1097]. Delambre, J. *Histoire de l'Astronomie moderne.* 2 Volumes. Paris, 1821.

[1098]. *Della origine et ruccessi degli Slavi, oratione di M. V. Pribevo, Dalmatino da Lesena, etc. et hora tradotta della lingua Latina nell'Italiana da Bellisario Malaspalli, da Spalato.* Venetia, 1595.

[1099]. *Der Marienschrein im Dom zu Aachen.* Die Publikation dieses Sonderheftes erfolgt durch die Grünenthal GmbH, Aachen. Domkapitel, 2000.

[1100]. *Description de l'Égypte. Publiée sous les ordes de Napoléon de Bonaparte. Description de l'Égypte ou recueil des observations et des recherches qui ont été faites en Égypte pendant l'expédition de l'Armée française publié sous les ordes de Napoléon Bonaparte.* Bibliothèque de l'Image. Inter-Livres. 1995.

[1101]. Desroches-Noblecourt, Christiane. *Life and Death of Pharaoh Tutankhamen.* London, Penguin Books, 1963.

[1101:1]. *Deutschland. Germany. Allemagne. Germania.* Euro Map. Halwag AG, Bern, Printed in Switzerland-Germany 4-26 AK.

[1102]. Dheily, J. *Dictionaire Biblique.* Ed. Desclec. Tournai, 1964. 193.

[1103]. *Dialogus Historicus Palladii episcopi Helenopolis cum Theodoro.* Patrologiae Cursus Completus. Patrologiae Graecae. T. LVII. J.-P. Migne, 1858.

[1104]. *Die Bibel. Oder die Ganze Heilige Schrift des Alten and Neuen Testaments.* Nach der Überzetzung Martin Luthers. Württembergische Bibelanstalt, Stuttgart. 1967.

1105. *Die Weihnachtsgeschichte. Nacherzählt in Bildern aus der Biblioteca Apostolica Vaticana.* Stuttgart, Zürich, Belser Verlag, 1993.

[1106]. *Dom Betrachtung.* Die Hochgräber im Kölner Dom. 4. Herausgeber, Dompfarramt – Dompfarrer Rolf Breitenbruch, Domkloster 3, 50667, Köln.

[1107]. Douais, C. *L'Inquisition, ses origines, sa procédure.* Paris, 1906.

[1108]. Dreyer, J. L. E. *On the Origin of Ptolemy's Catalogue of Stars.* Monthly Notices of the Royal Astronomical Society, No. 77 (1917): 528-539.

[1109]. Dreyer, J. L. E. *On the Origin of Ptolemy's Catalogue of Stars.* Second Paper. Monthly Notices of the Royal Astronomical Society, No. 78 (1918): 343-349.

[1110]. Duden. *Ethymologie: Herkunfswörterbuch der deutschen Sprache.* Mannheim, Wien; Dudenverlag, Zürich, 1989.

[1111]. Duncan, A.J. *Quality Control and Industrial Statistics.* NY, Irwin, 1974.

[1112]. Dupont-Sommer, A. *Les écrits essentiens decouverts près de la Mer Morte.* Paris, 1957.

[1113]. Dupuis, C. *The Origin of All Religious Worship.* New Orleans, 1872.

[1114]. Duvernoy, Jean. *Le catharisme.* Volume I: *La religion des Cathares.* Volume II: *Histoire des Cathares.* Toulouse, Private, 1976 and 1979. Re-published 1986.

[1115]. Duvernoy, Jean, Paul Labal, Robert Lafont, Philippe Martell, and Michel Roquebert. *Les Cathares en Occitanie.* Fayard, 1981.

[1116]. Van Ermen, Eduard. *The United States in Old Maps and Prints.* Wilmington USA, Atomium Books, 1990.

[1116:1]. Égypte. Large album with photographs. Paris, Molière, Art Image, 1998.

[1117]. Eichler, Anja-Franziska. *Albrecht Dürer. 1471-1528.* Cologne, Könemann Verlagsgesellschaft GmbH, 1999.

[1118]. *Encyclopaedia Britannica; or, a Dictionary of Arts and Sciences, compiled upon a new Plan. In which the different Sciences and Arts are digested into distinct Treatises or Systems; and the various Technical Terms, etc. are explained as they occur in the order of the Alphabet. Illustrated with one hundred and sixty copperplates. By a Society of Gentlemen in Scotland. In 3 volumes.* Edinburgh, A. Bell and C. Macfarquhar, 1771.

[1118:1]. *Encyclopaedia Britannica.* On-line version, 2001.

[1119]. Evans, James. *On the Origin of the Ptolemaic Star Catalogue*. Part 1. *Journal for the History of Astronomy*, Volume 18, Part 3, No. 54 (August 1987): 155-172.

[1120]. Evans, James. *On the Origin of the Ptolemaic Star Catalogue*. Part 2. *Journal for the History of Astronomy*, Volume 18, Part 4, No. 55 (November 1987): 235-277.

[1121]. Liebermann, F., and R. Pauli, Eds. *Ex Annalibus Melrosensibus*. MGH SS, T.XXVII. Hannoverae, 1885. 439.

[1121:1]. Winship, Betsy, and Sheila Stoneham, eds. *Explosives and Rock Blasting*. Field Technical Operations. Atlas Rowder Company. Dallas, Texas, Marple Press, 1987.

[1122]. Fatih, Cimok. *Hagia Sophia*. Istanbul, A turizm yayinlari, 1995.

[1123]. Fatih, Cimok. *Hagia Sophia*. Istanbul, A turizm yayinlari, 1985.

[1124]. Fergusson, G. I. *Reduction of Atmospheric Radiocarbon Concentration by Fossil Fuel Carbon Dioxide and the Mean Life of Carbon Dioxide in the Atmosphere*. London, Proc. Royal Soc., 243 A, pages 561-574. 1958.

[1125]. Filarete, Antonio Averlino. *Tractat über die Baukunst*. Vienna, 1890.

[1126]. Fischer, Fr. *Thucydidus reliquiae in papyris et membranis aigiptiacis servatae*. Lipsiae, 1913.

[1127]. Verlag, Dr. Ludwig Reichert. *Flüsse im Herzen Europas. Rhein-Elbe-Donau*. Kartenabteilung der Staatsbibliothek zu Berlin. Preussischer Kulturbesitz. Wiesbaden, 1993.

[1128]. Fomenko, A.T. *The Jump of the Second Derivative of the Moon's Elongation. Celestial Mechanics*, Volume 29 (1981): 33-40.

[1129]. Fomenko, A. T. *Some New Empirico-Statistical Methods of Dating and the Analysis of Present Global Chronology*. The British Library. Department of Printed Books. Cup. 918/87. 1981.

[1130]. Fomenko, A.T. *New Empirico-Statistical Dating Methods and Statistics of Certain Astronomical Data*. The theses of the First International Congress of the International Bernoulli Society for Mathematical Statistics and Probability Theory. Volume 2. Moscow, Nauka, 1986. 892.

[1131]. Fomenko, A.T. *Duplicates in Mixed Sequences and a Frequency Duplication Principle. Methods and Applications*. Probability theory and mathematical statistics. Proceeding of the 4th Vilnius Conference (24-29 June 1985). Volume 16. Utrecht, Netherlands, VNU Science, 1987. 439-465.

[1132]. Fomenko, A.T. *Empirico-Statistical Methods in Ordering Narrative Texts. International Statistical Review*, Volume 566, No. 3 (1988): 279-301.

[1133]. Fomenko, A. T., V. V. Kalashnikov, and G.V. Nosovskiy. *When was Ptolemy's Star Catalogue in "Almagest" Compiled in Reality?* Preprint. No. 1989-04, ISSN 0347-2809. Dept. of Math., Chalmers Univ. of Technology, The University of Goteborg. Sweden.

[1134]. Fomenko, A. T., V. V. Kalashnikov, and G.V. Nosovskiy. *When was Ptolemy's Star Catalogue in "Almagest" Compiled in Reality? Statistical Analysis*. Acta Applicandae Mathematical. Volume 17. 1989. 203-229.

[1135]. Fomenko, A. T. *Mathematical Statistics and Problems of Ancient Chronology. A New Approach.* Acta Applicandae Mathematical. Volume 17. 1989. 231-256.

[1136]. Fomenko, A. T., Kalashnikov V. V., Nosovskiy G. V. *Geometrical and Statistical Methods of Analysis of Star Configurations. Dating Ptolemy's Almagest.* USA, CRC Press, 1993.

[1137]. Fomenko, A. T. *Empirico-Statistical Analysis of Narrative Material and its Applications to Historical Dating.* Volume 1: *The Development of the Statistical Tools.* Volume 2: *The Analysis of Ancient and Medieval Records.* The Netherlands, Kluwer Academic Publishers, 1994.

[1138]. Fomenko, A. T., V. V. Kalashnikov, and G.V. Nosovskiy. *The dating of Ptolemy's Almagest based on the coverings of the stars and on lunar eclipses.* Acta Applicandae Mathematicae. Volume 29. 1992. 281-298.

[1139]. Fomenko, A. T., V. V. Kalashnikov, and G.V. Nosovskiy. *Statistical analysis and dating of the observations on which Ptolemy's "Almagest" star catalogue is based.* In: *Probability theory and mathematical statistics.* Proc. of the Fifth Vilnius Conference. Volume 1. Moklas, Vilnius, Lithuania. VSP, Utrecht, The Netherlands, 1990. 360-374.

[1140]. Fomenko, A. T., and S. T. Rachev. *Volume Functions of Historical Texts and the Amplitude Correlation Principle.* Computers and the Humanities. Vol. 24. 1990. 187-206.

[1141]. Manuel, Frank E. *Isaac Newton, the Historian.* Cambridge, Massachusetts, The Belknap Press, 1963.

[1142]. Franke, Peter Robert, and Ilse Paar. *Die Antiken Münzen der Sammlung Heynen. Katalog mit Historischen Erläuterungen.* Landschaftsmuseum Krefeld-Burglinn. Rheinland-Verlag, Köln, in Kommission bei Rudolf Habelt Verlag, Bonn. 1976.

[1143]. de Landa, Friar Diego. *Yucatan before and after the Conquest.* Translated with notes by William Gates. San Fernando, Atrio de San Francisco, 1993.

[1144]. Fricke, W., and A. Koff *FK4.* No.10. Heidelberg, Veröf. Astr. Inst., 1963.

[1145]. Fuchs, W. *Nach allen Regeln der Kunst. Diagnosen über Literatur, Musik, bildende Kunst. Die Werke, ihre Autoren und Schöpfer.* Stuttgart, Deutsche Verlags-Anstalt., 1968.

[1146]. Fuchs, W. *Mathematical Theory of Word-Formation.* London, 1955.

[1147]. Fulton, Alexander. *Scotland and her Tartans. The Romantic Heritage of the Scottish Clans and Families.* Colour Library Books Ltd., Sandbach, Cheshire; Godalming, Surrey, 1991.

[1148]. Fussbroich, Helmut. *St. Maria Lyskirchen in Köln.* Rheinische Kunststätten. Heft 60. Rheinischer Verein für Denkmalpflege und Landschaftsschutz. Köln, Neusser Druckerei und Verlag GmbH, 1992.

[1149]. Gabovitsch, Eugen. *Newton als geistiger Vater der Chronologiekritik und Geschishtsrekonstruktion (neben Hardoin).* Bemerkungen zum Artikel von Uwe Topper in Synesis Nr. 4/1999. Efodon-Synesis (Germany) Nov/Dez. 1999, Nr. 6/1999, S. 29-33.

[1150]. Gabovitsch. Eugen. *Die Grosse Mauer als ein Mythos: Die Errichtungs-geschichte der Chinesischen Mauer und ihre Mythologisierung.* Efodon-Synesis (Germany), Nov/Dez. 1999, Nr.6/1999, S. 9-21.

[1151]. Gadol, J. *Leon Battista Alberti.* Chicago, London, 1969.

[1152]. Gassendi. *Nicolai Coppernici vita.* A supplement to the edition titled *Tychonis Brahei, equitis Mani, astronomorum copyrhaei vita.* XDCLV.

[1152:1]. El Gayar, El Sayed, and M. P. Jones. *Metallurgical Investigation of the Iron plate found in 1837 in the Great Pyramid at Gizeh, Egypt.* In: *Journal of the Historical Metallurgy Society,* Volume 1 (1989): 75-83.

[1153]. Gingerich, O. *Ptolemy Revisited: A Reply to R. R. Newton.* Quarterly *Journal of the Royal Astronomical Society,* No.22 (1981): 40-44.

[1154]. Ginzel, F. K. *Spezieller Kanon der Sonnen- und Mondfinsternisse für das Ländergebiet der klassischen Altertumswissenschaften und den Zeitraum von 900 vor Chr. bis 600 nach Chr.* Berlin, Mayer & Müller, 1899.

[1155]. Ginzel, F.K. *Handbuch der Mathematischen und Technischen Chronologie.* Bd. I-III. Leipzig, 1906, 1911, 1914.

[1156]. Ginzel, F. K., and A. Wilkens. *Theorie der Finsternisse.* Encykl. der Wissenschaftten. Bd. VI, 2. S. 335. 1908.

[1157]. Girou, Jean. *Simon de Monfort.* Paris: La Colombe, 1953.

[1158]. Della Fina, Giuseppe M., *Luoghi e tempi Etruschi schede di ricerca.* Firenze: Fatatrac, 1989.

[1159]. Gladwin, H. *Men out of Asia.* NY, 1949.

[1160]. Goss, John. *Kartenkunst: Die Geschichte der Kartographie.* Deutsche Asgabe: Braunschweig, Georg Westermann Verlag, 1994. German translation of the English edition: Goss, John. *The Mapmaker's Art. A History of Cartography.* London, Studio Editions Ltd.

[1160:1]. Granier, J., and S. Gagnière. *Avignon. (The city at Sunset. The Popes' Palace. The Saint Benezet bridge).* English edition. Éditions du Boumian, Monaco.

[1161]. Grasshoff, Gerd. *The History of Ptolemy's Star Catalogue.* New York, Springer Verlag, 1990.

[1162]. Grienberger, C. *Catalogus Veteres affixarum longitudiues et latitudines cum novis conferens.* Romae apud B. Zannetum, 1612. (The Pulkovo Observatory Library.)

[1163]. Grierson, Philip. *Coinage and Money in Byzantine Empire.* Spoleto, 1961.

[1164]. Grierson, Philip. *Monnaies du Moyen Âge.* Fribourg, 1976.

[1165]. Grimme, Ernst Günther. *Der Dom zu Aachen. Architektur und Ausstattung.* Aachen, Einhard-Verlag, 1994.

[1166]. Grollenberg, L. N. *Atlas of the Bible.* NY, 1956.

[1167]. Gualberto, Zapata Alonzo. *An Overview of the Mayan World. With a Synthesis of the Olmec, Totonac Zapotec, Mixtec, Teotihuacan, Toltec and Aztec Civilizations.* Mexico, Merida, 1993.

[1167:1]. *Guide to Edo-Tokyo Museum* (English edition). Edited by Edo-Tokyo Museum. Japan Broadcast Publishing Co., Ltd. Printed in Japan by Toppan Printing Co., Ltd.

[1168]. *Gutenberg-Bibel. Geschichtliche Bücher des Alten Testaments.* Die biblio-
philen Taschenbücher. Dortmund, Harenberg Kommunikation, 1977.

[1169]. *Gutenberg Bibel (1452-1455).* Reprinted 1968 by Verlag Konrad Köbl.
8022 Grünwald bei München, Huberttusstrasse 13. Firma Elektra, Reprograf-
ischer Betrieb, Kjeld Höjring, Niedernhausen/Ts. Printed in Germany.

[1170]. Schneider, Dr. Cornelia. *Gutenberg-Dokumentation. Information Mittelalter. Das Buch vor Gutenberg (I).* Gutenberg-Museum Mainz, 1990.

[1171]. Schneider, Dr. Cornelia. *Gutenberg-Dokumentation. Information Mittelalter. Das Buch vor Gutenberg (II).* Gutenberg-Museum Mainz, 1990.

[1172]. *Haack Geographisch-Kartographischer Kalender.* Germany, Haack Gotha,
VEB Hermann Haack Geographisch-Kartographische Anstalt Gotha, 1983.

[1172:1]. *Haack Geographisch-Kartographischer Kalender.* Germany, Haack Gotha,
VEB Hermann Haack Geographisch-Kartographische Anstalt Gotha, 1988.

[1173]. Hagek, W. *Kronyka Czeska.* Prague, 1541.

[1174]. Hans, Peter. *Der Dom zu Köln. 1248-1948.* Düsseldorf, Verlag L.
Schwann, 1948.

[1175]. Hansen, P. *Ecliptische Tafeln für die Konjunktionen des Mondes und der
Sonne.* Leipzig, 1857.

[1176]. Hansen, P. *Theorie der Sonnenfinsternisse und verwandten Erscheinun-
gen.* Leipzig, 1859.

[1177]. Harley, J. B., and David Woodward. *The History of Cartography. Volume
1. Cartography in Prehistoric, Ancient and Medieval Europe and the Mediterranean.* Chicago & London, The University of Chicago Press, 1987.

[1178]. Harvey, Arden. *Who Owns Our Past? National Geographic,* Volume 175,
No.3 (March 1989): 376-393.

[1179]. Hauvette, A. *Herodote historien des guerres midiques.* Paris, 1894.

[1180]. Haveta, E. *La modernité des prophètes.* Paris, 1891.

[1181]. Hazirlayan, H. H. Aliy Yalcin (Hz. Yusa Camii Imam-Hatibi). *Hazreti
Yusa (Aleyhisselam).* Istanbul. Brochure written by the prior of the temple at
the grave of St. Iusha at the outskirts of Istanbul.

[1182]. Hearnshaw, J .B., and D. Khan. *An Analysis of the Magnitude Data in Ptolemy's Almagest.* Southern Stars. Journal of the Royal Astronomical Society of
New Zealand (Wellington), Volume 36, Nos. 5-6 (December 1955): 169-177.

[1183]. Heath, T. L. *Aristarchus of Samos, the Ancient Copernicus; a History of
Greek Astronomy to Aristarchus, together with Aristarchus' Treatise on the Sizes
and Distances of the Sun and Moon.* Oxford, Clarendon Press, 1913.

[1184]. Heine-Geldern, R., and G.Ekholm. *Significant parallels in the symbolic
arts of Southern Asia and Middle America.* In: *Selected Papers of the 29th
International Congress of Americanists,* Volume 1. Chicago, 1951. 306.

[1185]. Heinsohn, Gunnar. *Assyrerkönige gleich Perserherrscher! (Die Assyrien-
funde bestätigen das Achämenidenreach).* Gräfelfing, Mantis Verlag, 1996.

[1186]. Heinsohn, Gunnar, and Heribert Illig. *Wann lebten die Pharaonen?
(Archäologische and technologische Grundlagen für eine Neuschreibung der
Geschichte Ägyptens and der übrigen Welt.)* Gräfelfing, Mantis Verlag, 1997.

[1187]. Heintze, C. *Objects rituels, croyances et dieux de la Chine antique et de l'Amérique.* Antwerpen, 1936.

[1188]. Heis. *Die Finsternisse während des pelop. Krieges.* Progr. d. Fried. Wilh. Gimn. Köln, 1834.

[1189]. Herbert, Ewe. *Abbild oder Phantasie? Schiffe auf historischen Karten.* Rostock, VEB Hinstorff Verlag, 1978.

[1190]. [Herodotus]. *The History of Herodotus.* London, 1858.

[1191]. Hignett, C. *Xerxes Invasion of Greece.* Oxford, 1963.

[1192]. Hincks, E. *The Egyptian Dynasties of Manetho.* The Journal of Sacred Literature. London, 1864.

[1193]. Hipparchus. *Hipparchi in Arati et Eudoxi Phenomena Commentarium.* Ed. and German trans. C. Manitius. Leipzig, 1894.

[1194]. *Historiae bysantinae scriptores post Theophanem. Patrologiae cursus completus. Series graeca posterior.* T.CIX. J.-P. Migne, 1863.

[1195]. Hochart. *De l'authenticité des Annales et des Histoires de Tacite.* Paris, 1890.

[1196]. Hodge, K.C., and G.W.A. Newton. *Radiocarbon Dating. Manchester Museum Mummy Project. Multidisciplinary Research on Ancient Egyptian Mummified Remains.* Edited by A. Rosalie David. Published by Manchester Museum. Manchester, England, 1979. 137-147.

[1197]. Hofflit, D. *The Bright Star Catalogue.* New Haven Connecticut, USA, Yale Univ. Obs., 1982.

[1198]. Hoffman. *Sämtliche bei griechishen und lateinschen Schriftstellern des Altertums erwähnte Sonnen- und Mondfinsternisse.* Trieste, 1885.

[1199]. Horster, M. *Brunelleschi und Alberti in ihrer Stellung zur römischen Antike.* Florence, 1973.

[1200]. Horus. *The Enigma Surrounding the Sphinx.* An Egyptian Magazine, April/June 1999.

[1201]. Hoster, Joseph. *Der Dom zu Köln.* Köln, Greven Verlag, 1965.

[1202]. Huddleston, L.E. *Origin of the American Indian. European Concepts, 1492-1729.* Austin, 1967.

[1203]. Hütt, Wolfgang. Altdorfer. *Maler und Werk.* Eine Kunstheftreihe aus dem VEB Verlag der Kunst. Dresden, 1976.

[1204]. Hugot, Leo. *Aachen Cathedral.* Aachen, Germany, Einhard Verlag, 1988.

[1205]. Ideler, L. *Handbuch der mathematischen und technischen Chronologie.* Band 1-2. Berlin, 1825-1826.

[1206]. Ilhan Aksit. *The Topkapi Palace.* Istanbul, Aksit Kultur Turism Sanat Ajans Ltd., 1995.

[1207]. Ilhan Aksit. *The Museum of Chora. Mosaics and Frescoes.* Istanbul, Aksit Kultur Turism Sanat Ajans Ltd., 1995.

[1208]. Illig, Heribert. *Hat Karl der Große je gelebt? (Bauten, Funde und Schriften im Widerstreit).* Gräfelfing, Mantis Verlag, 1996.

[1208:1]. *Irish Dictionary.* Collins Gem. English-Irish. Irish-English. Seamus Mac Mathuna and O Corrain (University of Ulster). Harper Collins, 1999.

[1209]. Isidori Junioris. *Hispalensis episcopi: De responsione mundi.* 1472. (The Pulkovo Observatory Library.)

[1210]. Islam. *Kunst und Architektur.* Herausgegeben von Markus Hattstein und Peter Delis. Köln, Könemann, 2000.

[1211]. *Istanbul and the Marmara Region. A Tale of two Continents.* Turkey, The Ministry of Tourism, Istanbul, 1994.

[1212]. Janin, R. *Constantinople Byzantine.* Paris, 1950.

[1213]. Jirku, A. (Jurku, A.) *Ausgrabungen in Palästina-Syrien.* Halle, 1956.

[1214]. Johnson, Edwin. *The Rise of English Culture.* Williams and Norgate. London-New York, Putnam, 1904.

[1215]. Johnson, Edwin. *The Rise of Christendom.* London, Kegan Paul, Trench, Trubner, & Co. Ltd., 1890.

[1215:1]. Johnson, Paul. *The civilization of Ancient Egypt.* London, Seven Dials, Cassel & Co., 2000.

[1216]. Joubert, Pierre. *L'Heraldique. Les guides practiques.* Editions Ouest-France, 1984.

[1217]. Keegan, John. *A History of Warfare.* New York, Vintage Books, 1994.

[1218]. *Katalog dawnych map Rzeczypospolitej Polskiej w kolekcji Emeryka Hutten Czapskiego i w innych zbiorach.* Wroclaw, Warszawa, Krakow, Gdansk: Zaklad Narodowy im. Ossolinskich, Wyd. Polskiej Akademii Nauk. Instytut Geografii i Przestrzennego Zagospodarowania. Ossolineum. N.1. Mapy XV-XVI wieku. 1978.

[1219]. Keller, W. *Und die Bibel hat doch Recht.* Düsseldorf, 1958.

[1220]. Kenyon, K. M. *Digging in Jericho.* London, 1957.

[1221]. *Kings & Queens of England. A set of picture cards.* Great Britain, Fax Pax Ltd., 1988.

[1222]. Kinoshita, H. *Formulas for Precession.* Smithsonian Inst. Astrophys. Observatory. Cambridge, Massachussets, 1975.

[1223]. Sale, Kirkpatrick. *The Conquest of Paradise. Christopher Columbus and the Columbian Legacy.* New York, Penguin Books, 1990.

[1224]. Knobel, E.B. *British School of Archaeology in Egypt and Egyptian Research Account.* London, 1908.

[1225]. Knobel, E.B. *The Chronology of Star Catalogues.* Memoirs of the Royal Astronomical Society. No.43 (1877): 1-74.

[1226]. Kobold, H. *Finsternisse. Handwörterbuch der Astronomie.* Herausg. von W. Valentiner. Bd. I. Breslau, 1897.

[1227]. Koeva, Margarita. *Rila Monastery.* Sofia, Borina, 1995.

[1228]. *Köln in historischen Stadtplänen. Die Entwicklung der Stadt seit dem XVI Jahrhundert.* Berlin, Argon, 1995.

[1229]. *Kostbarkeiten der Buchkunst. Illuminationen klassischer Werke von Archimedes bis Vergil.* Herausgegeben von Giovanni Morello. Stuttgart-Zürich, Belser Verlag, 1997.

[1230]. Krishnaiah, P. and B. Miao. *Review about Estimation of Change-Points.* In: *Handbook of Statistics,* Volume 7. 1988. 375-402.

[1231]. *Krönungen, Könige in Aachen. Geschichte und Mythos.* Vom 12. Juni bis 3.Oktober 2000 in Rathaus, Domschatzkammer und Dom, Aachen. (Annette Fusenig M. A. und Barbara Jacobs M. A.). From 12th of June to 3rd October 2000 in Town Hall, Cathedral Treasury and Cathedral, Aachen. Kurzführer zur Ausstellung. Guide to the exhibition. Printed in Germany by Verein Aachener Krönungsgeschichte e. V.

[1232]. Mittelstädt, Kuno. *Albrecht Dürer.* Henschelverlag Kunst und Gesellschaft. Arkady, Warszawa-Berlin, 1977.

[1232:1]. *Kunst des Mittelalters in Armenien.* Burchard Brentjes, Stepan Mnazakanjan, Nina Stepanjan. (Kultur. Architektur. Plastik. Wandmalerei. Buchmalerei. Angewandte Kunst). Union Verlag, Berlin, 1981

[1233]. Lafuente, Jesús Precedo. *Visitor's Guide. The Cathedral of Santiago de Compostela.* Spain: Aldeasa, División Palacios y Museos, Estudios Gra'ficos Europeos, 1998.

[1234]. Kurth, Willi. *The Complete Woodcuts of Albrecht Dürer.* With an introduction by Campbell Dodgson, M.A., C.B.E. New York, Dover Publications, Inc., 1963.

[1235]. Lajta, Edit. *Malarstwo Francuskie od Gotyku do Renesansu.* Wydawnictwa Artystyczne i Filmowe-Warszawa. Drukowano na Wegrezech, 1979. Drukarnia Kossuth, Budapeszt. Wspolne wydanie wydawnictw Corvina, Budapest i WAiF, Warszawa.

[1236]. *L'art de vérifier les dates faites historiques.* Ed. par des Bénédictines. 1 ed., Paris, 1750; 2 ed., Paris, 1770; 3 ed., Paris, 1783, 1784, 1787.

[1237]. Laclotte, Michel (Director, Musée du Louvre). *Treasures of the Louvre.* New York, London-Paris, Abbeville, 1993.

[1238]. Langeteau, C. *Tables pour le calcul des syzygies ecliptiques, Connaissanse des Temps pour 1846.* Paris, 1843, 1850.

[1239]. Layamon. *Brut, or the Chronicle of Britain.* Ed. F. Madden. Volume II. London, 1847. 525-526, vv. 22589-22602.

[1240]. Stegena, Lajos, ed. *Lazarus Secretarius. The First Hungarian Mapmaker and His Work.* Budapest, Akademiai Kiado, 1982.

[1240:1]. Lecoq-Ramond, Sylvie, and Béguerie Pantxika. *Le Musée d'Unterlinden de Colmar.* Musées et Monuments de France. Paris, Schongauer & Albin Michel, 1991.

[1241]. Leland, C. *Fusang or discovery of America by Chinese Buddhist priests in the 5th century.* London, 1875.

[1242]. Dal Maso, Leonardo B.. *Rome of the Caesars.* Firenze, Bonechi Editioni Il Turismo, 1974, 1992.

[1243]. *Le Saint voyage de Jérusalem de seigneur d'Anglure.* Paris, F. Bonnardot and A. Longnon, 1878.

[1244]. *Le Wallraf-Richartz Museum de Cologne.* Munich, Scala, C. H. Becksche Verlagbuchhandlung (Oscar Beck), 1992.

[1245]. Lehmann, P. *Tafeln zur Berechnung der Mondphasen und Sonnen- und Mondfinsternisse.* Berlin, 1882.

[1245:1]. *Les Grandes Civilisations Disparues.* Sélection du Reader's Digest. Paris-Bruxelles-Montréal-Zurich, 1980.

[1246]. *Les Manuscripts de la Mer Morte. Aux origines du christianisme.* Les Dossiers d'Archéologie, No. 189 (Janv. 1994).

[1247]. de Austria, Leupoldus. *Compilatio de Astrorum Scientia,* cuts. 1489. (The Pulkovo Observatory Library.)

[1248]. Lhotsky, A. *Auf Satze und Vortrage.* Halle, 1970-1972.

[1249]. Lichtheim, Miriam. *Ancient Egyptian Literature.* Volumes 1-3. USA, University of California Press, 1975.

[1250]. Libby, W.F. *Radiocarbon dating.* 2nd edition. Chicago, Univ. of Chicago Press, 1955.

[1251]. Lilly, W. *An Introduction to Astrology.* London, G. Bell, 1939.

[1252]. Linde, A. v. d. *Gutenberg. Geschichte und Erdichtung.* Stuttgart, 1878.

[1253]. Linde, A. v. d. *Geschichte der Buchdruckerkunst.* Berlin, 1886.

[1254]. Lokotsch, K. *Etymologisches Wörterbuch der europäischen Wörter.* Heidelberg, 1927.

[1255]. Longhi, Roberto. *Caravaggio.* Die Italienische Malerei. Dresden: Editori Riuniti Rom, VEB Verlag der Kunst, 1968

[1256]. Lubienietski, S. *Theatrum Cometicum, etc.* Amstelodami, 1666-1668. (The Pulkovo Observatory Library.)

[1257]. Lubienietski, S. *Historia universalis omnium Cometarum.* Lugduni Batavorum, 1681. (The Pulkovo Observatory Library.)

[1258]. *Lucas Cranach d. Ä.* Herausgegeben von Heinz Lüdecke. Welt der Kunst. Henschelvarlag Kunst und Gesellschaft. Berlin, 1972.

[1259]. Magi, Giovanna, and Giuliano Valdes. *All of Turkey.* Firenze, Casa Editrice Bonechi, 1990.

[1260]. Manuel, Chrisoloras. *Manuels Chrisolorae Vita et scripta.* Patrologiae cursus completus. Series graeca posterior. T.CLVI. J.-P. Migne, 1866.

[1261]. Manuel II Palaeologus. *Laudatio funebris fratris sui Theodori Palaeologi Despotae.* Patrologiae cursus completus. Series graeca posterior. T. CLVI. J.-P. Migne, 1866.

[1261:1]. *Maps of the Ancient World. 2002 Calendar.* From The Huntington Library. Avalanche Publishing, Inc., 2001.

[1262]. *Mapy severni a jizni hvezdne oblohy.* Praha, Kartografie Praha, 1971.

[1263]. Marco Polo. *Le Livre des Merveilles.* La Renaissance du Livre. Collection Références. Extrait du Livre des Merveilles du Monde (Ms. fr. 2810) de la Bibliotheque nationale de France. 1999 Ultreya srl, Milan. 1996 Faksimile Verlag Luzern pour les textes et les images. 1999 La Renaissance du Livre, Tournai pour l'edition francaise. Belgique.

[1264]. Marco Polo. *The Travels of Marco Polo.* The Complete Yule-Cordier Edition. With a Total of 198 Illustrations and 32 Maps and Site Plans. Three Volumes Bound as Two. Volumes 1,2. Including the unabridged third edition (1903) of Henry Yule's annotated translation, as revised by Henry Cordier; together with Cordier's later volume of notes and addenda (1920). New York, Dover, 1993.

[1265]. Maria Da Villa Urbani. *Basilica of San Marco*. Milan, Editions KINA, 1993.

[1266]. Martin Behaim's 1492 *Erdapfel*. A paper version of our earliest surviving terrestrial Globe. First made in Nuremberg in 1492. Follow Marco Polo and the quest for spice on this unique medieval relic. Greaves & Thomas, London, England. Registered design & Patents Pending. Artwork & Globe Gores, 1997. (A selection of facsimile globes from the Greaves & Thomas collection. Spanning cartographic history from 1492 to the present day.)

[1267]. Maso Finiguerra. *A Florentine Picture-Chronicle*. Reproduced from the originals in the British Museum by the Imperial Press, Berlin. A critical and descriptive text by Sidney Colvin, M. A. Keeper of the prints and drawings of the British Museum. New York, Benjamin Blom, 1970.

[1268]. [Paris, Matthew] *The Illustrated Chronicles of Matthew Paris*. Cambridge, Corpus Christi College, 1993.

[1268:1]. McKenzie, John L., S. J. *Dictionary of the Bible*. G. Chapman, London, 1985 (1965 by Macmillan Publishing).

[1269]. Meier, H. *Deutsche Sprachstatistik*. Hildesheim, 1964.

[1270]. de la Garza, Mercedes. *The Mayas. 3000 years of civilization*. Mexico, Monclem Ediciones; Florence, Casa Editrice Bonechi, 1994.

[1271]. *Germany*. Michelin et Cie, 1996.

[1272]. *Paris*. Michelin et Cie, 1996.

[1273]. Michell, J. A. *Little History of Astro-Archaeology: Stages in the Transformation of a Heresy*. London, 1977.

[1273:0]. Michov, H. *Weitere Beiträge zur älteren Kartographie Russlands*. Mit 1 Textabbildung und 5 Karten. Sonderabzug aus den Mitteilungen der Geographischen Gesellschaft in Hamburg, Band XXII. Hamburg: L.Friederichsen & Co. Inhaber: Dr. L. Friederichsen, 1907.

[1273:1]. Migne, J.-P. *Patrologiae Cursus Completus etc*. Paris: Petit-Montrouge, 1800-1875.

[1274]. Miller, W. *The Latins in the Levant. A History of Frankish Greece in 1204-1566*. London, 1908.

[1275]. Mommsen, T. *Die Römische Chronologie bis auf Caesar*. Berlin, 1859, 2 Aufl.

[1276]. Montucla, J. E. *Histoire des Mathématiques*. T.IV. Paris, 1802.

[1277]. Montucla, J. E. *Histoire des Mathématiques*. 4 vols. Paris. 1799-1802.

[1278]. *Musée Royal de Naples: Peintures, bronzes et statues érotiques du cabinet secret, avec les explanations de M. C. F. (César Famin)*. Paris, 1857.

[1279]. *Museum. Gutenberg Museum Mainz*. Braunschweig, Georg Westermann Verlag, 1980. (3 Auflage 1994.)

[1280]. Myres, J. *Herodotus. Father of History*. Oxford, 1953.

[1281]. Ahmed Kardy. *Finding a Pharaoh's Funeral Bark*. National Geographic, Vol. 173, No. 4 (April 1988): 513-546.

[1282]. Peter Miller. *Riddle of the Pyramid Boats*. National Geographic, Vol. 173, No. 4 (April 1988): 534-546.

[1282:1]. Rick Gore. *The Eternal Etruscans. National Geographic*, Volume 173, No. 6 (June 1988): 696-743.

[1283]. *National Geographic*, Volume 176, No. 4 (October 1989).

[1284]. Nelli René. *Ecritures cathares*. Complete Cathar writings translated into French. Planete, 1968.

[1285]. Neugebauer, O. *Astronomische Chronologie*. Berlin and Leipzig, 1929.

[1286]. Neugebauer, O. *Specieller Kanon der Sonnenfinsternisse*. Ergänzungsheft, Astron. Nachr. 8, 4. Kiel, Verlag der Astronomischen Nachrichten, 1931.

[1287]. Neugebauer, O. *A History of Ancient Mathematical Astronomy*. 3 Vols. New York-Berlin, Springer-Verlag, 1975.

[1288]. Neugebauer, O. *The Exact Sciences in Antiquity*. 2nd edition. Providence, Rhode Island, Brown University Press, 1957.

[1289]. Neugebauer, Otto and Richard A. Parker. *Egyptian Astronomical Texts*. 3 vols. Providence and London: Lund Humphries for Brown University Press, 1960-1969.

[1290]. Neugebauer, O., and H. B. Van Hoesen. *Greek Horoscopes*. Philadelphia, The American Philosophical Society, 1959.

[1290:1]. Neugebauer, O., and R. A. Parker. *Egyptian Astronomical Texts*. Vols. 1-3. London, Brown University Press, 1964.

[1291]. Neugebauer, O., R. A. Parker, and D.Pingree. *The Zodiac Ceilings of Petosiris and Petubastis. Denkmäler der Oase Dachla. Aus dem Nachlass von Ahmed Fakhry*. Bearbeitet von J. Osing, M. Moursi, Do. Arnold, O. Neugebauer, R. A. Parker, D. Pengree und M. A. Nur-el-Din. Archäologische Veröffentlichungen 28 Deutsches Archäologisches Institut. Abteilung Kairo. Mainz am Rhein, Verlag Philipp von Zabern, 1982.

[1292]. Neugebauer, P. V. *Tafeln zur astronomischen Chronologie*. 3 Volumes. Leipzig, 1912.

[1293]. Neugebauer, P. V. *Abgekürzte Tafeln der Sonne und großen Planeten*. Berlin, 1904.

[1294]. Newcomb, S. *On the reccurence of solar eclipses with tables of eclipses*. Astronomical Papers (Washington). Vol. 1, No. 1 (1882).

[1295]. Newcomb, S. *Tables of the Motion of the Earth on its Axis and around the Sun*. Astronomical Paper. V.VI, Pt.1. 1898.

[1296]. Newmann, Dianne. *The Pergamon Altar*. Staatliche Museen zu Berlin, Preussischer Kulturbesitz, 1993.

[1297]. Newton, Isaac. *Abregé de la chronologie de I. Newton* fait par lui-même, et traduit sur le manuscript Angloise [par Nicolas Freret]. Paris: Gavelier, 1725.

[1298]. Newton, Isaac. *The Chronology of Ancient Kingdoms Amended. To which is Prefix'd, A Short Chronicle from the First Memory of Things in Europe, to the Conquest of Persia by Alexander the Great*. London: J. Tonson, 1728. Re-edited in 1988 by Histories and Mysteries of Man Ltd.

[1299]. Newton, Isaac. *La Chronologie des Ancien Royalmes Corrigée, Martin u.a.* Translation F. Granet. Paris, 1728.

[1300]. Newton, Isaac. *Kurzer Auszug aus der weltberühmten Isaac Newtons*

Chronologie derer alten Königreiche: worinnen 4 Haupt-Periodi veste gestellt u. aus d. Antiquität eruiert werden...; wobei zugl. gezeiget wird, wie d. dunckle Histoire d. alten verfallenen Königreiche... in e. richtige chronolog. Ordnung zu bringen sei... Aus d. Engl. Von Philipp Georg Hübner. Meiningen, 1741.

[1301]. Newton, Isaac. *Abrégé de la chronologie des ancien royaumes.* Trad. Deel Anglois de Mr. [Andrew] Reid. Geneve, 1743.

[1302]. Newton, Isaac. *Kurzer Auszug aus der I.Newtons Chronologie.* Von Pf. Georg Hübner, Hilburgshausen u. a. 1745.

[1303]. Newton, R. R. "Astronomical evidence concerning non-gravitational forces in the Earth-Moon system." *Astrophysics and Space Science,* Volume 16 (1972): 179-200.

[1304]. Newton, R. "Two Uses of Ancient Astronomy." *Philosophical Transactions of the Royal Society of London,* Series A., 276 (2 May 1974): 99-115. DOI: 10.1098/rsta.1974.0012.

[1305]. Newton, Robert R. *The Origins of Ptolemy's Astronomical Tables.* The Johns Hopkins University Applied Physics Laboratory. The Center for Archaeoastronomy, University of Maryland. USA, 1985.

[1306]. Newton, R. R. *Ancient Astronomical Observations and the Accelerations of the Earth and Moon.* Baltimore and London, John Hopkins University Press, 1970.

[1306:1]. Newton, R. R. *The Moon's Acceleration and Its Physical Origin.* Baltimore, John Hopkins University Press, 1979.

[1307]. Newton, Robert R. *On the fractions of degrees in an ancient star catalogue.* Quarterly Journal of the Royal Astronomical Society, Volume XX (1979): 383-394.

[1308]. Newton, Robert R. *The origins of Ptolemy's planetary parameters.* The Johns Hopkins University Applied Physics Lab. The Center for Archaeoastronomy. 1982. 86-90.

[1309]. *Nicolai Copernici Thorunensis de Revolutionibus Orbium Coelestium Libri VI.* Ex. auctoris autographio recudi curavit Societas Copernicana Thorunensis. Berolini, 1873.

[1310]. Nikulin, N. *Lucas Cranach. Masters of World Painting.* Leningrad, Aurora Art, 1976.

[1311]. Nilsson, M. P. *Primitive Time-Reckoning. A Study in the Origins and the First Development of the Art of Counting Time among the Primitive and Early Culture Peoples.* Lund, Gleerup, 1920.

[1312]. Noth, M. *Die Welt des Alten Testaments.* Berlin, 1957.

[1313]. Oertel, F. *Herodots ägyptischen Logos und die Glaubwürdigkeit Herodots.* Berlin, 1970.

[1314]. Olston, A. B. *The Story of Time.* Chicago, Jarvis Universal Clock Co., 1915.

[1315]. Oppolzer, Th. *Kanon der Sonnen- und Mondfinsternisse.* Wien: K. K.Hof- und Staatsdruckerei, 1887.

[1316]. Oppolzer, Th. *Tafeln zur Berechnung der Mondfinsternisse.* Wien, 1883.

[1317]. Oppolzer, Th. *Syzygientafeln für den Mond.* Leipzig, Astronomische Gesellschaft, 1881.

[1318]. Orbini, Mauro. *Origine de gli Slavi & progresso dell'Imperio loro.* Pesaro, 1606.

[1319]. Orontij, Finai Delphinatus. *Canonum Astronomicum.* 1553. (The Pulkovo Observatory Library.)

[1320]. Orontii, Finaei Delphinatis. *Fine Oronce, etc.* 1551. (The Pulkovo Observatory Library.)

[1321]. Orr, M. A. *Dante and the Early Astronomers.* London, Gall and Inglis, 1913.

[1321:1]. Otero, Gloria. *El Arte Romanico en España. Romanesque Art in Spain.* Subdireccion General de Promocion Exterior del Turismo. Turespaña, Spain, 1995.

[1322]. Otero, José Carro. *Santiago de Compostela.* Second edition. Leon, Spain, Editorial Everest S.A., 1999.

[1323]. Ostrowski, W. *The ancient names and early cartography of Byelorussia.* London, 1971.

[1324]. Owen, G. F. *Archaeology and the Bible.* NY, 1961.

[1325]. Page, E. S. *Continuous inspection schemes. Biometrika,* Volume 41, No.1 (1954): 100-115.

[1326]. Page, E. S. *A test for a change in a parameter occurring at an unknown point. Biometrica,* Vol. 42, No.4 (1955): 523-527.

[1327]. Paladilhe, Dominique. *Simon de Monfort et le Drame Cathare.* France: Librairie Académique Perrin, 1997.

[1328]. Pannekoek, A. *A History of Astronomy.* New York, 1961.

[1329]. *Paris. Tourist Guide.* Paris: Guide Michelin, 1992.

[1330]. Parker, Richard A. *Ancient Egyptian Astronomy.* Philosophical Transactions of the Royal Society of London, Ser. A, 276 (1974): 51-65.

[1331]. Pastoureau, Michel. *Traité d'Héraldique.* Bibliothèque de la Sauvegarde de l'Art Francais. 3e éd. Paris, Grands manuels Picard, 1997.

[1332]. Venetus, Paulus. *Philisiphiae naturalis compendium clarissimi philosophi Pauli Veneti: una libro de compositione mundi, etc.* Paris, J. Lambert (s. d.), n.d.

[1333]. Pearce, A. *The science of the stars.* London, Glen & Co., 1898.

[1334]. Pearce, A. *The text-book of Astrology.* London, Glen & Co., 1911.

[1335]. Pedersen, O. *A survey of the Almagest.* Odence, 1974.

[1335:1]. Pelloutier, S. *Histoire des Celtes.* Paris: Quillan, 1771.

[1336]. Perrier, Jacques. *Notre-Dame de Paris.* Association Maurice de Sully, Paris, 1996.

[1337]. Petavius, D. *De doctrina temporum.* Vol. 1. Paris, 1627. (Petau, D. *Opus de doctrina temporum, etc.* Volume 1. Antwerpiae, M. DCCV.)

[1338]. Petavius, D. *Petavii Avrelianensis e Societate Iesu, Rationarium Temporum in Partes Dvas, Libros tredecim distributum.* Editio Ultima. Parisiis, Apud Sebastianum Cramoisy, Regis, & Reginae Architypographum: Gabrielem Cramoisy. M.DC.LII. Cvm Pivilegio Regis.

[1339]. Peters, C. H. F., and E. B. Knobel *Ptolemy's Catalogue of Stars. A Revision of the Almagest*. Publ. No. 86. Washington, The Carnegie Inst. of Washington, 1915.

[1340]. Petrarca, Francesco. *Familiarum rerum libri*. Editione critica per cura di Vittorio Rossi. Firenze, 1968.

[1340:1]. Petrie, Flinders W. M. *Athribi* Mem. of British School of Archaeology in Egypt. Volume 14. 1902.

[1340:2]. Petrie, Flinders. *Wisdom of the Egyptians*. London, British School of Archaeology in Egypt and Bernard Quaritch Ltd., 1940.

[1341]. Pfeil, Ulrich. *Trier. A tour of the most famous sights*. Kunstverlag Weick. Passau, 1996.

[1342]. Philip, A. *The Calendar: Its History, Structure and Improvement*. Cambridge University Press, 1921.

[1343]. *Philipp Apian und die Kartographie der Renaissance*. Bayerische Staatsbibliothek. Anton H. München, Konrad Verlag, 1989.

[1344]. [Phrantzae, Georgius] *De Vita et Acriptus Georgii Phrantzae*. Patrologiae cursus completus. Series graeca posterior. T. CLVI. J.-P. Migne, 1866.

[1345]. Pingre, A. *Chronologie des eclipses qui ont été visibles depuis le pole boréal jusque vers l'equateur pendant les dix siècles qui ont précedé l'ère Chrétienne*. Paris, 1787.

[1346]. Pogo, A. *Additions and corrections to Oppolzer's Kanon der Mondfinsternisse*. Astron. Journal, V. 43 (1937): 45-48.

[1347]. Pokorny, J. *Indogermanisches etymologisches Wörterbuch*. In 2 Bd. Tübingen. Basel: Francke Verlag, 1994 (3. Aufl.).

[1348]. Goetz, Delia and Sylvanus G. Morley. *Popol Vuh. The Sacred Book of the Ancient Quiché Maya*. From the translation of Adrian Recinos. Volume 29 in the "Civilization of the American Indian" series. Norman and London, Univ. of Oklahoma Press, 1950. (13th edition in 1991).

[1349]. Portal, Charles. *Histoire de la ville de Cordes (Tarn), 1222-1799*. Toulouse, 1902.

[1350]. Priese, Karl-Heinz. *The Gold of Meroe*. The Metropolitan Museum of Art, New York. Mainz, Verlag Philipp von Zabern, 1993.

[1351]. Prowe, L. *Nicolaus Copernicus*. 3 Bde. Berlin, 1883-1884.

[1352]. [Ptolemaeus, Claudius]. *Phelusiensis Alexandrini philosophi et matematici excellentissimi Phaenomena stellarum 1022 fixarum ad hanc aetatem reducta, atque seorsum in studiosorum gratiam. Nunc primum edita, Interprete Georgio Trapezuntio*. Excessum Coloniai Agrippinae. Anno 1537, octavo Calendas 5 Septembers.

[1353]. [Ptolemaeus, Claudius]. *Geographia*. Ed. Sebastian Münster. Basel, 1540. Reprint: Series of Atlases in Facsimile. Amsterdam: Theatrum Orbis Terrarum Ltd., 1966.

[1354]. [Ptolemaeus, Claudius]. *Clavdii Ptolemaei Pelusiensis Alexandrini omnia quae extant opera, praeter Geographiam, etc*. Baseliae, 1551.

[1355]. Ptolemy. *The Almagest*. (Great Books of Western World, V. 16). Encyclopaedia Britannica, 1952.

[1356]. Ptolemy, C. *Claudii Ptolemaei opera quae exstant omnia*. Ed. J. L.Heiberg et al. 3 volumes. Leipzig, 1898-1903,.

[1357]. Ptolemy. *Tetrabiblos*. Ed. and trans. F. E. Robbins. Harvard, 1940.

[1358]. *Ptolemy's Almagest*. Transl. and annot. by G. J. Toomer. London, 1984.

[1359]. Putnam, James. *Mummy*. London, New York, Eyewitness Books. 1993.

[1360]. Putnam, James. *Pyramid*. London, New York, Eyewitness Books. 1994.

[1361]. Radini (Radinus), Tedeschi. *Sideralis abyssus*. Luteciae, Impressum opa T. Kees. (The Pulkovo Observatory Library). 1514 (1511?).

[1362]. Ramet, Henri. *Histoire de Toulouse*. Toulouse, Le Pérégrinateur Editeur, Queray, 1994.

[1363]. Ranson, C. L. *A Late Egyptian Sarcophagus*. Bulletin of the Metropolitian Museum of Art. 9 (1914): 112-120.

[1364]. Raska. *Chronologie der Bibel*. Berlin, 1878.

[1365]. Rawlins, Dennis. *An investigation of the ancient star catalog*. Publications of the Astronomical Society of the Pacific. Volume XCIV. 1982. 359-373.

[1365:1]. Reade, Julian. *Assyrian Sculpture*. British Museum. British Museum Press, London, 1983, 1988.

[1366]. Reeves, Nicholas. *The Complete Tutankhamun. The King. The Tomb. The Royal Treasure*. New York, Thames and Hudson, 1990, 1995.

[1367]. Reeves, Nicholas, and Nan Froman. *Into the Mummy's Tomb. The Real-Life Discovery of Tutankhamun's Treasures*. Toronto: A Scholastic/Madison Press Book, 1993, 1994. 1st published in the United States by Scholastic, 1992.

[1368]. *Rembrandt Harmensz van Rijn*. Tableaux dans les musées de l'Union Soviétique. Leningrad, Aurora, 1981, 1987.

[1369]. Robert, C. *Archäologische Hermeneutik*. Berlin, 1919.

[1370]. Roberts, J. M. *The Pelican History of the World*. England, Penguin Books, 1984.

[1371]. Robertson, J. M. *Pagan christs; studies in comparative hierology*. London, Watts & Co, 1911.

[1372]. Roche, Déodar. *Le Catharisme*. 2 Volumes. Narbonne, Cahiers d'Études Cathares, 1973 and 1976.

[1373]. Rogov, Alexander. *Alexandrov. (Alexandrovskaya Sloboda, or, literally, "The Freemen's Village of Alexander")*. *Museum Cities*. Leningrad, Avrora, 1979.

[1374]. Grafton, Anthony, ed. *Rome Reborn*. The Vatican Library and Renaissance Culture. Washington: Library of Congress; New Haven, London: Yale University Press; Vatican City: Biblioteca Apostolica Vaticana, 1993.

[1375]. Romero, Anne-Marie. *Saint-Denis. La montée des pouvours*. Caisse Nationale des Monuments Historiques et des Sites. Paris, CNRS, 1992, 1993.

[1376]. Roquebert, Michel. *Cathar Religion*. Toulouse, Editions Loubatières, 1994.

[1377]. Roquebert, Michel. *L'épopée Cathare, 1209-1229. (On the Crusade against the Albigeois)*. 3 volumes. Toulouse: Private, 1970, 1977 and 1986.

[1378]. Rosalba, Manzo. *New Castle Museum. Naples City Hall. Joint to the major for culture*. D. E. C. Artistical and Museums Patrimony Service. Naples, n.d.

[1378:1]. Rose-Marie, Rainer Hagen. *Egypt. People, Gods, Pharaohs.* Köln: Benedikt Taschen Verlag GmbH, 1999.

[1379]. Ross. *Tacitus and Bracciolini. The Annals forged in the XVth century.* London, 1878.

[1380]. Rostovzeff, M. *Social and Economic History of the Roman Empire.* Paris, 1957.

[1381]. Rowley, H. H. *The Old Testament and Modern Study.* Oxford, 1961.

[1382]. *Rundsicht der Stadt Wien zur Zeit der Türkenbelagerung, 1529, Niklas Meldemann, Nürnberg 1530.* HM Inv. Nr. 48068. Faksimile 1994, Museen der Stadt Wien Druckerei Gert Herzig, Wien. (Mediaeval plan of Vienna of the XVI c. depicting the siege of Vienna by the Turks in 1529.)

[1383]. Sacro, Bosco J. de. *Opusculum Johannis de Sacro busto spericum, cu figuris optimus ei novis textu in se, sive ambiguitate declarantibus.* Leipzig, 1494. (The Pulkovo Observatory Library.)

[1384]. Sacro, Bosco J. de. *Sphera materialis.* (The Pulkovo Observatory Library). Nürnberg, Gedruckt durch J. Getkneckt, 1516.

[1385]. Sacro, Bosco J. de. *Opusculu de Sphaera . . . clarissimi philosophi Ioannis de Sacro busto.* (The Pulkovo Observatory Library). Viennae Pannoniae, 1518.

[1386]. Sayce. *Herodotus I-III. The ancient empire of the East.* London, 1883.

[1387]. Scaliger, I. *Opus novum de emendatione temporum.* Lutetiac. Paris, 1583. (Thesaurum temporum, 1606).

[1388]. Schaarschmidt, K. *Die Sammlung der Platos Schriften zur Schreidung der echten von den unechten untersucht.* Bonn, 1866.

[1389]. Schäfer, Heinrich. *Ägyptische und heutige Kunst und Weltgebäude der alten Ägypter. Zwei Aufsätze.* Berlin, Walter de Greyter, 1928.

[1390]. Schlafke, Jakob. *La Cattedrale di Colonia.* Editione Italiana. Bonechi Verlag Styria, Casa Editrice Bonechi, Graz, Lahn Verlag, Limburg/Lahn, 1990.

[1391]. Schliemann, Heinrich. *Ilios. Stadt und Land der Trojaner. Forschungen und Entdeckungen in der Trojas und besonders auf der Baustelle von Troja.* Leipzig, 1881.

[1392]. Schliemann, Heinrich. *Troja. Ergebnisse meiner neuesten Ausgrabungen auf der Baustelle von Troja, in der Heldengräbern Bunarbaschi and an anderen Orten in der Trojas im Jahre 1882.* Leipzig, 1884.

[1393]. Schilgen, Jost, and Martina Wengierek. *So schön ist Trier.* Grasberg, Sachbuchverlag Karin Mader, 1994.

[1394]. Schjellerup, H. C. F. G. *Description des étoiles fixes composée au milieu du Xe siècle de notre ère par l'astronome persan abd-Al-Rahman Al-Sufi.* St. Petersburg, 1874.

[1395]. Schram, R. *Tafeln zur Berechnung der naheren Umstände der Sonnenfinsternisse.* Wien, 1886.

[1396]. Schram, R. *Reductionstafeln für den Oppolzerischen Finsternis Kanon zum Übergang auf die Ginzelschen Correctionen.* Wien, 1889.

[1396:1]. Schedel, Hartmann. *La chronique universelle de Nuremberg.* L'édition de

Nuremberg, colorée et commentée. (L'édition 1493, colorée et commentée). Introduction et Appendice par Stephan Füssel. Taschen GmbH. (Köln). Köln, London, Madrid, New York, Paris, Tokyo, 2001.

[1397]. Schram, R. *Kalendariographische und chronologische Tafeln.* Leipzig, 1908.

1398 Schroter, J. *Spezieller Kanon der zentralen Sonnen- und Mondfinsternisse.* Kristiania, 1923.

[1399]. Schulten, Walter. *Der Schrein der Heiligen drei Könige im Kölner Dom.* Luthe-Druck Köln, 1995.

[1400]. Schwahn, P. *Mathematische Theorie der astronomischen Finsternisse.* Leipzig, 1910.

[1401]. Schwegler, T. *Die Biblische Urgeschichte.* München, 1960.

[1402]. Serrus, Georges. *Montségur.* Toulouse, Editions Loubatières, 1994.

[1403]. Serrus, Georges, and Michel Roquebert. *Cathare Castles.* Toulouse, Editions Loubatières, 1993.

[1404]. Severy, Merle. *The world of Suleyman the Magnificent. National Geographic,* Volume 172, No.5 (1987): 552-601.

[1405]. Siebeck, H. *Zur Chronologie der platonischen Dialoge.* Halle, 1873.

[1405:1]. Simon, J. L., P. Bretagnon, J. Chapront, M.,Chapront-Touze, G. Francou, and J. Laskar. Software for the calculation of heliocentric coordinates, radial vectors and immediate speeds for the 8 main planets of the Solar System (the PLANETAP program, Fortran 77) *Astron. Astrophys.,* 282, 663 (1994).

1405:2 Sivaramamurti, Calambur. *The Art of India.* India Book House, Bombay, 1977. Published by Harry N. Abrams, Inc., New York.

[1406]. Shaban, S. *Change-point problem and two-phase regression: annotated bibliography. International Statistical Review,* Volume 48 (1980): 83-86.

[1407]. *Speyer. Die Kaiserstadt am Rhein.* KINA Italia Mailand, Kaiserdom-Pavillon Renate Hahn am Domplatz, ATD Mailand, 1994.

[1408]. *Speyer Cathedral.* Regensburg, Verlag Schnell & Steiner GmbH Regensburg, 1997.

[1409]. Spielberg, W. *Die Glaubwürdigkeit von Herodots Bericht über Ägypten.* Berlin, 1926.

[1410]. Staccioli, Romolo A. *Storia e cività degli Etruschi. Origine apogeo decadenza di un grande popolo dell'Italia antica.* Rome, Newton Compton editori, 1981.

[1411]. Stancheva, Magdalina. *Veliki Preslav.* Sofia, Zlatostrouy, 1993.

[1412]. Steeb, J. *Coelum sephiroticum Hebraeorum, etc.* (The Pulkovo Observatory Library). Mainz, 1679.

[1413]. Stephan, Beissel S. J. *Kunstschätze des Aachener Kaiserdomes. Werke der Goldschmiedekunst, Elfenbeinschnitzerei und Textilkunst.* M. Gladbach. Druck und Verlag von B. Kühlen. Anstalt für Christliche Kunst. 1904.

[1414]. Stevens, Henry N. *Ptolemy's Geography. A brief account of all printed editions down to 1730.* Amsterdam, Theatrum Orbis Terrarum Ltd. Meridian Publishing Company, 1972.

[1415]. Stierlin, Henri. *The Pharaohs Master-Builders*. Paris, Finest S.A./Éditions Pierre Terrail, 1992.

[1416]. *St. Lorenz. Sagen + Geschichten.* 73. Verein zur Erhaltung der St. Lorenz-kirche in Nürnberg (E.V.). Herausgegeben von Gerhard Althaus und Georg Stolz. Nürnberg. Nr. 15/3, unveränderte Auflage, 1998.

[1417]. *St.Lorenz. Türme + Glocken.* 81. Verein zur Erhaltung der St. Lorenz-kirche in Nürnberg (E. V.). Herausgegeben von Gerhard Althaus und Georg Stolz. Nürnberg. Nr.25/2, verbessterte Auflage, 1998.

[1418]. *St. Lorenz. Wappen in Fülle. Wappenkunde. Wappenkunst und Wappen-recht.* 86. Verein zur Erhaltung der St. Lorenz-kirche in Nürnberg (E.V.). Herausgegeben von Gerhard Althaus und Georg Stolz. Nürnberg. NF.Nr.31, 1986.

[1419]. *St. Lorenz. Ich bin das Licht der Welt. Grosse und kleine Lichter.* 90. Verein zur Erhaltung der St. Lorenzkirche in Nürnberg (E.V.). Herausgegeben von Gerhard Althaus und Georg Stolz. Nürnberg. NF.Nr.35, 1990.

[1420]. *St. Lorenz. Sand-Sandstein. Steinsand-Sand.* 91. Verein zur Erhaltung der St. Lorenzkirche in Nürnberg (E. V.). Herausgegeben von Gerhard Althaus und Georg Stolz. Nürnberg. NF. Nr. 36, 1991.

[1421]. *St. Lorenz. Behelmt, behütet und bedacht.* 92. Verein zur Erhaltung der St. Lorenzkirche in Nürnberg (E. V.). Herausgegeben von Gerhard Althaus und Georg Stolz. Nürnberg. NF. Nr. 37, 1992.

[1422]. *St. Lorenz. Mein Auge schauet was Gott gebauet.* 93. Was Verein zur Erh-altung der St. Lorenzkirche in Nürnberg (E. V.). Herausgegeben von Gerhard Althaus und Georg Stolz. Nürnberg. NF. Nr. 38, 1993.

[1423]. *St. Lorenz. Ecce Panis Angelorum. Das Sakramentshaus des Adam Kraft.* Verein zur Erhaltung der St. Lorenzkirche in Nürnberg (E. V.). Herausgege-ben von Gerhard Althaus und Georg Stolz. Nürnberg. NF. Nr. 39, 1994.

[1424]. *St. Lorenz. 500 Jahre Sakramentshaus: Erklärung – Verklärung, Deutung – Umdeutung.* 96. Verein zur Erhaltung der St. Lorenzkirche in Nürnberg (E. V.). Herausgegeben von Gerhard Althaus und Georg Stolz. Nürnberg. NF. Nr. 41, 1996.

[1425]. *St. Lorenz. Türen. Tore. Portale.* 97. Verein zur Erhaltung der St. Lorenz-kirche in Nürnberg (E.V.). Herausgegeben von Gerhard Althaus und Georg Stolz. Nürnberg. NF. Nr. 41, 1997.

[1426]. *St. Lorenz. Wandfresken. Bestand. Restaurierung. Erhaltung.* 98. Verein zur Erhaltung der St. Lorenzkirche in Nürnberg (E. V.). Herausgegeben von Gerhard Althaus und Georg Stolz. Nürnberg. NF. Nr. 43, 1998.

[1427]. *St. Lorenz. Im Blickpunkt das Kreuz. Kruzifix-Darstellungen.* 99. Verein zur Erhaltung der St. Lorenz-kirche in Nürnberg (E. V.). Herausgegeben von Gerhard Althaus und Georg Stolz. Nürnberg. NF. Nr. 44, 1999.

[1428]. Struve, O. *Libroram in biblioteca Speculae Pulcovensis catalogus systemat-icus.* Petropoli, 1860.

[1429]. Stryjkowski, Maciej. *O Poczatkach, wywodach....* Of the Beginnings, Sources, the Deeds of the Knights and the Home Affairs of the Glorious Peoples of Lithuania, Zhmuda, and Russia, an Original Tale Inspired by the Lord and the Author's Own Experience. Warszawa, 1978.

[1430]. Suckow, Hähel. *Stadtführer Halle. Sehenswertes in Halle*. Halle, Druck-haus Schütze, 1998.

[1431]. Suess, H. *Secular variations. Journal of Geophysical Research*, Volume 70, No. 23 (1965).

[1432]. Suess, H. *Bristlecone Pine. Radioactive Dating and Methods*. Vienna, 1968.

[1433]. Suess, H. *Bristlecone Pine Calibration of the Radiocarbon*. XII Nobel Symposium on Radiocarbon Variations and Absolute Chronology. Uppsala, 1969.

[1434]. Sueton. *Die zwölf Caesaren, nach der Übersetzung v. A. Stahr neu hrsg*. München, Leipzig, 1912.

[1435]. Suhle, A. *Mittelalteriche Brakteaten*. Leipzig, 1965.

[1436]. Swerdlow, N. M., and O. Neugebauer. *Mathematical Astronomy in Copernicus' De Revolutionibus*. 2 vols. Berlin, 1984.

[1437]. *Sztuka Egipska. Piramidy i mastaby*. Mala Encyklopedia Sztuki. 23. Warszawa, Arkady, 1976.

[1438]. *Sztuka Egipska. Luksor*. Opracowal Kazimierz Michalowski. Mala Encyklopedia Sztuki. 25. Warszawa, Arkady, 1976.

[1438:1]. Tabov, Jordan. *Chronological Distribution of Information in Historical Texts*. Computers and the Humanities, 2003, Volume 37, pages 235-240.

[1439]. Targuebayre, Claire. *Cordes en Albigeois*. Toulouse, Editions Privat, 1988.

[1440]. Tesnierio, Ioanne. *Opus Matematicum octolibrum*. (The Pulkovo Observatory Library.) Coloniae Agrippinae, apud J. Birckmannum & W. Richwinum, 1562.

[1441]. Teutsch Astronomei. *Astronomia*. Woodcuts, 1545. (The Pulkovo Observatory Library.)

[1442]. *The Anglo-Saxon Chronicle*. London: Everyman's library, J. M. Dent. Sons Ltd., 1990.

[1443]. Wright, G. E., ed. *The Bible and the Ancient Near East. Essays in Honour of W.F.Albright*. NY, 1961.

[1444]. *The Cambridge medieval history. IV. The Byzantine Empire*. Cambridge Univ. Press, 1966-1967.

[1445]. *The Cathedral of St.Stephen in Vienna*. Graz, Verlag Styria, Casa Editrice Bonechi, 1992.

[1446]. Gransden, A., ed. *The Chronicle of Bury St. Edmunds, 1212-1301*. London-Edinburgh, 1964.

[1447]. *The Concise Columbia Encyclopedia*. USA, Columbia University Press, 1983.

[1448]. *The Egyptian Book of the Dead. The Book of Going Forth by Day*. The first authentic presentation of the complete papyrus of Ani. Featuring full color images. Transl. by Dr. R. Faulkner. San Francisco, Chronicle Books, 1994.

[1449]. *The English version of the polyglot Bible with a copies and original selection of references to parallel and illustrative passages*. London, S. Bagster and Sons.

[1450]. *The Holy Bible, containing Old and New Testaments: Translated out of the original tongues; and with the former translations diligently compared and revised, by His Majesty's special command. Appointed to be read in Churches.* London, British and Foreign Bible Society, Instituted in London in the Year 1804.

[1451]. *The Holy Bible, containing Old and New Testaments: Translated out of the original tongues; and with the former translations diligently compared and revised, by His Majesty's special command. Authorized King James version.* Salt Lake City, Utah, Church of Jesus Christ of Latter-Day Saints, 1992.

[1452]. *The New Encyclopaedia Britannica.* Volume 16. 1987.

[1453]. *The place of astronomy in the ancient world.* A discussion organized jointly for the Royal Society and the British Academy. Philos. Trans. of the Royal. Soc. of London, Ser. A., Volume 276 (1974): 1-276.

[1454]. Farid, Shafik, ed. *The Pyramids of Giza.* Book 1. Simpkins Splendor of Egypt. Salt Lake City, Utah, Simpkins Souvenirs, 1982.

[1455]. *The R. C. Church of St. Karl. Vienna.* Salzburg, Christiche Kunststätten Österreichs, Nr.20 E. Verlag St. Peter, 1994.

[1456]. Werber, Eugen. *The Sarajevo Haggadah.* Svjetlost, Sarajevo. Printed by Mladinska Knjiga, Ljubljiana, 1999.

[1457]. *The Shrine of Torreciudad. Guide.* Oficina de Información, 22391 Torreciudad (Huesca), España.

[1458]. Farid, Shafik, ed. *The Temple of Luxor.* Book 3. Simpkins Splendor of Egypt. Salt Lake City, Utah, Simpkins Souvenirs, 1982.

[1458:1]. *The Treasures of the Valley of the Kings. Tombs and Temples of the Theban West Bank in Luxor.* Edited by Kent R.Weeks. The American University in Cairo Press. Cairo, Egypt, 2001. White Star, S. r. l. Vercelli, Italy.

[1459]. *The World Encompassed.* An exhibition of the history of maps held at the Baltimore Museum of Art October 1 to November 23, 1952. Baltimore, Maryland, The Trustees of the Walters Art Gallery, 1952.

[1460]. Thierry, Amedee. *St. Jean Chrysostome et l'impératrice Eudoxie.* Paris, 1872.

[1460:1]. Thoren, Victor E. *The Lord of Uraniborg. A Biography of Tycho Brahe.* With contributions by John R. Christianson. Cambridge, New York, Port Chester, Melbourne, Sydney, Cambridge University Press (1994?).

[1461]. Thorndike, L. H. D. *A History of Magic and Experimental Science. (During the first thirteen centuries of our era).* Volumes 1,2. NY, 1923., New York, Columbia University Press, 1943, 1947, 1958.

[1462]. Topper, Uwe. *Die Große Aktion. Europas Erfundene Geschichte. Die planmäßige Fälschung unserer Vergangenheit von der Antike bis zur Aufklärung.* Tübingen, Grabert-Verlag, n.d.

[1463]. Topper, Uwe. *Erfundene Geschichte. Unsere Zeitrechnung ist falsch. Leben wir im Jahr 1702?* München, F. A. Herbig Verlagsbuchhandlung GmbH, 1999.

[1464]. Turhan, Can. *Istanbul, Gate to the Orient.* Istanbul, Orient, 1995.

[1465]. Turhan, Can. *Topkapi Palace.* Istanbul, Orient, 1995.

[1466]. Eco, Umberto. *Serendipities. Language and Lunacy.* Weidenfeld & Nicolson (UK). NY, Orion/Columbia Univ. Press. 1999.

[1467]. *Venice.* Venezia, Storti Edizioni, 1993.

[1468]. Vesconte, Pietro. *Seekarten.* Mit einem Geleitwort von Otto Mazal. Einfürung von Lelio Pagani. Edition Georg Popp Würzburg. 1978. Grafica Gutenberg, Bergamo, 1977.

[1469]. Vidal-Quadras, José A. *Torreciudad.* Imprenta Moises Barbasto, Spain, 1987.

[1470]. Vidal-Quadras, José A. *Torreciudad. A shrine to Our Lady.* Office of Information Torreciudad, Spain, n.d.

[1471]. Villehardouin, Geoffroy de. *La conquète de Constantinople.* Historiens et chroniqueurs du Moyen Âge. Ed. A. Pauphilet. Paris, 1963.

[1472]. Virgil, Mocanu. *Tintoretto.* Clasicii Picturii Universale. Bucuresti, Editura Meridiane, 1977.

[1473]. Vries, Hesselde. *Variation in concentration of radiocarbon with time and location on Earth.* Koninkl. Nederlandse Akad. Wetensch. Proc. 1958, ser. B. 61, pages 1-9.

[1474]. *Wallraf-Rischartz-Museum der Stadt Köln. Vollständliges Verzeichnis der Gemäldesammlung.* Köln/Mailand, 1986.

[1475]. Waterfield, R. L. *A Hundred Years of Astronomy.* NY, Macmillan, 1938.

[1476]. Wehli, Tünde. *A Középkori Spanyolország Festészete.* Budapest, Corvina Kiadó, 1980.

[1477]. Wenzler, Claude. *L'Héraldique.* Rennes, Éditions Ouest-France, 1997.

[1478]. Werner, H., and F. Schmeidler. *Synopsis der Nomenklatur der Fixsterne.* Wissensch. Stuttgart, Verlags-Gesellschaft 1986.

[1478:1]. Wigal, Donald. *Anciennes Cartes Marines. A la Découverte des Nouveaux Mondes. 1290-1699.* New York, Parkstone Press, 2000.

[1479]. Williams, John. *Observations of Comets from B.C.611 A.D. to 1640, extracted from the Chinese Annals.* 1871.

[1480]. Willis, E. H., H. Tauber, and K. O. Münnich. *Variations in the atmospheric radiocarbon concentration over the past 1300 years. Radiocarbon,* Volume 2 (1960): 1.

[1481]. Wissowa, Pauly. *Real-Encyclopädie der Klassischen Altertumwissenschaft in alphabetischer Ordnung.* Hrsg. von Kroll. Stuttgart, 1839-1852.

[1482]. Wittkower, R. *Architectural Principles in the Age of Humanism.* Paris, 1960.

[1483]. Wolf, R. *Handbuch der Astronomie, ihrer Geschichte und Literatur.* Bd. II. Zürich, 1892.

[1484]. Wooley, L. *Excavation at Ur.* NY, 1955.

[1485]. Woronowa, Tamara, and Andrej Sterligov. *Westeuropäische Buchmalerei des 8. bis 16. Jahrhunderts in der Russischen Nationalbibliothek, Sankt Petersburg. (Frankreich. Spanien. England. Deutschland. Italien. Niederlande).* Augsburg: Bechtermünz. Genehmigte Lizenzausgabe für Weltbild Verlag, 2000. England, Parkstone/Aurora, 1996.

[1486]. Wright, G. E. *Biblical Archaeology.* Philadelphia, London, 1957.

[1487]. Altet, Xavier Barral. *Compostelle de Grand Chemin.* Découvertes Gallimard Réligions. Gallimard, 1993.

[1488]. Zadkiel. *The Grammar of Astrology.* London, J. Cornish, 1849.

[1489]. Zarnecki, George, Florence Deucher, and Irmgard Hutter. *Neue Belser Stilgeschichte. Band IV. Romantik, Gotik, Byzanz.* Stuttgard, Zürich, Belser Verlag, 1986.

[1490]. Zech, J. *Astronomische Untersuchungen über die wichtigeren Finsternisse, welche von den Schriftstellern des klassischen Altertums erwähnt werden.* Leipzig, 1853.

[1491]. *Zeitensprünge.* Interdisziplinäres Bulletin. Sonderdruck. September 1996. Thema Absolutdatierung. Mantis Verlag, Germany.

[1492]. Zevi, B., E. Battisti, E. Garin, and L. Malle. *Alberti. Enciclopedia universale dell'arte.* Vol. I. Venezia, Roma, 1958.

Made in the USA
Middletown, DE
20 October 2023

41135935R00156